Charles Morris

The War with Spain

A complete history of the war of 1898 between the United States and Spain

Charles Morris

The War with Spain
A complete history of the war of 1898 between the United States and Spain

ISBN/EAN: 9783337115623

Printed in Europe, USA, Canada, Australia, Japan

Cover: Foto ©ninafisch / pixelio.de

More available books at **www.hansebooks.com**

THE WAR WITH SPAIN

A COMPLETE HISTORY
OF THE WAR OF 1898

BETWEEN

THE UNITED STATES AND SPAIN

BY
CHARLES MORRIS
AUTHOR OF "THE NATION'S NAVY," "HISTORY OF THE UNITED STATES,"
"HISTORICAL TALES," ETC.

WITH MAPS AND ILLUSTRATIONS

PHILADELPHIA
J. B. LIPPINCOTT COMPANY
1899

Copyright, 1898,
BY
J. B. Lippincott Company.

PREFACE.

THE true mission of the United States may be held to be peace, not war; production, not destruction; industry, not rapine. But even to the most peacefully inclined of nations occasions come which irresistibly demand that the sword shall be drawn and blows be struck, and through one of these periods of violence this country has just passed. It has had to deal with a nation not yet in the nineteenth century, a belated relic of the mediæval age, and has found it necessary to employ forcible methods. War is an evil, but there are greater evils only to be met by war, national diseases which only the strongest remedies can cure. Spain's colonial system has been such a disease, one with which only heroic treatment would avail. It has been a system of despotism and enslavement, of the suppression of insurrection by massacre and starvation, and of obstinate adherence to methods long since outlived by other civilized nations. The state of affairs had grown intolerable when the United States took up the sword for the relief of a starving and perishing people, and began a war based upon the highest of motives, that of humane sympathy and the succor of the oppressed.

This country has been accused of a selfish greed for the territory of Spain; but it may be safely said that no purpose of territorial aggrandizement was among the motives that inspired the war. All wars yield unpremeditated results, and the principal result of this has been to place under the control of the United States certain island possessions which obviously cannot be handed back to Spain, to be misgoverned as before, and whose people are incapable of self-government. The United States must retain them or hand them over to land-greedy nations which stand ready to seize every shred of unappropriated soil. Some of them she has decided to hold ; but it may be repeated that this result of the war was not included among its motives.

The war has been regarded with interest by foreign nations from another point of view. For years past the powers of instruments of destruction have been steadily on the increase, until it began to appear as if war would become wholesale butchery, and must cease as something too terrible to be contemplated. This war has, therefore, been looked upon as an object-lesson in the destructive powers of magazine rifles, rapid-fire guns, torpedo-tubes, and other death-dealing implements. The result has been to prove that in the rush, the turmoil, the nerve-strain of combat, modern weapons are apt to waste their projectiles upon the empty air, and that infantry may still charge earthworks and rifle-pits with no greater loss of life than in former wars. In naval combat the value of coolness and training, as compared with the opposite qualities, has received a wonderful demonstration in the quick and complete destruction of the Spanish fleets and the remarkable immunity of American ships and men. The "man behind the gun" seems of more importance than the gun itself.

But a preface should not be an argument or an example of special pleading, and we may conclude by saying that in these less than four months of war the

United States has taken a new position before the world, a higher and nobler attitude. Europe has suddenly discovered that we are more than a nation of shopkeepers; that we are a people who can strike shrewdly for the right, and one that is destined to be a leader in the van of human progress, an example to the world of the value of free institutions, peaceful industries, high aspirations, and moral energies.

CONTENTS.

CHAPTER I.

SPAIN AND HER COLONIES.

PAGE

Cruelty of the early Spaniards—Annihilation of the natives —How Cuba was colonized—Later history of Cuba— Spain's methods of administration—Commerce forbidden —Character of office-holders—Insurrections begin—The cruelties of the Spanish army—The Captain-General of Cuba given despotic powers—Cuban hatred of Spain— Attempts at insurrection—The Lopez invasion—The Quitman project—Revolt in Spain—Condition of affairs in Cuba—Oppression of the islanders—Large salaries and perquisites of the Spanish officials—Frauds and fees— The share of Spain—Disregard of Cuban interests—The revolt of 1868—A guerilla war—The character of the country—The machete as a weapon—Bush fighting—The rainy season—Desultory warfare—Official bulletins—The trocha and reconcentration—Outrages in Havana—Massacre of the students—The treaty of El Zanjon—Promises of reform not kept 21

CHAPTER II.

RELATIONS OF THE UNITED STATES TO CUBA.

Early difficulties with Spain—Threatened interference of the Holy Alliance between Spain and the revolting colonies—This leads to the Monroe doctrine—The United States gives warning to European powers—Mexico and Colombia warned to keep out of Cuba—The United States guarantees Spain's title to Cuba—Secretary Everett's ultimatum—Offer to purchase Cuba—The Black Warrior affair—The Ostend conference—Buchanan's views—The Virginius affair—Protest and indemnity—President Grant's attitude—Injuries to American commerce 47

CHAPTER III.

CUBA IN INSURRECTION.

Cubans in exile—The work of the clubs—Marti's efforts—The outbreak of revolt—Maceo and Gomez reach the island—Death of Marti—Campos appointed governor-general—His methods—How the insurgents fought—Their horsemanship—Life in a Cuban camp—Gomez in command—His troubles and despondency—Camaguey invaded—Gomez's plan of campaign—A war of skirmishes—The battle of Bayamo—A Cuban constitution and government—Maceo's activity—Progress of the war westward—Its destructive character—Pinar del Rio invaded—Campos replaced by General Weyler—Weyler's reputation for cruelty—His inefficient campaigning—Destruction of plantations—Maceo's operations—His death—The province of Pinar del Rio pacified—Operations of Weyler in Santa Clara—Gomez's waiting game—General Garcia's capture of Victoria de las Tunas—Indignation at Weyler's cruelty—He is recalled and replaced by General Blanco—A reform administration—How the Cubans received it 58

CHAPTER IV.

THE FORTS AND THE TROCHAS.

The Spanish ill-success due to their method of warfare—This method of advantage to the insurgents—Guerilla warfare a Spanish habit—The trocha trusted to—Successive trochas built—Gomez and Maceo treat them with disdain—Weyler's trocha from Mariel to Majana described—The trocha from Jucaro to Moron—The multitude of forts—The Spanish held the towns and forts, the Cubans the country—Spain on the defensive; no energetic offensive operations—Their system of returning to dinner—War bulletins—Falsehoods with a purpose . . 82

CONTENTS.

CHAPTER V.

THE RECONCENTRADOS AND THE MILITARY PRISONS.

PAGE

Weyler's barbarity—The reconcentrado order—Its disastrous effect—Pacification by starvation—The reconcentrados at Jaruco—McKinley's denunciation of the cruelty displayed—What Senator Proctor and others saw in Cuba—Incomunicado imprisonment—General Lee's protests—Murder of Dr. Ruiz—No more Americans imprisoned—The sufferings of Cuban exiles—The story of Evangelina Cisneros—Spanish compared with Turkish barbarity—A butcher of men feasted in Sagua—The endless conflagrations—An intolerable situation 92

CHAPTER VI.

EVENTS LEADING TO INTERVENTION.

Efforts to prevent expeditions to Cuba—The Competitor prisoners—President Cleveland's message—Spain's reply—General Lee sent to Havana—His report—President McKinley's action—Spain's reply to Minister Woodford—Intervention for charity—Spain's financial condition—The hopeless state of the war—Lee's opinion of the insurgents—Increase of irritation—The riot in Havana—The Key West squadron—The De Lome letter—The Maine in Havana harbor—The explosion and its result—Wide-spread indignation—The Court of Inquiry and its verdict—Active preparations for war—Emergency fund voted—New ships bought and ordered—Senator Proctor's speech—The feeling in Congress—McKinley's pacific action—Lee leaves Havana—The message to Congress—The consular reports—Warlike resolution of Congress—Its immediate results—Spanish methods—War inevitable—Concentration of the army—The attitude of the powers of Europe 103

CHAPTER VII.

CUBA UNDER BLOCKADE.

PAGE

The waiting fleet at Key West—A night of signalling—The start for Cuba—The first prize—Establishment of the blockade—Peril of the Paris—Blanco and the Havanese—Prizes of the fleet—Lieutenant Rowan's daring journey—The question of privateers—Spain's declaration—Secretary Sherman retires—The Matanzas ports bombarded—The Cape Verde fleet—The flying squadron—Bombardment of forts at Cienfuegos and Cardenas—The journey of the Oregon—Complaints from Tampa—Attitude of the powers of Europe—Friendliness of Great Britain . 134

CHAPTER VIII.

THE SEA-FIGHT AT MANILA.

The Philippine Islands—The natives rebel against Spain—Admiral Dewey's squadron sent to Manila—First news of a victory—General Augustin's proclamation—The squadron in the bay—Passing Corregidor Island—Manila in view—The Spanish ships at Cavite—How they were stationed—The battle begins—Submarine mines—Fierce firing on both sides—Poor gunnery of the Spanish—Terrible results of the American fire—The Reina Cristina attacks the Olympia—Fatal result—Fate of the torpedo-boats—The Spanish ships in flames—Dewey withdraws for breakfast—Returns and completes the destruction of the Spanish ships—Wonderful result—No American killed—Heavy loss on the Spanish side—Great accuracy of American fire—Dewey asked not to bombard the city—Corregidor Island taken—Dewey's despatch—Work of the Petrel—The natives in Cavite—Dewey thanked and rewarded by the President and Congress—Ships and troops sent to his aid 150

CONTENTS.

CHAPTER IX.

UNDER FIRE AT CARDENAS AND CIENFUEGOS.

Sailing of the Cape Verde fleet—Preparations along the coast—The mosquito fleet—An affair at Matanzas—In the Bay of Cardenas—The Winslow disabled—Death of Ensign Bagley and his companions—Escape of the Winslow—Burial of the victims—Grappling for the cables at Cienfuegos—Sharp fire and return—The cables cut—The lighthouse demolished—Other efforts to cut cables 170

CHAPTER X.

THE SEARCH FOR THE SPANISH FLEET.

Admiral Sampson's squadron seeks San Juan—Defences of the town—The rounds of the ships—The bombardment—The Terror at work—Results of the engagement—The lessons learned—The hospital ship Solace—News of the Spanish fleet—In search of coal—Schley's squadron leaves Key West—Reaches Cienfuegos—No trace of the Spanish ships—The Hawk brings news—Evidence of Cervera's movements—The collier Restormel captured—Schley sails for Santiago—Location of this city—Admiral Cervera's ships—Bombardment of the batteries—Presence of the ships proved—Admiral Sampson arrives—The voyage of the Oregon—Accident of the Columbia—Failure of the Gussie expedition—The newspaper censorship—The Florida lands supplies for the Cubans 180

CHAPTER XI.

THE HEROES OF THE MERRIMAC.

The Merrimac—Hobson's scheme—Preparation—Hosts of volunteers—A premature start—The actual start—Powell and the launch—The collier goes in—The picket boat—Opening of the battery fire—The catamaran—Hobson's narrative—Saved by Cervera—News sent to the fleet—Prisoners in the Morro—Schley's opinion—Aid from British consul—The exchange—Enthusiastic reception of Hobson and his men 199

CHAPTER XII.

THE FIRST FIGHT ON CUBAN SOIL.

PAGE

Schley's scouts—Lieutenant Blue's exploit—A torpedo-boat attack—Torpedoes afloat—The forts bombarded—Marines landed in Guantanamo Bay—A Spanish attack—Fighting day and night—Death of Surgeon Gibbs—The Sunday attack—A picturesque scene—Cuban allies—The Spanish camp attacked—Tricks of the bush-fighters,—Shelling of Caimanera—Work of the dynamite guns—The channel open—A conference on Cuban soil 215

CHAPTER XIII.

THE ARMY OF INVASION.

Organizing an army—Commanding officers—Treatment of the soldiers criticised—General Alger's remarks—Character of the army—The Rough Riders—The invading force—The transports sail and are called back—The final start—Santiago reached—A landing place chosen—The Spanish retreat—Landing under difficulties—The army on shore—Its unready condition—An advance movement—Skirmishing—Garcia's army moved 227

CHAPTER XIV.

THE RAID OF THE ROUGH RIDERS.

Advance of the dismounted cavalry—Wheeler's reconnoissance—The country and the roads—Spaniards in ambush—Plan of attack—The climb of the Rough Riders—Fighting by both columns—A dangerous situation—Wood and Roosevelt charge—The block-house taken—Fight of the regulars—Incidents of the battle—Its results—A Spanish comment. 238

CONTENTS. 15

CHAPTER XV.

THE BATTLE OF SANTIAGO.
PAGE

The Cuban roads—A reconnoissance—The American position and supplies—Condition of the troops—The lines of the enemy—Shafter orders battle—The lines on July 1—The balloon and its results—The Spanish positions at El Caney and San Juan—The wire-clipping advance-guard—Lack of artillery—Attack on the El Caney fort—The Spanish rifle-pits—Chaffee's charge—Fort and town taken—Exposure of the troops—Aguadores attacked—The fight at San Juan—Advance of the troops—Wading the San Juan—Grimes's battery at work—Exposure and loss of the Americans—An impetuous charge—The hill taken—Exhaustion of the men—The July 2 fight—The Spanish repulse—Dastardly work of guerillas—Positions on the 3d—Shafter an invalid—Gallantry of the American soldiers 247

CHAPTER XVI.

THE FATE OF CERVERA'S FLEET.

The doings of the Terror—A larger blockade—The fight at Manzanillo—The journey of Camara's squadron—An eastern squadron formed—The guard on Santiago harbor—Bombardment of July 1 and 2—Cervera's plan of escape—Positions of American ships July 3—The flight of the Spanish ships—Clearing for action—Rapid work of the fleet—The hot fire on the Brooklyn—Terrific return—All the fleet in action—The Maria Teresa on fire and beached—Fate of the Almirante Oquendo—The Vizcaya in flames—Chase of the Colon by the Brooklyn and Oregon—The Colon beached—The Gloucester sinks the torpedo-boats—Lessons from the battle—The effort to save the crews—Work of the Iowa and the Gloucester—Admiral Cervera on the Iowa—The Reina Mercedes sunk—Brave deed of American sailors 267

CHAPTER XVII.

THE SIEGE AND FALL OF SANTIAGO.

The surrender of Santiago demanded and declined—Non-combatants leave the city—Food supplied them—The wounded seek Siboney—The refugees follow—Preparations for bombardment—The American lines—General Toral's offer to capitulate "with honor"—Declined and bombardment begins—Unconditional surrender refused—A tropical rain-fall—General Miles arrives—The burning of Siboney—Shafter's offer to send the Spanish soldiers back to Spain—Appeal of General Linares—Toral accepts the terms—Basis of capitulation signed—Correspondence—The territory surrendered—Entering the harbor—Slight results of bombardment—Ceremonies of the surrender—Toral's demeanor—Stars and Stripes float over Santiago 286

CHAPTER XVIII.

EVENTS AFTER THE SURRENDER.

Return of the refugees—Good feeling between the victors and the vanquished—Castilian cunning—Cleansing the city—Contempt for the Cubans—Garcia takes offence—Shafter's explanation—Naval events—Capitulation of garrisons—A Spanish contract—The problem of the sunken ships—The Santiago prison record—Condition of the army—Treatment of the wounded—Their exposure to the weather—Rapid increase of sickness—Dr. Senn's statement—Testimony of Drs. McCook and Krauskopf—The War Department order—Roosevelt's letter—The Round Robin communication—The Porto Rico expedition—Comments of the press—Convalescent camp—Scandalous condition of the transports—State of affairs at Camp Alger—Who was responsible?—Roosevelt and Secretary Alger 307

CONTENTS.

CHAPTER XIX.

THE INVASION OF PORT RICO.

Dominating influences in the war—The expedition to Porto Rico—The Gloucester in the harbor of Guanica—The town occupied—The port of Ponce surrenders—Welcome to the American flag—The city of Ponce occupied—Enthusiastic greeting—General Miles's proclamation—A skirmish at Yauco—Business revives at Ponce—Mayor Magia's proclamation—The military road mined—Change of plan—Guayama taken—General Stone's advance—Capture of Coama and its garrison—A fight near Mayaguez—Cape San Juan—The advance on Aibonito—An artillery duel—News of peace stops hostilities—An affair at Manzanillo—The daring of the Mangrove—A shell in the San Francisco 334

CHAPTER XX.

THE SIEGE OF MANILA.

The Philippine rebels—Investment of Manila—General Augustin in doubt—Aguinaldo's proclamations—A declaration of independence—Desperate situation of the Spaniards—Dewey's demeanor—A Ladrone island taken—Attitude of the Germans—The Irene incident—American expeditions arrive—Want in the city—General Merritt arrives—An attack by the Spaniards—Their repulse—The Monterey arrives—Notice sent General Jaudenes—Surrender demanded and refused—Clearing for action—The bombardment—Attack by the troops—A show of resistance—The American flag floats over Manila—Terms of surrender—Flight of Augustin—The final event of the war 347

CHAPTER XXI.

FROM WAR TO PEACE.

Singular character of the war—Its effect on the countries concerned—Events in Spain—A revolution threatened—The financial status of the United States—The loan and tax—Great development of commerce—The Hawaiian annexation—Sailing of the Philadelphia—Admiral Miller raises the flag—Attitude of the powers—Thoughts of intervention—Great Britain's attitude—Spain's only hope—The request for peace—M. Cambon represents Spain—The terms accepted—A protocol prepared—Its text—The ceremony of signing—The news sent around the world . 361

CHAPTER XXII.

FINAL CONSIDERATIONS.

Hostile relations of natives and Spaniards—The future of Cuba—The commission and its work—The demands of the Philippine natives—Naval demonstration—Rewards to the heroes—Proposed increase of the navy—A larger army demanded—The treatment of the sick soldiers—Effect of her colonial dominion on Spain—Possible benefit from the loss of her colonies—The war but an incident in United States history—The new position of this country before the world—Its future mission 375

ILLUSTRATIONS

	PAGE
The Wreck of the Maine	*Frontispiece.*
Map of the West Indies	25
Map of the Island of Cuba	40
Cuban Leaders	60
Spanish Commanders	80
United States Naval Commanders	120
Map of Atlantic Ocean	131
President McKinley and Secretaries Long and Alger	142
Map of the Philippine Islands	150
Plan of the Battles at Manila	157
The Annihilation of the Spanish Fleet in the Harbor of Manila	164
Panoramic View of the Harbor of Santiago	192
Map of Santiago and Vicinity	195
Lieutenant Hobson on the Merrimac	202
The Marine Bombardment of Santiago	210
Soldiers Going on Transports at Tampa	232
Massachusetts Volunteers Landing at Siboney	237
Infantry Camp at Las Guasimas	242
The Country near Santiago	252
Plan of the Battle of Santiago	262
How the American Soldiers Fought at Santiago	266
Cervera's Fleet Endeavoring to Escape. American Ships Firing	274

ILLUSTRATIONS

	PAGE
Wreck of the Spanish Cruiser Almirante Oquendo, showing Effect of American Fire	280
The Oregon, just after her Chase of the Cristobal Colon	284
Wounded at Siboney. After the Rough Riders' Charge	292
United States Army Commanders	297
Soldier Life: Washing Clothes in Stream	310
Map of the Island of Porto Rico	334
At the Front, near Arroyo, Porto Rico	342
Ox-Train Disabled in the Rough Mud Road to Adjuntas, Porto Rico	344
Map of Manila and Vicinity	354

THE WAR WITH SPAIN.

CHAPTER I.

SPAIN AND HER COLONIES.

ON Sunday, October 28, 1492, Christopher Columbus, sailing southward through the placid Western seas, gazed with eyes of delight upon the shores of a rich and charming island, "the most beautiful land," he said, "that the sun ever shone upon or that the eyes of man ever beheld." Cubanacan, the land "where gold is found," the natives called it. The Spanish were liberal with names, calling it successively Juana, Fernandina, Santiago, and Ave Maria. None of these titles, however, took hold. Cuba, half the native name, prevailed, —about the only relic of the natives that survived a half-century of Spanish rule. It has been poetically designated the "Pearl of the Antilles," though it is a pearl whose lustre has been sadly dimmed.

It is not without warrant that we begin our history four centuries back, for the causes of the nineteenth-century war of which we propose to treat began with the advent of the Spaniards to this continent, and have grown with the growth of their dominion in the New World. Cruelty and oppression marked their coming to America, and to cruelty and oppression was due their final departure from its shores. The whole record of Spain on this continent, in fact, has been one of inhumanity and tyranny, with the result that her colonies have, one after another, been driven into rebellion and won independence. At the opening of the nineteenth century much more than half the Western Hemisphere was held by the strong hand of Spain. At its close the final remnants of this splendid colonial dominion were falling from her enfeebled grasp, while hardly a throb of pity beat for her in the heart of the world, for her misfortunes were felt to be the inevitable consequences of her faults. We are constrained, therefore, to place Spain in witness against herself by a brief review of her policy in America, seeking to show that the war of 1898 was the culmination of a chain of related events due to her persistently oppressive colonial policy.

It was a brief respite from suffering for the natives of Cuba that the Spaniards made their first settlement in the neighboring island named by them Hispaniola, but now known as Hayti. This island was peopled by a race of innocent and happy natives, who welcomed the white strangers as deities, though they were soon to regard them as demons. Under the cruel rule of the new-comers their happy lot suddenly ended. Their liberty was quickly exchanged for slavery, and so ruthlessly were they driven to severe and unaccustomed toil that within a generation they had all disappeared. The entire population of the island was sacrificed to the cruelty and greed of its new lords.

In the year 1502, ten years after the discovery of America, Nicolas de Ovanda became governor of Hispaniola. He was a small, fair-haired man, mild of speech and courteous in demeanor; yet the seven years of rule of this cultured Spaniard were so filled with horrors that one shudders at his very name. To invite independent chiefs to an entertainment, then seize, bind, and burn them to death, was a mild proceeding under the rule of the soft-voiced Ovanda. Such a crew of wretches surely never came together as those that desolated that fair island while under his control. The life of an Indian slave was of no value. The natives were plentiful and could easily be replaced. It was cheaper to work one to death and get another than to treat the first with humanity; and the whip of the taskmaster rapidly did its work. At times the natives rose in rebellion, but their revolts were subdued with frightful savagery. Some were burned alive at the stake, others were torn to pieces by fierce bloodhounds. The murder of a Spaniard was revenged by chopping off the hands of fifty or sixty Indians. The masters of the isle made a sport of cruelty. On one occasion thirteen natives were hanged so that their toes just touched the ground, and then were slowly pricked to death by the sword-points of the Spaniards. Other tales of almost unmentionable cruelty might be given, but it must suffice to say that, fortunately for the natives, they soon disappeared under this rigorous discipline, and the Spaniards were obliged to replace them with negro slaves, who, as they had to be paid for, were treated with more humanity.

This, and much more of the kind, we may read in the pages of Las Casas, the gentlest and most humane of his race, whose pen fairly trembles with indignation as he writes. This apostle of humanity spent his life in vain attempts to alleviate the condition of the natives of New Spain, and died after a life of earnest but largely useless appeal. It was not the cruelties shown in Hispaniola alone of which he had to speak, for the progress of Spain in the New World was everywhere marked by a trail of blood. The courage of Cortes and Pizarro was sadly vitiated with treachery and cruelty, and two flourishing empires were overthrown, hosts of their people slain, and the remainder reduced to slavery, that a handful of adventurers might rise to power upon their misery. De Soto, in our own southern territory, with his bloodhounds and chains, was as faithless and cruel; and the whole story of the conquest of New Spain is one that it is best not to dwell upon too minutely. In the history of Mexico we are told that the rapacious laws depopulated towns, and that it mattered little whether a tribe was an ally or an enemy, since the work of the scourge and the sword led to the same end. Revolt only intensified cruelty. Death in the mines or inhumanity worse than death in the fields, we are told, was the lot of the natives under the rule of Spain.

In 1511, Don Diego Columbus, son of the discoverer, determined to take possession of Cuba, Hispaniola having become nearly exhausted of laborers within less than twenty years. No opposition was made to the invasion except by a chief named Hatuey, a fugitive who had lived under the amenities of Spanish rule in Hispaniola. His opposition was useless, and he was soon in the hands of the invaders, who, instead of treating him as an honorable captive, condemned him to be burned alive as a fugitive slave. While the fagots were being heaped around him, a Franciscan friar stood by the pile and, cross in hand, besought him to accept Christianity, in order that the flames which consumed his body might waft his soul to realms of endless bliss.

"Are there any Spaniards in those happy realms?" asked the chief.

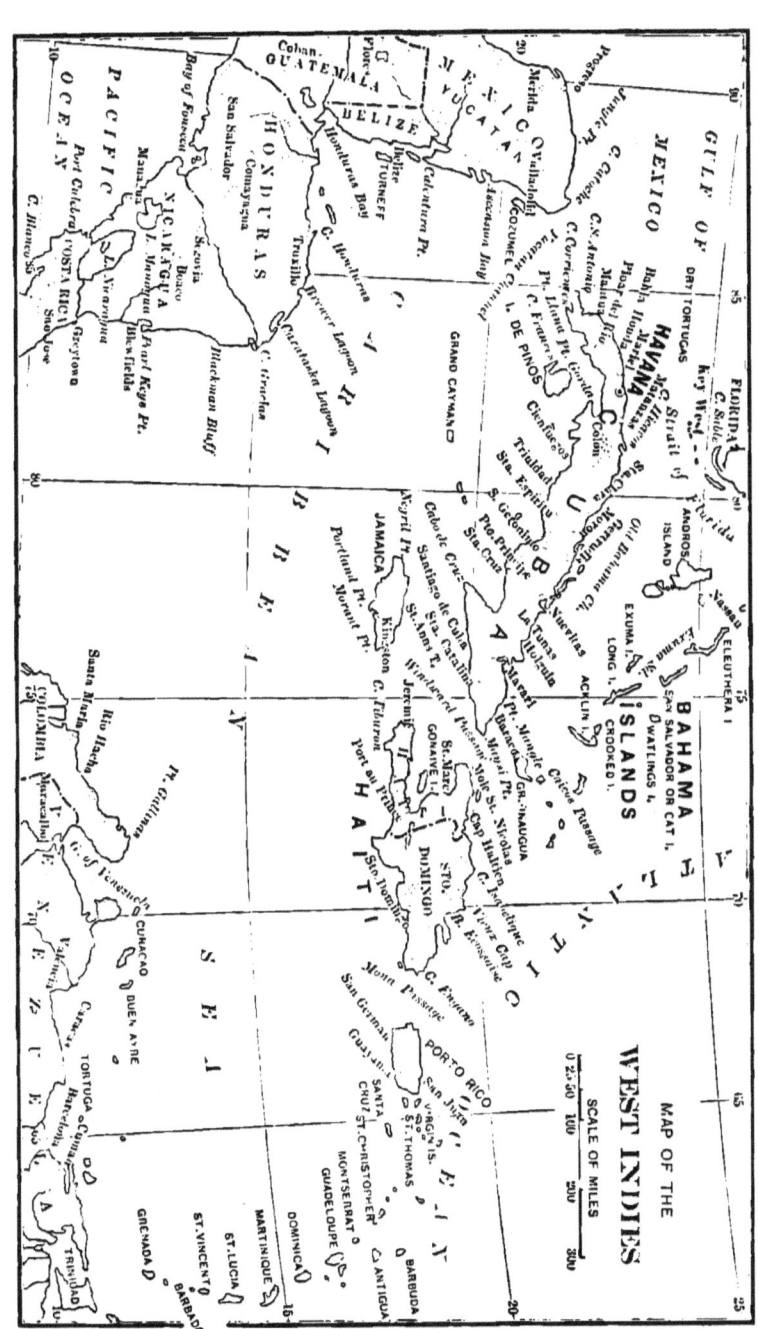

THE WAR WITH SPAIN. 25

"Yes," was the reply.

"Then I will have nothing to do with your religion. I will not go to a place where I may meet one of that accursed race."

No long period passed before all the native Cubans followed their intrepid chief. At the time of settlement they are said to have numbered more than three hundred thousand. Forty years afterwards it is doubtful if one of them survived. The wars they waged with the Spaniards ended in blood and torture. Their lot in peace was worse than in war. The sword and the lash soon did the work, and the natives vanished from the land. The methods by which a whole population can be exterminated in a generation need not be commented upon; they may be left to the imagination of the reader.

The subsequent history of Cuba, up to the early years of the nineteenth century, may be epitomized in a few words. Negro slaves succeeded the natives as laborers, and grew numerous after 1580, at which time the cultivation of tobacco and sugar-cane began. For a century and a half after 1600 almost perpetual fear brooded over the island. The French, English, and Dutch, and the pirates who infested the waters of the West Indies, invaded it at will. Even before that date Havana had been twice taken and burned by the French. In 1762 it was besieged by the English, and taken after an obstinate resistance of more than two months. Cuba was restored to Spain in the following year, and then first began to be prosperous. At its first census, in 1773, its population, black and white, numbered only 171,620. At its latest census it had a population of over 1,600,000.

The history of Cuba as a colony is at one with that of

the Spanish colonies as a whole. Much as the inhabitants of the British colonies in America objected to the methods of the home country, they enjoyed a high state of freedom as compared with the people of New Spain. The latter were destitute of even the shadow of liberty, being deprived of all privileges, civil, political, and religious. While the British colonists made their own laws, and in several colonies chose their own governors, the Spanish colonists were under the absolute dominion of governors appointed by the crown, and were as destitute of actual liberty as the slaves in their fields. Spanish officials filled every place of power or profit, monopoly and restriction were the principles of administration, and the people were kept in submission by a powerful army and navy, which they were heavily taxed to maintain. The "taxation without representation" which led to the revolt of the British colonists was but a mild measure of oppression as compared with that under which the people of Spanish America groaned.

A more detailed account of the character of this tyranny may be given, in view of the fact that it continued in Cuba and the Philippine Islands until the year 1898. It was of the most crushing character. The viceroys and captain-generals who were appointed by the king of Spain to rule over his dominions in America were invested with despotic power, their word having the force of absolute law. How they governed may be deduced from the fact that each of them went back to Spain immensely rich.

Spain looked upon her colonies as sources of revenue only, and rivalled the rapacious policy of her captain-generals and other colonial officials. Heavy duties were laid alike on imports and exports, and trade with any other nation than Spain was forbidden under the severest penalties. Any merchant captain not hailing from a Spanish port, and even Spanish merchants who sought to trade without official permission, were punished with death if they dared to enter a colonial harbor of Spain. The sole right of trading with his colonies was sold, near the end of the eighteenth century, by the king to the Philippine Company, an association of merchants trading with the West and the East alike, and privileged to fix the rates at which all goods might be sold. To trade without license from these merchants was a crime whose penalty was death. The colonists were forced to sell and buy their goods at prices fixed for them by this company, whose net profits were usually three hundred per cent.

The tyranny exercised was not restricted to trade, but covered every detail of life. Literature was under a strict censorship, and no book could be imported without the permission of the priests. In 1810, when the revolution in Chili and Peru began, these two colonies owned between them a single printing-press. Every effort was made to prevent intercourse with other countries, and even a native of Spain could not visit the colonies unless the king chose to grant him a passport. The colonists were under a similar restriction. They could not visit Europe, they could not even enter a neighboring colony, without special permission from the captain-general of their province. At home they were discriminated against in favor of Spanish-born immigrants, who occupied all the official positions and held them with the sole purpose of filling their pockets. Robbery, under the disguise of fees and charges, was the prevalent practice, from the captain-general down to the pettiest official. "*Robamos todos*" ("we are all thieves"), a functionary of high rank is said to have openly remarked; and it may well be questioned if any other colonies in the history of the world have been so shamefully misgoverned as those of Spain. This state of affairs yielded its natural result. In the year 1800 Spain was the unquestioned owner of all South America except Brazil and Guiana, and of all North America except the United States east of the Mississippi and the British possessions of the north. In 1825 her sole possessions consisted of Cuba and Porto Rico, two islands whose combined area is about equal to that of the State of Pennsylvania. Tyranny had driven the colonists into general revolt, and they had won their liberties by the sword,—such of them as remained alive after Spain had worked her will.

The effort of Spain to subdue her insurgent colonists was marked by a savage cruelty unknown in any other wars of the century. The Spanish official records admit that eighty thousand persons were executed, many of them being put to death with the refinements of cruelty. The records of the insurgents claim that fully a quarter of a million were thus dealt with, in addition to the multitude slaughtered in cold blood by the Spanish soldiers, who destroyed every city and town the people of which were suspected of sympathy with the rebels. We have a striking example of the Spanish method of suppressing insurrection in an official despatch of General Morillo, in which he refers to his dealings with the inhabitants of the city of Santa Fé de Bogota.

"Every person of either sex," he writes, "who was capable of reading or writing was put to death. By thus cutting off all who are in any way educated I hope effectually to check the spirit of the revolution."

THE WAR WITH SPAIN.   29

Fortunately for the people of this city, the Spanish restrictions on education and literature had prevented the arts of reading and writing from being widely disseminated. We are further told that all who had held official positions in the local administration, who were related to insurgents, or were distinguished for their talents and attainments, were thrown into prison, from which they were taken only to be hanged or shot,—husbands being thus put to death in the presence of their wives, and children in the presence of their parents. All this might be difficult to believe but for the fact that we have had similar examples in our own day in General Weyler's methods of suppressing insurrection. The spirit that finds enjoyment in the bull-fight seems to have infected the whole nature of the Spanish race.

The loss of all her colonies upon the mainland might have taught Spain that her colonial policy was a false one. Great Britain learned this lesson well, but Spain seemed past profiting by experience, and maintained in her few remaining possessions the mediæval methods that had cost her a continent. In 1808 Cuba gained the title of "The Ever-faithful Isle," in consequence of the members of its provincial council taking an oath to preserve the island for their sovereign, who had been deposed by Napoleon. This sovereign rewarded them in the true Spanish manner, by making the powers of the captain-general more autocratic, if possible, than before, giving him an authority equal to that of the Sultan of Turkey or the Russian Czar.

In 1825, the Spanish king issued a decree which put Cuba practically under martial law. Incensed by the loss of all his dominions upon the mainland, and even of Hispaniola, the earliest possession of Spain in the New

World, he took a step for the prevention of rebellion in the "Ever-faithful Isle" that seemed studiously designed to drive the colonists into revolt. We may quote from this astonishing decree:

"His Majesty, the King, our Lord, desiring to obviate the inconveniences that might, in extraordinary cases, result from a division of command, and from the interferences and prerogatives of the respective officers, for the important end of preserving in that precious island his legitimate sovereign authority and the public tranquillity through proper means, has resolved, in accordance with the opinion of his council of ministers, to give to your Excellency the fullest authority, bestowing on you all the powers which by the royal ordinances are granted to the governors of besieged cities.

"In consequence of this, His Majesty gives to your Excellency the most ample and unbounded power, not only to send away from the island any persons in office, whatever their occupation, rank, class, or condition, whose continuance therein your Excellency may deem injurious, or whose conduct, public or private, may alarm you, replacing them with persons faithful to His Majesty and deserving of all the confidence of your Excellency; but also to suspend the execution of any order whatsoever, or any general provision made concerning any branch of the administration, as your Excellency may think most suitable to the royal service."

This is, with few alleviations, the supreme law in Cuba to-day, whose governor has the absolute power of the commander of a besieged city. We need hardly ask what effect such a decree would have had upon the people of any Anglo-Saxon colony. In Cuba its result has been to produce a bitter spirit of revolt and an incurable hatred of Spanish rule. One writer tells us that "there is no hatred in the world to be compared to that of the Cuban for Spain and everything Spanish." The Creole detests the Spaniard, whom he looks upon as an alien thief, coming to rob him of the revenues of his island and to oppress and annoy him by petty and illegal exactions for which he has no redress. The Spaniard, on the other hand, treats the Creole with disdain, taunts him with cowardice and thriftlessness, and looks upon him as a degenerate being, born but to fill the coffers of Spain and swell with gold the purses of her officials. Feelings and acts like these are the seeds of rebellion, and we cannot be surprised that Cuba has made successive efforts to gain her liberty.

As early as 1823 an insurrection was attempted by a secret political society known as the "Soles de Bolivar." But the plot was discovered, and its leaders—such of them as did not escape by flight—were taught how Spain deals with rebels. In 1826, a plan to invade Cuba was laid by Cuban refugees in Mexico and Colombia, Simon Bolivar, the South American liberator, being asked to lead it; but, for reasons to be given in the next chapter, nothing came of it. In 1827–29, a secret society known as the "Black Eagle" was organized by the refugees in Mexico, who sought to gain recruits in the United States. This also failed, and its supporters in Cuba fell into the tender hands of Spain.

The next attempt at insurrection took place in 1844. This was a movement of the slaves on the sugar plantations around Matanzas, or rather the suspicion of a movement, for nothing was known about it except such evidence as could be obtained from witnesses under torture. It is well known what evidence of this kind is worth, yet it led to the conviction of more than thirteen hundred people, of whom seventy-eight were shot and the rest otherwise punished. Only a few of these were slaves.

A few years afterwards the celebrated Lopez invasion took place. Narciso Lopez was a Venezuelan by birth who had risen to a high rank in the Spanish army and had lived long in Cuba, for whose freedom he gained an ardent desire. He organized an insurrection in the island, but was obliged to flee for his life. Seeking New York, he made that city a centre for sympathetic appeals, and in 1849 sought to return with a small party to Cuba. He was prevented by the United States authorities, but in the following year he succeeded in reaching the island with a force of six hundred volunteers. He landed at Cardenas, but no aid and support came to him from the Cubans, and he was driven back to his ship, which a Spanish man-of-war chased to Key West.

In 1851, Lopez started again, now with four hundred and fifty men, sailing in the steamer Pampero from New Orleans. He landed at Playitas, thirty miles from Havana. It was his hope to find support from Cuban rebels, some of whom had taken to the field, but he quickly found himself confronted by a superior force of Spanish troops. With the main body of invaders Lopez sought the interior, leaving his second in command, a Kentuckian named Crittenden, to bring up the supplies with the rear-guard. Both parties were in a short time vigorously attacked. Crittenden's party, reduced by the fire of the foe to fifty men, were captured and shot. Lopez and his followers succeeded in reaching the interior, where, no longer able to fight, they wandered miserably in the thick woods without food or shelter, suffering severely from the pursuit of the foe and finding no Cuban aid. One by one the fugitives fell into Spanish hands, Lopez among the last. He was executed, but his American followers, after a term of imprisonment, were set free.

A second invasion was planned in 1854, General Quitman, of Mississippi, being its leader. This was organized in connection with a revolutionary movement in Cuba, but, like all previous movements of the kind, it came to grief. The leaders in the island were betrayed into the hands of their enemies, seized, and incontinently put to death, and the would-be invaders deemed it wise to stay at home. And thus affairs went on until 1868, when the long-repressed rebellious sentiment in the island finally broke out in open insurrection.

For the inciting cause of this revolt we must go to Spain. For years that country had presented a dismal picture of faction and intrigue, while its queen, Isabella II., had won the abhorrence of the people by the unblushing dissoluteness of her life. A strong party of reform grew under these conditions, and at length, not able to put an end to the disorders by quiet means, overturned the government by a successful revolt. The queen, on September 30, 1868, fled to France, from which she was never to return to the throne, and several years passed before a settled government was established in the Spanish realm. This state of affairs offered an opportunity to the revolutionists in Cuba of which they were quick to take advantage. On October 10, ten days after the flight of the queen, they issued a declaration of independence, and took to the field prepared to fight for their freedom.

Before speaking of the incidents of the war that followed, a fuller review of the influences leading to it seems in place. These were of two kinds,—financial and political. Cuba had been, under the despotic decree of 1825, for nearly half a century in a state of siege. Spain in Cuba was like an army encamped in the midst of a conquered people. All the soldiers were Spanish except the members of the body known as Cuban Volunteers, the National Guard of the island, and these were carefully recruited from Spanish sympathizers. The people of Cuba became divided into two parties,—the *Insulares* and the *Peninsulares*,—the Islanders and the Spaniards, or those in sympathy with them. Out of the latter grew the Volunteers, nearly all of them active politicians and of great power and influence in the affairs of the island. Even the captain-general stood in some awe of this powerful body; and in 1870 the Volunteers went so far as to arrest and send back to Spain Captain-General Dulce, of whose actions they did not approve.

As for the people of Cuba, they were completely disfranchised. After 1825 no legislative assembly, either provincial or municipal, existed in the island. At an earlier date the officials of the cities held some control over taxes and expenditures, but these powers were now all lost. No vestige remained of a popular assembly, trial by jury, independent tribunals, the right to vote, or the right to bear arms; in fact, no right of any kind was left; the will or the whim of the captain-general was the absolute law. And the Cubans were not alone disfranchised; they were rarely permitted to hold any office of honor, trust, or emolument in the island. Some Cubans did hold office, but they gained their positions through utter servility to the ruling powers.

This preference given to Spaniards over Cubans was a bitter pill for the natives of the island to swallow. All the power was wielded by the people of one country over those of another, the sole interest of the ruling class being that of the highwayman in his victim. The officials went to Cuba with the one purpose of filling their purses and returning to Spain to enjoy their gains. Some small offices in remote districts might be filled by natives of the island, but those of higher emolument were wanted for the sons of Spain. It was in this way that the statesman or politician at the head of affairs in the home government paid his political debts. Spain did not provide offices enough for these worthies, and Cuba was filled with them. Doubtless it was deemed presumptuous on the part of the natives to expect positions which cabinet officers at home needed for their useful friends.

The financial causes of the insurrection were immediately connected with the political. The office-holders sought only to retrieve their broken fortunes, and in this they usually succeeded—by fair means or foul. They had given important services to the leaders in Spain, and could demand large salaries. The captain-general was paid $50,000 a year, double the salary, at that time, of the President of the United States. The governor of each province had $12,000, twice the sum paid to the prime minister of Spain. The archbishops of Havana and Santiago each received an annual stipend of $18,000. And so downward in the same extravagant ratio ranged the salaries.

But the officials were not so easily satisfied. The "perquisites" often more than doubled the salaries. Wholesale robbery, in the form of illegal fees and charges, everywhere prevailed. All this was no secret, but no captain-general ever sought to prevent it. He was either the leader of the robbers himself or was powerless to overcome the deeply intrenched system. These official brigands went to Cuba for booty, and were not to be balked in their design.

It was openly known that at least forty per cent. were added to the custom-house charges at Havana by illegal fees. The officials at Santiago were less scrupulous; they exacted fully seventy per cent. These officials were changed with discouraging frequency. At every ministerial crisis in Spain—which came at times semi-annually—a new batch of hungry political servitors was sent to make their fortunes in Cuba by rapacity and corruption of every kind. The custom-house was but one of their fields of industry. Fees were everywhere to be picked up. We may instance one of the methods employed. A planter might make his return for the income-tax at ten thousand dollars. The tax-collector would blandly give him to understand that this was too low a rating, and that he proposed to assess him at fifteen thousand dollars. The planter, afraid to protest too strongly against this arbitrary assessment, might suggest a compromise at twelve thousand five hundred dollars. The result of the operation would be a rating on the books at ten thousand dollars and a fee for the astute collector of the tax on the extra two thousand five hundred dollars. Possibly the assessment of fifteen thousand dollars might not have been too much. Under such a system the government is sure to be one of the chief sufferers, for its interest is the last thing considered.

Spain was as rapacious as her officials. Cuba had long served her as a money-bag. In the effort to suppress the revolutions on the mainland, the "ever-faithful isle" has been obliged to supply a lion's share of the funds. The tariff, alike on imports and exports, was kept high enough to yield the largest revenue of which the island was capable, if not increased to an extent that threatened to put an end to commerce altogether. Spain could no longer keep the trade of Cuba for her own merchants and manufacturers by the old method of putting to death any foreign navigator who dared to enter a port of her colonies, but she sought to achieve the same result by a system of differential duties which discriminated severely against foreign goods.

As for the revenue produced, we have seen where much of it went. The sovereign of Spain would have preferred to keep a large share of it for himself, but he was powerless in the hands of the officials, with their strong political "pull," and had to content himself with what they left unappropriated. Yet, whatever these harpies might absorb, it was felt necessary that the crown should have a fairly liberal share, and this could best be secured by more sharply tightening the screws on the island. In 1857 the revenue yielded by Cuba was $17,960,000. By 1867 it had been largely forced up, and it was proposed to increase it to over $40,000,000. This was more than the islanders could possibly pay, and only a portion of it was collected. Yet every effort was made to squeeze the last drop of life-blood from the suffering colony.

Some further statistics may be of service. The people of Cuba were forced to pay the interest on the public debt of Spain at the rate of $6.39 per capita, while the rate paid by the home people was only $3.23. The cost of living was so increased by the high duties that, while four hundred pounds of bread per capita were annually consumed in Spain, fifty-four pounds were all that a

Cuban could afford to buy. A letter from Europe, even if prepaid, had to pay twenty-five cents at the Cuban post-office, and if delivered, twelve and a half cents more were exacted.

One necessary result of the methods of administration pursued was that the home interests of the island had to be sadly neglected. The cities were overloaded with debt and unable to meet the most essential expenses. The streets remained uncleaned, garbage was not collected, a dozen important functions were left undone. No money could be diverted to pay teachers, and the schools were closed. Havana had the only asylum for the insane on the island, and elsewhere this class of unfortunates had to be kept in the cells of the common jails. In every way the revenues of Cuba were employed for the benefit of Spain and her needy sons, and the interests of the islanders were left out of the account.

It was this state of affairs in Cuba which gave rise to the revolution of 1868. A revolt had been secretly planned months before the revolution in Spain, but the outbreak in that country and the flight of the queen precipitated it. On October 10, 1868, Carlos M. de Cespedes, a lawyer of Bayamo, issued a declaration of independence from Spain, and took to the field at the head of an army amounting to one hundred and twenty-eight half-armed men. But he had the country at his back. His appeal to the people that "we are in danger of losing our property, our lives, and our honor under further Spanish dominion" struck home to the Cuban heart, and at the end of a few weeks Cespedes headed a force of fifteen thousand men, ill supplied with arms and equipments, it is true, but stout of heart and earnest in purpose. A constitution was drawn up and promulgated on April 10, 1869. This provided for a republican government and the immediate abolition of slavery. A legislature was chosen, which met and elected Cespedes president.

The war that followed was one that cannot be dealt with in the ordinary manner. We can give no picturesque description of marches, battles, and campaigns. It was a war of irregulars, not of regulars; of bush fighting, not of contests in the open field; of guerrilla skirmishes, not of set battles. "The pomp and circumstance of glorious war" were sadly wanting, and forest ambushes, sudden attacks and retreats, and sharp affrays that led to nothing formed the staple of the affair. The Cubans were bold and daring, and for the first two years proved successful in nearly every engagement. But they had no expectation, with their lack of arms and dearth of supplies, of triumphing over Spain, whose power of furnishing fresh troops, armed with the best modern weapons, gave her the ascendency in the open country and kept the patriots confined to the bush. Their one hope was to wear out their enemy, and make the war so costly for Spain that sheer lack of means would in the end force her to retire from the contest in despair.

That we may better understand the character of this war, something must be said of the country in which it was fought. Despite the fact that Cuba has been settled for nearly four centuries, two-thirds of it remain uncultivated, and half its area is covered with forest and thicket. The lowlands of the coast in the wet season are turned into swamps of tenacious black mud, impassable to the traveller. Underbrush everywhere fills the forest, so thick and dense that it can be traversed only with the aid of the machete. High bushes and thick grasses cover much of the dry plains, forming a close jungle that also calls for the sharp edge of the machete, that tool of the Cuban farmer and weapon of the Cuban warrior.

The machete is a formidable instrument in the hands of the countrymen of Cuba. Its handle, usually of horn, fits upon a perfectly straight blade from twenty-four to thirty inches long, as heavy as a cleaver, and with an edge kept almost at razor sharpness. The corn-scythe of the American farmer is not unlike it, but the machete is heavier, and its outer instead of its inner edge is the cutting one. To the Cubans skilled in its use as an implement to hew a way through the jungle and undergrowth it is a weapon that takes the place of the sword in war, and with which they can decapitate an enemy as easily as they can shear through a sapling.

Through the centre of the island passes a mountain range, broken at intervals, but extending from end to end, and in the east turning and following the southern coast past Santiago de Cuba to Cape Cruz. The range is highest in the eastern section, where it presents rugged summits over six thousand five hundred feet in height, though its average elevation is not over two thousand two hundred feet. The wooded heights of the mountains, the recesses of the densely-grown forests, and the depths of the grassy jungle have furnished secure lurking-places for the Cuban insurrectionists in all their outbreaks, to which they could retire at will and from which they could break at unexpected points upon the foe. To retire to the "long grass," to use a common Cuban phrase, was to gain safety from pursuit, and an ambushed host might lie unseen and unheard in these

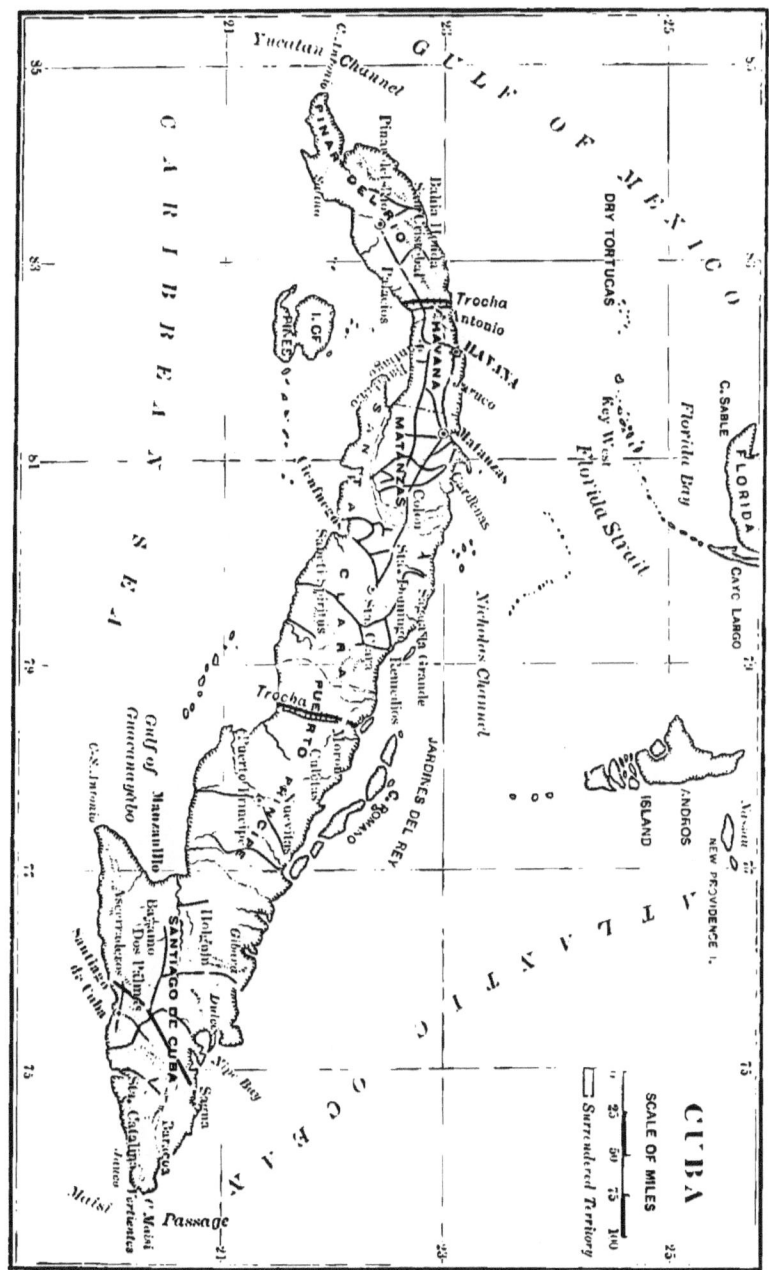

secure retreats while an army passed by not many feet away. In short, Cuba is a paradise for the bush-fighter, and all the contests in that island have taken the form of guerrilla warfare, with its unpremeditated affrays and lack of definite results.

The war with which we are concerned took, in part, the form of a hunt for the insurgents, in which the Spanish soldiers were, perhaps, none too eager to find them, since they usually learned that they had "caught a Tartar." In this exercise the Cuban Volunteers took little part. They employed themselves in police and garrison duties, leaving the work in the field to the Spanish soldiers, of whom during the ten years of war not less than one hundred and fifty thousand were sent to the island. Of these more than one-half met their death, largely through disease.

While Cuba is very ill adapted by nature to regular warfare, it was rendered more so by the inefficiency of the military authorities. The roads are abominable; even those near Havana itself being mere tracks with deep ruts and holes. For half the year, during the hot and rainy season, campaigning was pursued under frightful difficulties, and from May to November warlike operations in great part ceased. At the opening of a campaign the custom was to convey a force by land or sea to a point near which the insurgents were supposed to lurk; then, drawing up the force in narrow columns, to cut a pathway into the forest. If the insurgents were met, a few shots were apt to end the affray,—the troops finding it judicious to retire or the rebels seeking some new retreat.

Often the enemy could not be found at all, and the troops wandered for days or weeks in vain search for a rebel in arms. Their spies served them poorly, while the sympathy of the people kept the insurgents well advised of every movement of the troops. As for starving out the rebels, that was out of the question. The wild fruits of the earth, the yams, sweet potatoes, bananas, and other productions which they could readily cultivate in forest clearings, kept them well supplied. The soil of Cuba is so prolific that a crop planted to-day may yield food in plenty within two months, while the country-people were ever ready to supply their friends in the field.

The only way to overcome the insurgents would have been to intersect their haunts with a net-work of roads, laying bare their lurking-places, and to pursue them with remorseless energy from lair to lair. But this was not the Spanish idea of campaigning; it was certainly not that of the officers, to whom the allurements of the towns were too enticing to be long deserted; while the leaders doubtless found an inducement to prolong the war in their share of the Cuban spoils.

The Spanish official bulletins during this war were curious affairs. One officer with his battalions had "come up with an insurgent band far away in some spot above Guantanamo, in the district of Santiago de Cuba. To attack the rebels and to completely rout them was for the heroic Spanish troops one and the same thing. They killed many of them, wounded many more, and took fourteen horses and one rifle." Again, an affray yielded the Spaniards "six prisoners and a mule." In another affair the valiant troops captured two prisoners and three fire-arms, while forty women and children were taken. This is neither magnificent nor is it war. Nor were the outrages which were perpetrated on the non-combatants war in any modern sense of the word.

It cannot be said that the insurgents were any more daring than the troops. Only once in four years of war did they make an open attack. Then they swooped down suddenly upon Holguin, an inland town of Santiago de Cuba. But here they contented themselves with plundering the inhabitants, and withdrew without waiting for the troops.

The government adopted methods similar to those with which we have recently become very familiar. The *trocha*, of which so much has been said of late years, was tried,—a military cordon being drawn across the island from side to side with the hope of hemming in the insurrection. It proved as useless then as it has done since. *Reconcentration*, General Weyler's later system of warfare, was also attempted,—the whole population of one large district being huddled together under guard in the little town of St. Espiritu. The result was, as it has been since: a dozen diseases assailed the poor captives, and they as well as their guards died in multitudes. Thus the population was murdered, the country was devastated, the cattle were slaughtered, the crops and dwellings were burned, everything was done but to put down the rebellion, which held its own despite these measures of repression.

Outrages were common. The rule on both sides was to kill their prisoners without discrimination. Powder and shot could not be wasted for such purposes; the machete did the work,—unless torture was preferred. Women fared as badly as men; even children were not spared: a carnival of cruelty and bloodshed ravaged the island. In March, 1869, a party of young men, who had foolishly displayed the Cuban flag and sung patriotic songs at a theatre and a café in Havana, were set upon by the Volunteers, who poured volleys into both places, heedless of whom they might kill. In 1871 an affair took place which attracted wide attention. The graves of some soldiers at the cemetery had been defaced, and a number of students were seized as the criminals, dragged before a lynch-law tribunal of Volunteers, and ordered to be shot. Fifteen thousand Volunteers turned out and executed the eight boys in defiance of the captain-general. Indignation at this outrage spread through the world; even the Spanish Cortes censured it; but no one was punished. The Volunteers were too powerful to be called to account. There were eighty thousand of them in Cuba.

The insurrection continued active until 1871, in which year a large number of the insurgents in Central Cuba surrendered on condition that their lives should be spared. General Agramonte, their leader, refused to yield, and kept up the war for two years more, when he was killed. President Cespedes was deposed in 1873, and was soon after killed by the Spaniards. He was succeeded by Salvador Cisneros (formerly the Marquis de Santa Lucia), who was elected president again in the revolt of 1895. The war dragged on until 1878. By that time both parties were thoroughly worn out, and neither saw any hope of success. General Martinez de Campos, commander of the Spanish forces, finding hostilities unavailing, now resorted to negotiation. Terms of peace were offered and accepted, and the war came to an end in February, 1878. The treaty is known as that of El Zanjon, from the place near which it was concluded.

The terms of this treaty were the following: Full pardon was granted to all who had been engaged in the war, and freedom to the slaves who had taken part in it.

Every one who wished was at liberty to leave the island, the Spanish government agreeing to furnish him with the means. Under this clause, Maximo Gomez, one of the Cuban leaders, sought a new home in San Domingo, there to bide his time until 1895. Many others left their native land, not caring to remain within Spanish reach. The island of Cuba was to be granted the same privileges as were enjoyed by the island of Porto Rico, —namely, the right of representation in the Spanish Cortes.

Radical reforms in the administration of Cuba were promised and expected; the island was divided into its present provinces; provisional assemblies were instituted, and, as has been said, representation in the Cortes was granted. But the captain-general remained an irresponsible despot, and all these so-called reforms were manipulated in the interest of the Spanish party. Everything soon fell back into its old state. The debt continued to grow, taxation was as heavy as ever, the officials were as corrupt, the salaries and perquisites as high. The debt of Cuba began in 1864 with an issue of $3,000,000. In 1891 it had increased to $175,000,000. Of this great sum hardly a dollar had been spent on the island. The peculations continued. In 1895 it was asserted by a Spanish newspaper that the custom-house frauds in Cuba since 1878 had amounted to $100,000,000.

There has been only one substantial measure of reform in Cuba within the century. A bill was passed in 1870 providing for the gradual abolition of slavery. The work of abolition was completed in 1886 by an act which finally put an end to this long-established institution. This reform was hardly a free-will offering, but a necessary result of the conditions arising from the war; and though the blacks were set free, the whites were as stringently controlled as ever. The decree of 1825, which likened Cuba to a besieged city, was revoked about 1870; but the captain-general (or the governor-general, as he was now entitled) retained all his old power, and could play the autocrat as much as ever. In 1895 another measure of reform was passed, a council of administration being established, half chosen by the crown, half elected by the provinces. But as the governor was given the power to suspend any member likely to make trouble, or to suspend the whole council if he chose, this was not likely to serve a very useful purpose, except as a handy tool of tyranny.

If it had possessed any element of value, it came too late. The Cubans, incensed at the broken promises of Spain and seeing no hope of redress under Spanish rule, again declared for liberty and once more raised the standard of revolt.

CHAPTER II.

RELATIONS OF THE UNITED STATES TO CUBA.

CUBA, as was long ago said by an American statesman, is by nature an outpost of the United States, and it has long been held that "manifest destiny" demands its annexation to this country. Seventy-five years ago Jefferson said that "the addition of Cuba to our confederacy is exactly what is wanted to bound our power as a nation to the point of its utmost interest," and this sentiment has been widely entertained. The relations of amity between the United States and Spain have frequently been strained through the aggressive acts of Spanish colonial agents. As long ago as the beginning of the nineteenth century the efforts of the authorities at New Orleans to close the Mississippi to American commerce almost precipitated war. At a later date border troubles with Florida caused a suspension of diplomatic relations with Spain, lasting from 1808 to 1815. In the end, West Florida was taken by force, the uncivilized methods of Spanish colonial administration having rendered the situation intolerable. In 1819, Florida was obtained by purchase, and the long-existing border difficulties were brought to an end. Meanwhile, in 1810, the revolution in Spanish America had begun. Injury was done by Spain to the commerce of the United States during the war, but redress was stoutly resisted, and only granted after seven years' negotiations. Payment of the indemnity was made in the usual dilatory fashion of Spain.

In July, 1818, Richard Rush, United States minister to England, was told by Lord Castlereagh that Spain had requested that country to mediate between her and her rebellious colonies, with the co-operation of the Holy Alliance,—a compact of the despotic powers of Europe formed after the fall of Napoleon, though it was never made manifest in what the holiness of this alliance consisted. Rush said in reply that the United States would take no part in any intervention for peace "if its basis were not the independence of the colonies."

This plain declaration ended the matter until 1823, in which year Rush found reason to believe that the Holy Alliance was laying plans to aid Spain in her struggle with her colonies. England had now shifted in the opposite direction, refused to join the alliance in these plans, and suggested opposition on the part of the United States. This was the state of affairs which led to the celebrated Monroe Doctrine, in which this country first clearly formulated the policy in relation to European interference in America which it has since vigorously maintained.

Monroe began by asking Jefferson for his opinion as to what was proper in the crisis. The venerable author of the Declaration of Independence replied briefly but forcibly, saying that it should be a leading principle of the United States "never to suffer Europe to interfere with cisatlantic affairs." Monroe placed this opinion before his cabinet, by which body it was fully indorsed. This it was that led to the doctrine which later events have made famous. It will suffice here to quote one of its most significant passages:

THE WAR WITH SPAIN. 49

"We declare that we should consider any attempt [of the allied powers] to extend their system to any portion of our hemisphere as dangerous to our peace and safety."

This general declaration of principles was followed by statements of American policy directly relating to Cuba. The close of the struggle for independence in Spanish America left Spain devoid of any colonies in this part of the world except Cuba and Porto Rico. Avaricious eyes were being turned upon these. There was reason to distrust France and England, while Mexico and Colombia made open preparations for invasion, as mentioned in the preceding chapter. It was time for the United States to act.

There was no hesitation or loss of time in doing so. The opinion was everywhere held in this country that the interests of the United States demanded the maintenance of the *status quo* in Cuba. This was officially indicated in 1825 in the decided declaration that the United States could not see with equanimity the island pass into the possession of any European power whatever. Henry Clay, secretary of state, put this declaration into plainer language still, sending a despatch to our minister to Russia in which it was distinctly stated that the United States would not "allow and permit" Cuba to pass into the hands of any foreign power. This threatening ultimatum put an end to all projects of interference on the part of England, France, or the Holy Alliance.

American powers remained to be warned off. In 1821, a congress had been suggested for the purpose of forming a close union between the Spanish states of Central and South America. This, known as the Panama Congress, met in 1825. The freeing of the islands of Cuba and Porto Rico from Spain was openly placed upon the platform of the congress, in consequence of which Mexico and Colombia began, as has been stated, to organize an expedition for the invasion of Cuba. This the United States was not willing to permit. The horrors of the San Domingo massacre were fresh in memory, and those countries were informed, in polite phrase, that if an invasion should lead to a race war between blacks and whites, the United States would feel obliged to interfere. They were, therefore, requested to delay the expedition that they were fitting out.

In Congress it was declared by Senator Hayne that the United States would not permit the Spanish American states to "take or to revolutionize" Cuba. Other members suggested that threats should be tried if advice or remonstrance failed. No overt action was needed, however. Diplomacy ended the difficulty. Mexico and Colombia deemed it wise to withdraw from their projected enterprise.

The United States had thus virtually guaranteed to defend the title of Spain to Cuba against any other power in Europe or America. The guarantee as regarded American states was made openly in 1830, when Martin Van Buren, secretary of state under Jackson, declared that Mexico would not be allowed to acquire Cuba. As for European powers, a similar declaration was made by every secretary of state from Clay to Webster. The latter, under date of October 22, 1851, wrote to the Spanish Minister Sartiges as follows: "The government of France and those of other European countries were long since officially apprised by this government that the United States could not see without concern that island transferred by Spain to any other European state."

In 1852, a proposition was made to the United States, on the part of France and Great Britain, to the effect that each of those three parties should bind itself not to acquire Cuba, nor suffer any other power to do so. The United States declined to enter into any such convention, and Secretary Everett, in a despatch to Minister Crampton, decisively laid down the position of this country as regarded Cuba. His statement contained three clauses: First, that the United States would permit no foreign interference, European or American, in the island of Cuba; second, that it would join in no agreement with European powers respecting the island; third, that it would not bind itself not to take the island if this should become necessary through its condition under Spanish rule.

"But," he continued, "the President would consider its acquisition by force, except in a just war with Spain (should an event so gravely to be deprecated ever take place), as a disgrace to the civilization of the age."

This was certainly plain enough. Nearly half a century ago the United States had definitely formulated its position, and Spain had accepted it as a guarantee to her title in Cuba,—viz., that the destiny of the island must be determined by the United States, and could be left to no foreign power whatever. This country had also virtually pledged itself not to interfere, unless the character of Spanish rule in the island or other sufficient cause should lead to a just war with Spain.

Previous to this declaration, however, a strong feeling in favor of the acquisition of Cuba had arisen in the Southern States, whose leaders were moved by a desire to gain more slave territory. For the same reason this movement met with opposition in the North. In 1848, James Buchanan, secretary of state under President Polk, authorized in the name of the President an offer to Spain of $100,000,000 for the purchase of Cuba. This offer was indignantly refused by Spain, and the negotiation ended almost as quickly as it had begun. Soon afterwards the Lopez invasion took place. It found sympathizers and adherents in the South, many Americans joining the expedition. The execution of Crittenden's fifty men led to such a show of indignation that when the remainder of the party was captured the military authorities in Cuba found it convenient to confine their executions to Lopez and his Cubans, the Americans being released after a term of severe imprisonment.

Another event that aroused much excitement in this country took place in 1850. The Black Warrior, a steamer plying between New York and Mobile, which was in the habit of stopping at Havana to land and receive passengers and mail, but not to take on or discharge freight, was seized on a charge of violating the customs regulations She had on board nine hundred and sixty bales of cotton, and in strict accordance with the stringent revenue laws at that port should have shown a manifest of her cargo. But this would have been a mere form, as none of it was moved; and therefore, to save time and trouble, she was entered and cleared as "in ballast." This had taken place no less than thirty-six times before, the revenue officers knowing the facts and consenting, and it was in accordance with a written general order of the Cuban authorities.

Yet on the occasion in question the vessel was seized for alleged violation of law, its cargo confiscated and taken on shore, and a fine of twice its value laid against the vessel. Captain Bullock refused to pay any fine, protested against the whole proceeding, and when the customs authorities forcibly opened the hatches, he hauled down his colors, took them with him, and left the vessel in the hands of the authorities as a Spanish prize. He and his crew and passengers made their way home by other vessels to the United States.

This violent and uncalled-for action raised a storm in the United States. The feeling was strongly warlike; but the difficulty was settled by negotiation, Spain agreeing to pay an indemnity of $300,000, and doing so after five years' delay. The feeling of resentment was added to by the action of England and France after the failure of the Lopez invasion. They sent orders to their admirals in the West Indies to prevent by force any new attempt of filibusters to land on the island. Mr. Crittenden, then acting secretary of state, emphatically intimated that any attempt by these countries to exercise police powers in American waters might lead to serious complications. The orders to the admirals were withdrawn.

The Black Warrior affair and the attitude of the European powers named had their natural effect in creating a strong annexation sentiment in this country, which was greatly strengthened by the desire then entertained in the South to extend the area of slavery. It gave rise to a second attempt to take the island by force, —the General Quitman enterprise of 1854, already referred to. A secret society devoted to the same purpose, the "Order of the Lone Star," was organized in New Orleans, its membership early in 1853 being twenty-eight thousand.

But the chief method depended upon to gain the island was that of purchase, and in this two Presidents from the North, Pierce and Buchanan, took a leading part. President Pierce proposed the annexation of Cuba by purchase early in his term. The most decided move in this direction, however, was the celebrated Ostend Conference. Under the inspiration of the President's desire, three leading American statesmen, Mr. Buchanan, Mr. Mason, and Mr. Soulé, United States ministers respectively to England, France, and Spain, met at Ostend, the result of their deliberations being the Ostend Manifesto, in which the purchase of Cuba for $120,000,000 was strongly recommended, with the further declaration that in no event should the island be permitted to become subject to any other European power than Spain.

Buchanan, on reaching the Presidency, continued to advocate the acquisition of Cuba, asking for an appropriation for its purchase in his first message, and continuing to do so in later messages. "It is required," he said in 1860, "by manifest destiny that the United States should possess Cuba, not by violence, but by purchase at a fair price." If the offer was not accepted, he did not see how a collision could be avoided. But neither Pierce, Buchanan, nor the Ostend *confrères* could induce Congress to act, and no offer was made to Spain. After 1860, more vital interests at home put an end to the scheme until 1868, when the subject of Cuban annexation was discussed in the American Senate, but no action was taken.

The insurrection of 1868–78 again brought the subject of Cuban annexation into prominence. The shooting of the students at Havana in 1871 sent a thrill of indignation throughout the United States, which was succeeded by a decidedly warlike feeling in 1873 in consequence of the celebrated Virginius affair. The Virginius had been a blockade-runner during the Civil War. She was captured and sold at New York to John F. Patterson, an American citizen. From 1870 to 1873 this vessel was engaged in West Indian waters, under control of a Cuban junta, in whose interest she occasionally visited the coast of Cuba. On October 31, 1873, while hovering off the Cuban coast with a cargo of arms for the insurgents, she was chased and captured by the Spanish cruiser Tornado, and brought the next day into the harbor of Santiago de Cuba. There were one hundred and fifty-five persons on board, mainly with Spanish names, though a considerable number of them had American names.

The Virginius carried the flag of the United States, and was chartered and cleared as an American vessel. She had, therefore, the right to protection as such until her claim to show these colors had been disproved. Mr. Schmitt, the American vice-consul at Santiago, made a prompt assertion of this right, and also demanded proper treatment for any American citizens on board; but the provincial governor treated him with great lack of courtesy, and declared that the prisoners were pirates, and should be dealt with as such. He even refused to the consul the use of the cable to Kingston, Jamaica.

A court-martial to try the prisoners was hastily summoned. They were as hastily condemned, and a series of shootings began, fifty-three of them having been tried and executed by the morning of the 8th of November. On that morning the British war-ship Niobe, which had been summoned in haste from Kingston by the British consul, entered the harbor of Santiago, and, so it is said, Captain Lorraine threatened to bombard the town unless the executions were stopped at once. There was no more shooting.

The tone assumed by the governor of Santiago was copied by the Spanish minister of state when General Sickles, United States minister to Spain, entered his protest against these sanguinary proceedings. The minister was so defiant that General Sickles demanded his passports, whereupon Señor Carvajal changed his tone, and agreed to give up the vessel and the surviving prisoners, salute the American flag, and punish the perpetrators of the massacre. This ended the affair. The Virginius had no right to fly the American flag, but could not well be called to account for her fraud, since she and all on board went to the bottom in a storm off Cape Fear on their way to the United States. Indemnity was paid to the families of American and British citizens who had been executed, but the sanguinary governor was never punished.

Citizens of the United States suffered in other ways from the arbitrary methods of the Spaniards, and much irritation was occasioned, but the government showed no disposition to interfere. Hamilton Fish, secretary of state, in a letter to Caleb Cushing, minister to Spain, in 1875, spoke strongly of the barbarous and useless character of the warfare, saying further, "No effective steps have been taken to establish reforms or remedy abuses, and the effort to suppress the insurrection by force alone has been a complete failure." He hinted that the time was at hand when it might be necessary to intervene.

President Grant, in his message of 1875, reviewed the

situation, but without recommending any definite action, and the government seemed disposed to move with great caution. The mild suggestions made were wasted on Spain. No attention was paid to them, and the insurrection dragged on until both parties, worn out with the useless struggle, consented to peace.

Some further injuries were done to American commerce. Three whaling vessels were fired upon and held for a time, their crews being treated with the usual brutality by Spanish officials. But these troubles, like former ones, were settled by the payment of an indemnity, and the two countries continued in a state of irritation, but without a show of open hostility, until the El Zanjon treaty of peace put an end to the cause of dissatisfaction. From that time until 1895 things went on smoothly. The blank disregard of its engagements on the part of Spain was not satisfactory to the American sense of honor, but however the Cubans themselves might chafe under the injustice done them, the people of this country settled down and watched calmly the course of events, with its slow but unseen drift towards war.

CHAPTER III.

CUBA IN INSURRECTION.

THE end of the war of 1868–78 was followed by the exile, voluntary or involuntary, of a large number of Cubans, many of whom found new homes in the United States, others in the Spanish-American republics and non-Spanish West India Islands. Among these were Maximo Gomez, the brothers Antonio and José Maceo, and others of the prominent leaders in the rebellion. Despite the pacific terms of the capitulation, these men deemed it safest not to remain within reach of Spain, particularly after seeing how that country juggled with its promised reforms. The number of Cubans in the United States is said to have been forty thousand, while there were large numbers elsewhere, all inspired by active hostility to Spain.

The spirit of revolution was never permitted to die out in the hearts of these exiles. Revolutionary clubs or juntas were formed, until about one hundred and forty of these existed in North and South America and the West Indies. For several years before 1895 these clubs were busily engaged in collecting money, buying war-supplies, and laying plans. Cuban workmen in the United States offered to give one-tenth of their earnings towards the fund. There were fire-arms on the island, concealed since 1878. Others were smuggled in. Every available step of preparation was made, and the revolutionists impatiently awaited a suitable opportunity to institute a new rebellion.

The chief organizer of these movements was a Cuban named José Marti, then in New York. Born in Cuba, he had studied at Seville, graduated at Madrid, and become a political convict at Havana, finally finding a refuge in the United States. Taking advantage of the business depression of 1894 in Cuba and the lack of employment on the sugar estates, hundreds of men being idle through the closing of the mills, Marti fixed the date of February 24, 1895, for the outbreak of the proposed rebellion, and notified the clubs in Cuba of his plan. He promised to bring them aid from outside, and for this purpose chartered three vessels, the Lagonda, the Amadis, and the Baracoa, which were loaded with war-material. This expedition failed, being stopped by the United States authorities at Fernandina, Florida. About the end of January, 1895, Marti made his way to San Domingo, where he entered into communication with the old soldier Maximo Gomez, who had taken a leading part in the previous war, and was now over seventy years of age. Consultations were also held with the Maceos, then in Costa Rica, and with other leaders of the late rebellion.

On the appointed day, February 24, 1895, the citizens of Havana were startled by the report that the public order had been disturbed,—a band of rebels, twenty-four in number, having appeared in arms at Ybarra, in the province of Matanzas. Other small bands defied the authorities in other sections of the island. Yet the affair at first seemed no more serious than a negro riot, and very unlikely to make way against the twenty thousand Spanish troops in the island and the sixty thousand Volunteers enrolled. Governor-General Calleja hastened to declare martial law in the provinces affected, and the outbreaks in Matanzas and Santa Clara were soon put down. This was not the case in the province of Santiago de Cuba, a thinly-settled, mountainous, and densely-wooded district, admirably adapted for the guerrilla warfare which the insurgents proposed to wage.

The plans of the conspirators in this province included wide-spread conflagrations and the extermination of the Spanish officials and soldiery, including the resident governor. Though these sanguinary plans were not carried out, the activity of the rebels in arms soon convinced the authorities that the affair was more serious than they had supposed, and early in March seven thousand troops were sent over from Spain to reinforce those in the island, of whom less than half were effective. Of the thirteen gunboats on patrol duty along the coast, no more than seven were in condition for use. The commissary arrangements were so bad as seriously to hamper the movements of the troops, and for a time the insurgents had it largely their own way, raiding and plundering the plantations of loyalists, and vanishing into the woods and mountains on the appearance of the troops. Many of the plantation hands joined them, and their numbers rapidly increased until there were several thousand men in arms.

They were as yet, however, without experienced leaders; but early in April, Antonio Maceo, with his brother and twenty-two others of the exiles who had taken part in the former war, arrived from Costa Rica, landing near Baracoa, not far from the eastern extremity of the island. Their progress inward proved a danger-

Gen. Maximo Gomez

Gen. Calixto Garcia

Gen. Antonio Maceo

CUBAN LEADERS

ous one. Intercepted by a party of Spanish cavalry, they had a brisk fight, Maceo finally getting away with a bullet-hole through his hat. For ten days the party made its way through the country, now seeking places of concealment, now forced to fight, and trusting to the wild fruits of the woodland for food. So alert were the Spanish patrols that in the end Maceo was left with only two or three of his original companions. With these he fell in with a band of rebels, by whom he was enthusiastically received.

Maceo, an educated mulatto, had gained a high reputation for daring and ability during the former conflict, his influence being great with the negro contingent of the rebellion. He was the only one of the leaders who had refused to concur in the capitulation of Zanjon, continuing in arms for two months, and finally leaving the country without signing the treaty of peace. He now put himself at the head of the insurgents in the district he had reached, and in several sharp brushes with the Spanish, in which he more than held his own, he proved that the rebellion had at length gained an able leader.

Shortly afterwards José Marti, the acknowledged head of the insurrection, reached Cuba from San Domingo, Maximo Gomez and several others coming with him. They landed on the southern coast, in a district filled with the pickets and patrols of the enemy, and for two days they were in great danger, hiding in caves on the coast. On the evening of the third day, with five followers, they reached a camp of the rebel army, where they were received with an enthusiasm equal to that which had greeted Maceo.

The arrival of these experienced leaders inspired the Cuban patriots, many of whom now joined the ranks, until the patriot army numbered more than six thousand men, and bolder operations became possible. It was arranged that Marti should return to the United States and seek further aid for the revolutionists, leaving the command in the able hands of Gomez, who was to advance to his old battle-ground of Camaguey, the Cuban name for the province of Puerto Principe, while Maceo and the others remained in Santiago de Cuba to recruit their forces.

Marti accompanied Gomez some distance on his way, and on seeking to return was met by a body of troops, before whose fire he fell dead. Gomez, who came to his aid, was slightly wounded, and was borne by his men from the field. The corpse of Marti was embalmed by the Spaniards and taken to the city of Santiago de Cuba, where it was given honorable burial. Thus early in the war perished the fomenter and organizer of the insurrection, for which he, with his associates, is said to have collected a fund of more than a million dollars.

The rapid growth of the insurrection soon satisfied the Spanish authorities in the home government that Calleja was not the man for the situation, and Premier Canovas had him removed, appointing in his place Martinez Campos, who had the prestige of having put an end to the previous war, and was looked upon as the ablest general of Spain. He reached the island about the middle of April, landing at the port of Guantanamo with reinforcements numbering twenty-five thousand men.

Great hopes were entertained by the Spanish party that the new governor-general would quickly end the war. He took hold of affairs with energy, while at the same time he sought to conciliate the people, giving employment to the laboring population on the roads, and otherwise trying to alleviate the prevailing distress. His standard of action, however, was above that of his agents, and things soon went wrong. As for the revolutionists, they quickly made it apparent that they were not to be disarmed by a show of leniency, and their numbers increased until over ten thousand were in the field, perhaps three-fourths of them armed with rifles, though cartridges were not abundant. The war went on in the fashion of 1868. There was no such thing as a battle, though skirmishes were of almost daily occurrence. In most of these affairs the Spaniards largely outnumbered their opponents, and were far superior to them in equipments. The insurgents, therefore, fought principally from ambush, being little affected in their consciences by the constant reproach of the Spaniards that they would not stay still long enough to be killed. They were past-masters in the act of vanishing, and were so thoroughly familiar with all the by-paths and mountain fastnesses of the island that pursuit was usually idle. It was their purpose to wear out and worry out their foes, and in this they showed excellent skill.

It may be said here that the strength of the insurgents lay largely in their horses. They were admirable horsemen, riding like Cossacks or cowboys, and far superior in this respect to the Spanish cavalry, few of whom were trained to the saddle. Many stories are told of women who rode in their ranks and wielded the machete even more fiercely than the men, and there is little doubt that these stories have some foundation in truth. The favorite mode of fighting by the insurgents was to harass the Spanish troops with a skirmish fire, in which they sought to pick off the officers by sharpshooting; then, if the opportunity presented, they would dash forward in a wild cavalry charge, machete in hand, and seek to make havoc in the ranks of the foe. The Maceos excelled in this mode of fighting.

As regards the character of their horses, we are told by a newspaper correspondent who visited one of their camps: "Horses are tethered about everywhere, and stand unsheltered, rain or shine. They are fed on rushes, or colla, for no other grain is to be had, and a sore-backed, sorry lot they are, though tough and tireless as our own bronchos."

A further extract may fitly be made from the picturesque account given by this writer, Mr. Grover Flint, correspondent of the New York *Journal*. He says:

"CAMP SABANAS, near Sagua, April 1, 1896.—This is a real insurgent camp. About me, as I write, are standing its swarthy guards, with the silver star on their hat-rims and rifles in their hands. It is a permanent camp, with a little hospital. Dr. Francisco Domingues, of Havana, is stationed here as a special agent of General Maximo Gomez, not only to attend to the wounded, but to forward despatches to the chiefs of insurgent divisions throughout the Matanzas province.

"The camp lies in a forest among the foot-hills that rise from either side of the valley, reaching from the coast to the interior of the island. High mountains and swamps, green with rushes and cane, protect it on all sides but one. On this side a narrow trail zigzags for a league in the woods, barely missing morasses and pitfalls. Twenty well-armed men could hold that trail against a regiment. The camp itself is tropical and picturesque. It is a plateau, thickly overgrown with stunted trees and towering palms, reached by little paths cut with the machete.

"The insurgents live in small huts or wikyups,—'jackals' they call them here,—built of boughs and saplings and thatched with palm-leaves. Rebels against Spain must sleep in hammocks, for the ground sweats in the Cuban jungle, and white men cannot sleep on it and live. At night strange birds sing, queer animals, like overgrown rats, look at you from the trees, and great land-crabs scurry into their holes at your approach. . . .

"The camp-guard consists of fifty men, exclusive of negro camp-servants, armed only with machetes. . . . Guards and patrols watch the trail leading from the valley, and no one is allowed to leave without a pass from the commander. Squads of men ride through the country at night in search of the 'plateados,' those blood-thirsty robbers who were the terror of the country early in the war, but who have been almost suppressed by the insurgents. When the plateado is caught, he is brought into camp and hanged to the nearest tree.

"It is odd to find soldiers with camp-servants to fetch water, cut wood, and perform the acts of personal service; but the men are active and quick to take the saddle on sudden alarm, as I have seen on several occasions since my arrival. For simplicity, the life is like that of Marion's men in our American Revolution. No coffee, no bread; heated sugar and water at daybreak, sweet potatoes and stewed beef at noon, and stewed beef and sweet potatoes at night. Beans and rice are luxuries. Sugar-cane, sweet and nutritious, does for bread. We eat with our fingers and knives down here, with bits of palm-bark for plates. Food is plentiful or scarce according to the country and to circumstances. That there is no scarcity now is proof that the sympathy of the native population is with the insurrection. No man is so poor that he cannot cheerfully give food for the army. This proves, also, the truth of the saying here that the Spaniard owns only the ground he stands on. The news of every movement of the Spaniards is quickly reported."

The death of Marti left Gomez at the head of the insurrectionary movement. But the old rebel leader did not find himself in comfortable surroundings. After the death of Marti, he wrote despondently: "From that moment my position became considerably worse. I was without health, without troops, without arms." Though determined on the invasion of Camaguey, he made the movement "sick not only in body, but in soul as well." He had abundant reason for depression. "The people of Camaguey," he was informed, "wanted no war." To rid themselves of their unwelcome visitor, they offered to find him the means to leave the country, and proposed to make him re-embark by force if he would not do so of good will.

A still more dangerous phase of the situation was the attitude assumed by his men, who did not relish being led out of their province into new and strange districts. One morning his escort drew up their horses to a halt, declaring that they would go no farther, and demanding to be led back to their native province.

"It cost me trouble to reduce them to obedience," writes Gomez. "Three days later," he continues, "a traitor presented himself to the enemy and informed him of my situation, and again my escort insisted upon their proposition not to follow me. In vain their own officer in command interposed his authority; the soldiers refused to obey. Then, indignant, I rebuked them severely, calling them disloyal and bad companions. 'Return to the East,' said I to them. 'I alone will go to Camaguey.'"

General Borrero addressed them still more indignantly. "General Gomez is a foreigner," he said, "who has come to help us in this holy war, and you wish to abandon him while sick and pursued by the enemy. If that is the way you act, then the whole world can say with reason that you are cowards."

This and more of the same kind of argument finally induced the soldiers to go on; but Gomez was "troubled with the most terrible doubts." His hopes revived on learning that Campos had "urged that his march should be stopped at all hazards," for, if he entered Camaguey, Spain might consider her cause lost.

The period spoken of was that of the greatest depression in the old soldier's career. His invasion of Camaguey proved highly successful, the Spaniards being beaten at every point, while abundant spoil fell into the hands of the patriots, and they had every reason for encouragement.

Gomez now developed his plan of campaign. The patriot bands were given the following general orders: They were, first, to attack the small posts held by the Spaniards, making every effort to obtain arms, and setting free every prisoner who would deliver his weapons; second, they were to cut all railway and telegraph lines; third, they were to keep on the defensive, and to retreat in small groups unless they had the advantage; fourth, all forts or buildings from which any resistance was made were to be destroyed; fifth, all crops of sugar-cane and all sugar-mills were to be destroyed unless their owners contributed to the Cuban war-fund ; sixth, the farmers were forbidden to send any food to the cities without paying taxes on the same to the insurgents.

Campos took steps to counteract the insurgent plan by ordering the division of certain regiments into detachments to protect the sugar-estates, while other detachments were stationed along the railroads and placed on every moving train. He further ordered an attack to be made on every band of rebels encountered that did not more than three times outnumber the troops, directing his officers to set free all who surrendered, and to provide convoys for food sent to the towns.

The war in 1895 was one of skirmishes innumerable, only a single affair reaching the dignity of a battle. This was of interest from the fact that Maceo and Campos were the opposing leaders. Maceo had greatly annoyed his foes by attacks on train-loads of supplies for the fortified town of Bayamo, in the district of Santiago de Cuba, and it was deemed necessary to drive him from the field. Several Spanish columns were put in movement against him from different quarters. Campos led one of these, a force of fifteen hundred men, from Manzanillo, and on July 13 came upon the foe, about two thousand seven hundred strong, well posted on a stock-farm several miles from Bayamo. The plan of Maceo was to attack the centre division, under Campos, but by an error the assault was made on the advance guard, led by General Santocildes, upon which fell a sharp fire from the wooded hill-sides. Santocildes fell dead, and a rebel bullet tore the heel from the boot of the governor-general.

The confusion in the Spanish ranks, due to the fall of

Santocildes, convinced Maceo that they had lost some important officer, and he at once made a vigorous machete charge, hoping to win a decisive victory. He was repulsed. But Campos, finding the situation critical, felt obliged to draw up his whole force into a hollow square, using as breastworks the wagons and the dead horses and mules. For several hours the Cubans raged around this strong formation, the Spaniards being saved from a disastrous rout only by the presence and the generalship of Campos. An assault had been made on the rear-guard early in the affray, Maceo hoping to capture the ammunition-train. But these troops defended themselves vigorously and fought their way to the main body, where they aided in the formation of the square. The Spaniards finally succeeded in reaching Bayamo, having suffered heavily in the fight and been pursued to the environs of the town. Maceo's lack of artillery saved them from total destruction, and Campos did not venture to leave his place of refuge until he had gathered around him a powerful force.

The advance of Gomez into Camaguey brought him into communication with the venerable Salvador Cisneros, who had discarded his title of Marquis de Santa Lucia to accept the presidency of the Cuban republic during the former insurrection, and was as ardent a revolutionist as ever. Marti had, upon landing in Cuba, issued a call for a constitutional convention, in consequence of which Cisneros and other Cuban leaders had come together, twenty representatives being sent from the provinces and twenty from the army. The convention met on September 13, 1895, adopted a constitution on the 16th, and on the 18th elected the following executive officers :

PRESIDENT, Salvador Cisneros Betancourt.
VICE-PRESIDENT, Bartolome Maso.
SECRETARY OF STATE, Rafael Portuondo.
SECRETARY OF WAR, Carlos Roloff.
SECRETARY OF THE TREASURY, Severo Pina.
GENERAL-IN-CHIEF, Maximo Gomez.
LIEUTENANT-GENERAL, Antonio Maceo.

Cuba was divided by this constitution into five states. Laws were passed regulating various government affairs, establishing post-offices, providing for the collection of taxes, etc., the whole forming a fairly complete government on paper, though one few of whose functions could be exercised. The tradition is that the seat of government was fixed at Cubitas, a mythical station on a mountain-top, approachable only by a spiral track, which a corporal's guard could defend against an army. But this stronghold probably existed only in imagination, and the government seems to have been a perambulatory one, though having its head-quarters in the Cubitas mountain district.

At the end of the constitutional two years' term of office, in October, 1897, a new government was elected, Bartolome Maso being now chosen President, Dr. Domingo M. Capote Vice-President, and José B. Aleman Secretary of War. Various other departmental officers were chosen, General Gomez was reappointed Commander-in-Chief, and Calixto Garcia was appointed Lieutenant-General.

In November, 1895, Maceo left Santiago de Cuba to join Gomez, who had made his way westward into the province of Santa Clara, where, on November 19 and 20, he fought a severe battle at Taguasco, in which he gained a decided advantage over General Valdez and his men. The much-vaunted trocha lay in Maceo's way, but he made short work of it. He simulated an attack on this line of defence, and, as soon as the Spaniards were concentrated upon the threatened point, he crossed an unprotected part of the line without firing a shot or losing a man.

Campos had concentrated twenty-five thousand troops in Santa Clara, but these failed to keep back the insurgents, who shrewdly availed themselves of their old guerrilla tactics, advancing in small columns, which held the enemy in check by pretended attacks, while the main body slipped onward with its pack-trains. In this way the provinces of Santa Clara and Matanzas were successfully crossed and that of Havana entered, the war being by this daring movement brought nearly to the gates of the capital. Gomez had succeeded in obtaining a few pieces of artillery, and the insurgent army no longer felt obliged to lurk in the woods and the long grass.

During the year 1895 the Spanish government had sent more than one hundred thousand troops across the ocean, to which the Volunteers added a strong contingent available for garrison duty. But there had been heavy losses through disease and combat, and the hospitals were full of the sick. It is impossible to say how many rebels were in the field. They have been variously estimated at from thirty thousand to fifty thousand, but may have been considerably less in number. This is certain, the present war was a far more serious affair than the former one, while the methods adopted by the Cuban leaders were more destructive of the Spanish strength and less easy to overcome. As the year progressed towards its end, the orders of Gomez were more fully carried out. Trains were wrecked and bridges blown up with dynamite, tracks were torn up and telegraph lines cut, contributions were forced from the planters to secure their crops from the torch, and taxes were collected upon food-supplies sent to the cities.

Fighting went on almost daily, but it was of the old kind. The insurgents would not fight unless they had the advantage in number or position. Every foot of ground was known to them, while nearly the whole population served them as spies. All the negroes and most of the whites were their friends, and they had timely warning of every movement of their foes. The Spanish outposts and columns were perpetually exposed to sudden and sharp assaults, the Cuban soldiers making off before an effective blow could be dealt them in return.

By the end of the year the Cuban forces were firmly established in Havana province, where they gained reinforcements from the negro field-hands and Cuban youths. The bandits, of whom a considerable number had arisen, taking toll from both parties alike, were hanged by the insurgents wherever captured. The fighting was principally done by Maceo, Gomez occupying himself in the more effective work of depriving Spain of the sinews of war by burning cane-fields and destroying railroads.

In January, 1896, a still further advance was made, Maceo leading his men into Pinar del Rio, the most westerly province of Cuba, into which insurrection had never before made its way. Thus within a year the Cuban revolution had spread from end to end of the island, the Spanish being left in possession only of the cities, while all the country was in insurgent hands or in a state of turmoil and insecurity. Gomez marched where he would and burned the crops of planters who sought to grind their cane, until the sky around the capital was filled with smoke by day and lurid at night with the flames of blazing fields.

The campaign of Campos had proved an utter failure. But, despite the severe criticism to which he was exposed, he refused to depart from his humane policy and make war upon non-combatants. In consequence, the demand for his recall and replacement by a man who would conduct the war with less regard to the feelings of the people grew urgent, and at length was responded to. He was ordered home, and sailed for Spain January 17, 1896, leaving General Sabis Marin in temporary authority until his successor should arrive.

We may somewhat briefly conclude our record of the events of the war before describing more particularly the system upon which it was conducted and the peculiarly Spanish method of dealing with a colonial revolution. The new governor-general, General Valeriano Weyler y Nicolau, Marquis of Tenerife, to give him his full title, reached Havana February 10, 1896, greatly to the satisfaction of the ultra-Spanish party, who now looked to see vigorous methods introduced and the island quickly swept clear of the scum of rebellion which had swept over it from end to end. They were destined to disappointment. The Weyler trumpet was blown very loudly, but its noise proved only empty air.

General Weyler had won the deep hatred of the Cubans by the atrocious deeds which he was said to have committed in Camaguey during the former war. In his military career during the disturbances in Spain and in the African war against the Moors he was a favorite lieutenant of the brutal chief Valmaseda, under whom he gained a reputation for barbarous cruelty. His fame in this direction preceded him to Cuba, and his career there fully sustained his reputation, the cruelty exercised towards the helpless non-combatants having rarely been surpassed in the history of war.

At present, however, we propose to deal only with warlike events, leaving methods to be considered later. Governor-General Weyler began by promising to clear the provinces near Havana of rebels in arms and let peaceful industry take its course. He was not long in discovering that he had a bold and active enemy to deal with. Hardly had he entered upon his office when Maceo returned from Pinar del Rio and swooped down on the city of Jaruco, which he looted and burned. Gomez joined him, and the two resumed their former course, burning cane, exacting tribute, and otherwise disturbing the enemy. The Cuban leaders had announced in December, 1895, their purpose to stop production and commerce, and thus deprive the Spanish government of the revenues of the island. In carrying out this policy Gomez had made his march through the rich sugar districts, destroying as he went and leaving ashes and desolation behind him. Maceo had wreaked similar ruin in the wealthy tobacco districts of Pinar del Rio, burning and destroying and forcing the helpless laborers either to join his ranks or seek subsistence in the cities. The work of "concentration" was thus began by the insurgents themselves.

Weyler's warlike energy proved to be more show than substance. He sent his infantry to pursue the cane-burning insurgents, but beyond the murder of non-combatants little was accomplished. He sent troops into Pinar del Rio, where they met no great opposition, and the world was informed that this province was pacified. Yet his proclamation had hardly been made before Maceo was back there again. On March 13, 1896, the dashing mulatto leader had entered and burnt the port of Batabano, on the southern coast, and before Weyler's troops could reach him he was in the "pacified" province. Here he made his head-quarters in the mountains and bade defiance to all the power of Spain.

Now was the time for Weyler to show his military skill, but in this he signally failed. Instead of pursuing his defiant foe persistently with cavalry and using bodies of infantry to occupy the country and cut off his retreat, he wasted his strength in the old exercise of trocha-building, extending a defensive line across the island from Mariel to Majana, a work which it took two months to construct and fifteen thousand soldiers to guard, a force sufficient, one would think, to have cleared the province of insurgents.

Meanwhile, Maceo held the province almost unopposed. By May 1 only four fortified cities were left to Spain in its southern part, and these were crowded with refugees. Weyler refused to do anything to aid these unfortunates, and the operating columns which he sent into the province were defeated in almost every engagement. Gomez meanwhile withdrew his forces to Camaguey, where, with five hundred followers, he met and defeated General Castillanos with two thousand troops. Two hundred men were killed and wounded on the side of the Spaniards, while the insurgents had but ten killed in this affair.

Though Maceo showed a humane disposition, Bermudez, one of his lieutenants, an ex-bandit, established a reign of terror in the district controlled by him, murdering men on the slightest pretext, and forcing the inhabitants to seek refuge in the fortified places until the country was practically depopulated. The autumn campaign was opened by Weyler in person, he marching into Pinar del Rio at the head of thirty thousand men, with the determination of starving or driving out the foe. While he did not succeed in this purpose, the province, through the double destruction achieved by the Cubans and the Spanish, was rendered incapable of supporting a large force, and Maceo's negro followers dwindled away. In consequence, leaving his slender following under Rius Rivera, the daring leader passed in a boat around Weyler's trocha into Havana province, having sent orders in advance for a concentration of the Cuban forces in this and Matanzas province. While waiting for these forces, on December 4, 1896, he, with his few followers, was fired on by soldiers in ambush, and fell, mortally wounded. Dr. Zertucha, of his staff, is charged with having treacherously led him into this ambuscade, though this is far from certain. Thus perished the most daring warrior of the Cuban conflict. His eight brothers had all died before him in the struggle for Cuban freedom. His body was recovered from the enemy after a desperate fight; his valiant soul was lost to the cause.

The death of Maceo and the capture of Rivera, which soon after took place, practically put an end to military operations in Pinar del Rio, and on January 11, 1897, Weyler proclaimed that the three western provinces were pacified and the rebellion confined to the eastern section of the island. Gomez had withdrawn into Camaguey, where he held his own, the members of the Cuban government being with him. After announcing that the provinces were "pacified," Weyler set out to pacify them. Pinar del Rio was actively patrolled by his troops, and he entered upon a campaign through Matanzas. Here he met with no insurgents in arms, but treated the country-people as rebels, ruthless devastation marking his line of march. The decree of concentration which he had issued was vigorously enforced, the country-people being driven into the towns, their dwellings burned, and everything destroyed that could in any way aid or shelter the insurgents. All those against whom the shadow of suspicion rested were killed on the spot and set down as rebels slain in battle in the absurd bulletins which Weyler constantly issued. Eventually, disturbed by the protests in the United States against his barbarity, he issued an order that no sentence of death should be carried out without his signature. But this did not put an end to the bulletins of battles in which a Spaniard or two were wounded and ten or more rebels killed, and which at once excited the derision of the world and the indignation of those who believed that these so-called engagements were really massacres of unarmed "pacificos." Weyler was rapidly earning contempt by his rodomontade and hatred by his cruelty.

The Spanish army reached the city of Santa Clara in February, 1897. Here, finding no large body of insurgents to oppose his progress, Weyler sent out columns of infantry to burn and destroy, afterwards crossing the province back and forth to see if his orders had been well obeyed. By the end of the month his troops had reached the fertile valleys of the mountains between Santa Clara and Trinidad, a region in which the Cubans had large supplies. Their system of government embraced a *prefectura*, it being the duty of the prefect in each district to claim control of all supplies, using them for the troops as needed and paying the owners in receipts for the goods taken. This system had been well organized in the district mentioned, and the troops found here herds of cattle, which they drove away; coffee- and potato-plants, which they destroyed; and hospitals, which they burned. Non-combatants were forced to take to the woods. If captured, they were killed or taken with the women and children to fortified towns, there to suffer the slower death of starvation.

Gomez, meanwhile, was playing a waiting game, knowing that the fury of Weyler's assault would soon subside. He had no commissary department, and his men were divided up into small bands, coming and going much as they pleased, planting and gathering their rapidly growing crops, and simply keeping within call that they might concentrate in the main camps if any movement in force should be undertaken. During their longer marches, they had to trust to their chance of living off the country. The two eastern provinces of Santiago de Cuba and Puerto Principe continued in their hands throughout the war. The only district held by the Spaniards in Santiago province was that of Bayamo, and this was retained only at severe cost in lives and strenuous effort. The cutting of the railroad to the north more than once reduced the garrison of Bayamo to the verge of starvation, while the supplies which it obtained by boat up the Rio Cauto were interfered with by the insurgents, who in January, 1897, blew up a Spanish gunboat in that river with a torpedo operated by means of an electric wire from the bordering woods. It was the effort to hold this town that led to the battle between Maceo and Campos, already described.

The principal demonstrations of the insurgents during 1897 were made by the forces under General Calixto Garcia, like Gomez a veteran of the ten-years' war, and now second in command. He had reached Cuba from the United States in the spring of 1897. The only military operation of the year on the part of the insurgents that calls for particular attention was the capture by Garcia of the strongly fortified post of Victoria de las Tunas, northwest of Bayamo, September 30. The siege of this place continued for three days, during which the Spanish commander was slain and forty per cent. of the garrison were killed or wounded, the remainder surrendering. Garcia's success must be attributed to his possession of artillery, he having two heavy and six rapid-fire guns, which were handled by American artillerymen. One of the latter estimated the spoils of the victory to be "twenty-one forts, over a thousand rifles, a million rounds of ammunition, and two Krupp cannon." The post had been declared impregnable by Weyler, and its fall exposed him to severe criticism in Madrid.

In truth, Weyler had been losing ground with the home government throughout the year. The indignation roused in the United States by his cruelty had produced a feeling of uneasiness in Spain, whose people seemed far more affected by this protest than by the cruelty itself. And it was growing evident that Weyler's severity was little more effective than Campos's clemency. The rebels continued unsubdued, the high-sounding war-bulletins were being derided in foreign newspapers as transparent fictions, and there was imminent danger that the era of Weylerism might provoke armed intervention from the United States.

Canovas, the prime minister who had appointed Weyler, continued to sustain him, but the Liberal party in Spain was gaining power at the expense of the Conservatives, and on August 6, 1897, the assassination of Canovas by an Anarchist left Weyler without support in the administration. After a brief interval the Liberals came into power on October 4, under their leader Sagasta, one of whose first acts was to order Weyler home. The chief reason offered for this step was "the deplorable condition of the sick and wounded soldiers arriving from Cuba." In fact, the principal losses to Spain during the war in Cuba had been from disease, the field operations being largely a series of inconsequential skirmishes with little loss to either side.

Weyler's successor was General Ramon Blanco, late governor-general of the Philippine Islands, and a man of very different character from his predecessor. He reached Havana October 31, 1897, and at once attempted to put into effect the milder policy which had been decided upon at Madrid. He had announced, "My policy will never include concentration. I fight the enemy, not women and children. One of the first things I shall do will be to greatly extend the zones of cultivation, and allow the reconcentrados to go out of the towns and till the soil."

But it was easier to promise than to perform. The starving reconcentrados were in no condition to wait until nature should return food in exchange for their labor. The amnesty proclamation issued by Blanco was unheeded by the insurgents. They had lost all faith in Spanish clemency, and did not propose to lay down their arms. The autonomous administration which he sought to establish was a similar failure. The insurgents would

Adm. Patricio Montojo

Adm. Pascual Cervera

Gen. Linares

Gen. Ramon Blanco

Gen. Valeriano Weyler

Gen. Martinez de Campos

SPANISH COMMANDERS

THE WAR WITH SPAIN.

have no autonomy. "Independence or death" was their sole demand. Gomez issued a warning that any person coming to his camps with offers of autonomy should be shot as a spy; and this severe order was carried out in the case of Lieutenant-Colonel Ruiz, who sought the camp of General Aranguren and persisted in offering autonomy to the men after being warned of the consequences. Aranguren, although his personal friend, ordered him to execution. That decisive event put an end to the scheme of home rule under a Spanish governor-general.

With the offers of amnesty and home government was mingled an attempt to bribe the Cuban leaders to desert their men. This met with a still less favorable reception, and several of those who sought to tempt the leaders to dishonor were dealt with as Ruiz had been.

Meanwhile the war had fallen back into its old condition of outpost skirmishes and indecisive conflicts, and to all appearance the task of putting down the insurrection was no more advanced than in the spring of 1895, though Spain had sent two hundred thousand soldiers to Cuba and had almost fallen into bankruptcy through her futile efforts. Thus events drifted on into the year 1898.

CHAPTER IV.

THE FORTS AND THE TROCHAS.

THE account of the leading events of the insurrection given in the preceding chapter is but half the story. The methods of conducting the war by the Spaniards were there little more than hinted at, it being deemed advisable to reserve them for a more detailed separate description. This it is proposed to give in the present chapter. Why it is that an army of more than two hundred thousand regulars, with a contingent force of some sixty thousand volunteers, could be held at bay for three years by a body of insurgents certainly never numbering over fifty thousand, and most of the time, in all probability, far below that number, and this in an island of comparatively small dimensions, is a mystery which has sorely puzzled the lookers-on. It seems evident that there has been something radically wrong in the conduct of the war by its three successive generals, for such strenuous efforts on the part of Spain to yield such meagre results. A consideration of the mode in which the war was conducted may serve to make more apparent the cause of Spain's signal failure.

Certainly, no very decisive result can ever be looked for from guerrilla warfare. As a defensive expedient, adopted to protract a combat, it has its uses, and the Cubans, with their inferior forces, were wise in employing it. They had no hope of mastering Spain in the field, but entertained a reasonable expectation of wearing her out in the bush, and of forcing her at length to retire from the contest through sheer lack of money and men. These hardy bush-rangers preferred to let disease do its work on the unacclimated lives of Spain and save their small supply of cartridges for sheer necessity. The yellow fever could be trusted as a more effective ally of their cause than the Mauser rifle.

But why the Spanish commanders adopted the same mode of warfare is difficult of comprehension, unless it be that this is the intuitive Spanish idea of war. In the early years of the nineteenth century, during the Napoleonic contests, the Spanish forces conducted war in the guerrilla method. In its closing years they adopted the same method in their contest with the Cuban insurrectionists. In all their wars of the century, in fact, the guerrilla system seems to have held predominance; and it may be that Spain's loss of all her American colonies was due to a lack of breadth, boldness, and energy of movement in dealing with the rebel forces. The Spanish soldier does not want in courage, but the Spanish commander seems sadly lacking in military genius.

With a quarter of a million of men at their command, Campos or Weyler should, one would think, have been able to construct a net-work of military roads from end to end of the island with no more effort than was expended in building forts and trochas. And with such facilities provided for rapid movements in force they should certainly have succeeded in keeping the small bodies of insurgents in check and in penetrating all their lurking-places. It is easy, of course, for civilian generals to win battles on paper, and the easier the less they are familiar with the facts of the situation; yet it may be taken as beyond question that if the Spanish troops had been replaced by an American, British, German, or French army, with almost any one of the skilled commanders now in those armies, the mode of campaigning and the result would have been far different from those which Spain has to show.

The trocha and the fort, trusted to by Spain as her principal means of success, seem to have been her principal causes of failure. An account of these expedients, upon which so much dependence was placed, comes next in course. The trocha is simply a passage-way made across a country without regard to its topography or its other roads. The word trocha means trench, and sustains this meaning in some of the military lines constructed in Cuba, though not in all. The idea of the trocha was first conceived in the insurrection of 1868–78 as a military cordon across the island, with detached forts at short intervals, its purpose being to hem in the insurrectionists and confine them to a limited region of the island,—a purpose in which it signally failed.

This original trocha crossed the island between the provinces of Puerto Principe and Santa Clara, the distance across at this point being less than fifty miles and the country elevated but little above sea-level, the mountains here sinking into the plain. The flanks of this military line rested in the tangled mangrove swamps of the coast. The forts were garrisoned, and small detachments of troops occupied the spaces between; but the device proved of little value, Gomez, as if in derision, crossing it with his wife and servants.

Campos no sooner took command in 1895 than he revived the idea of confining his foes by a trocha, constructing it across the same region as before, fifty thousand men being employed in the task. It was barely finished when Gomez crossed it at Sancti Spiritus and carried the war into Santa Clara. Maceo followed him, as already stated, by means of a feigned attack, and Campos, thinking his trocha too far from the capital, built a second, this extending between Las Cruces and Las Lajas and skirting the great salt marsh of Zapata. It proved as ineffectual as the former, and Campos found it expedient to continue his retreat, defending his rear by a third trocha, which crossed the island between Matanzas and La Broa Bay, a distance of only twenty-eight miles. This line had a new means of defence, it being traversed by the railroad from Havana to Batabano, on whose tracks were placed a series of perambulatory forts in the form of freight-cars plated with boiler iron and pierced with loop-holes for rifles. All the railroads were provided with similar cars, which were sent with all passenger trains and kept in motion night and day. But Gomez and Maceo showed their appreciation of the Spanish general's device by crossing the "iron dead-line" with all their forces without firing a shot. Then they rode back and tore up some three miles of the railroad track, "Just to let the Spaniards know," said Gomez, "that we have noticed their toy."

Weyler, on coming into power, accepted the idea of the trocha as a valuable inheritance from his predecessor, and soon after reaching the island set his men to constructing one to the westward of Havana, with the expectation of shutting up Maceo in Pinar del Rio. This extended from Mariel, about twenty-five miles from the capital, to Majana, on the southern coast, a distance of about twenty miles. He also made one on the old line between Jucaro and Moron, in the western part of the province of Puerto Principe.

The trocha upon which Weyler depended to cut the rebel army in two and shut up Maceo effectually in Pinar del Rio can be described in a few words. In constructing this military line the forest and dense underbrush were cut down through a width of from one hundred to eight hundred yards. Along this passage-way a barbed-wire fence nearly four feet high was erected, behind which the sentinels were posted. Forty yards back of it was a trench three feet wide and four feet deep, with a breastwork of palmetto logs. Fifty yards farther back were the log houses which served as quarters for the troops. These were built at intervals of from five hundred to eight hundred yards, being constructed of logs with dressed lumber on the outside. A narrow opening ran round the fort to permit firing, and near the top was an opening three feet wide to admit the air. Each fort had a garrison of about one hundred men, the whole line being guarded by about fifteen thousand soldiers. A platform of palm-boards, eight feet wide, was built where the line penetrated the swamp, the huts being there erected on piles. The soldiers never left the forts or platform to explore the swamp, but fired upon every person they saw near the line, taking it for granted that all intruders were enemies. It was through the swamp that the insurgents usually passed the line. Maceo made the passage that led to his death by aid of a boat.

The trocha from Jucaro to Moron presented some differences, the ditch being absent. The cleared space through the tropical forest was here some fifty miles long and about two hundred yards wide, the felled trees being piled up along the two sides of the roadway in parallel rows to a height of six feet or more. No man could cross this breastwork of jagged roots and branches without difficulty, and no horse could make its way across. A military railroad extended the whole length of the cleared space, on one side of which was the line of forts, and beyond this the barbed-wire fence. On the two sides were the barriers of fallen trees, with the jungle beyond.

There were three kinds and sizes of forts along the trocha,—large ones half a mile apart, smaller blockhouses midway between these, and in each of the quarter-mile intervals three little forts of mud and planks, each surrounded by a ditch and holding five men. The barbed wire was closely interlaced, there being over four hundred yards of wire to every twelve yards of posts. Entrance to the larger forts was obtainable only by the aid of ladders, which could be raised from the inside; and there was provided an overhanging story with loop-holes through which the defenders could fire down upon a foe below. The Spaniards also distributed bombs along the trocha, each with an explosive cap to which five or six wires were attached, so that they might be exploded by any one striking a wire. This was a device that seemed likely to prove as dangerous to the defenders as to their enemies.

As to the utility of the trochas, Consul-General Lee tells us that they cost a large amount of money and were in the end practically abandoned as useless. They had the serious defect of absorbing a large force of men for their defence, to this extent diminishing the effective Spanish army.

A second Spanish military measure, the fort (aside from those along the trochas), added seriously to the depletion of the force effective for field duty. In the words of Richard Harding Davis,* the Spaniards, as soon as the revolution broke out, "began to build tiny forts, and continued to add to these and improve those already built, until now the whole island, which is eight hundred miles long and averages eighty miles in width, is studded as thickly with these little forts as is the sole of a brogan with iron nails. . . . These forts now stretch all over the island, some in straight lines, some in circles, and some zigzagging from hill-top to hill-top ; some within a quarter of a mile of the next, and others so near that the sentries can toss a cartridge from one to the other."

Within these forts and the fortified towns and cities the Spaniards held absolute possession. Outside them— that is, in all the rest of the country—the Cubans were masters of the situation, not in fixed possession, but able to make it uncomfortable for any intruders on their domain. The towns were surrounded by successive circles of forts, with detached ones farther out, no person being allowed to leave a town without a pass, or to enter one without giving a satisfactory account of himself. Any one venturing outside the circle without authority rendered himself a rebel, and was likely soon to be made "food for powder."

In all, Cuba possessed two thousand or more such forts, structures impervious to rifle-shots and loop-holed for service. They stood upon every commanding place and formed a feature in the landscape hardly second to the royal palm, that dominating characteristic of Cuban scenery. With the long range of their rifles the Spanish soldiery could command a wide reach of territory from

---

* "Cuba in War Time."

these strongholds, but they were such wretched marksmen that the insurgents had little fear in venturing close up. The marksmanship on either side, indeed, had little to boast of.

It will be seen that the Spaniards were specially active in defensive measures. These were well enough in themselves, but of little value in suppressing an insurrection unless supplemented by active offensive operations. From their forts one would think it should have been their policy to follow the enemy and give him battle wherever found, but this is an idea that does not seem to have deeply penetrated the Spanish cerebrum. Bodies of guerrillas and columns of troops left the forts often enough, but they seemed to regard it as their duty to fall back upon their strongholds every night. If they encountered a body of the enemy, a fusillade would follow; but to pursue a flying enemy did not form a part of their policy, and instead of encamping on the ground and following the retreating foe the next day, they invariably retreated after the battle to the shelter of a neighboring town or circle of forts. Their excuse for this was that they were afraid of being decoyed into an ambush, or that they could not forsake their wounded to pursue the enemy. A force of as many as a thousand soldiers might carry back a few wounded men, making this their sole pretense for a return.

In truth, there is good reason to believe that the Spanish officers were not eager to end the rebellion, and that much of the failure of Campos and Weyler was due to the character of the tools they had to handle. The officers preferred to have the war go on, as they received double pay while on foreign service, while promotion was much more rapid than in times of peace. Orders and crosses are also freely distributed, often for small service. They seem to have emulated the civil officials in forcing loans or fees from planters and others, and are believed to have kept for themselves a large part of the pay of their men. The government suffered from their peculations, it being a common practice to report a considerable consumption of rations and expenditure of cartridges "in service," when perhaps only a few huts had been burned and the command had come back in time for dinner. The officers played constantly into one another's hands in thus hoodwinking the government. Such is the strange Spanish sense of honor. A soldier may be quite ready to die for his country, but is quite as ready to rob it.

In illustration of the character of the officers' reports, some extracts from war-bulletins may be of interest. Here is a typical Spanish story:

"The Guadalajara battalion, while marching to San Miguel, met a party of six hundred rebels, commanded by Aguirre and Morejon. A fierce fight ensued, resulting, it is said, in the rebels being so thoroughly beaten that they fled demoralized from the field. The rebel loss was stated to have been sixty, including fourteen killed. The Spanish troops were reported to have lost one officer and three soldiers wounded."

The Cubans tell this story with a difference:

"The affair was similar to others in which 'Pacificos,' or peaceful citizens, have been killed by Spanish troops. Fourteen of the dead are said to have been employés on estates, and not insurgents. On the Spanish side none were killed and only three wounded, while the Cuban dead exceeded thirty."

Numerous examples of this kind might be quoted in

which the discrepancy of losses was so great as to become ridiculous. It was easier to lie than to fight. We quote again :

"Colonel Hernandez reports having a fight with the rebel bands of Masso and Acea near San Felipe. The enemy occupied strong positions, but were attacked with great vigor by the troops, and finally fled, leaving seven dead upon the field. The troops had five men wounded."

"Colonel Moncado reports having had several engagements with rebel bands near Cienfuegos, in which the enemy had four men killed and seventy wounded, and the Spanish troops had five wounded."

"The official report of the fight on the Fermina ranch, near Jovellanos, states that the rebels lost eight killed ; the troops lost seven wounded. The Spaniards pursued the rebels and in skirmishes killed eighteen, without loss to themselves."

These preposterous stories were probably not told through sheer love of lying and trust in human gullibility. The officers probably had another object in view in reporting so few of their troops killed, that of keeping the names of the dead on the pay-rolls and pocketing their pay. Such is said to have been one of the methods in which those who were chiefly responsible for protracting the war managed to make it profitable to themselves.

CHAPTER V.

THE RECONCENTRADOS AND THE MILITARY PRISONS.

In the present chapter we propose to consider the principal causes of American interposition in the war, this being the savage Weylerian policy of concentration and the barbarous treatment of American citizens in Spanish prisons. General Weyler paved the way for intervention in his famous "Reconcentrado" order. Finding the rebels when he came to the government stationed in every part of the island, and failing to dispossess them as he had engaged to do, he sought to starve them out by cutting off what he supposed to be their main source of food-supply. By laying waste the country, and depriving them of the food they had been obtaining from the country-people, he fancied that he could through sheer starvation force them into submission.

The result was one without a parallel in the military history of the nations,—the deliberate enforcement of a plan of action which brought starvation to the bulk of the inhabitants of a country, and which had no just claim of efficacy to warrant it. All the pacificos, as the non-combatants were called, were ordered into the cities and towns,—namely, the old men, women, and children, as the brutal order forced most of the young men into the rebel ranks. All their food-plants were then uprooted, their dwellings burned, and their animals driven away. The helpless people were gathered within a line drawn one hundred and fifty yards around a town, or were collected around the forts. They were thus in a great measure prevented from tilling the ground; they had no means of obtaining food beyond the little the town-people could spare in charity; death by bullet was their lot if they ventured to cross the dead-line, and death by disease or starvation was inevitable if they remained.

"War is war," was Weyler's excuse for this barbarous order; but the order was in no proper sense a war necessity, since its effect was to drive the able-bodied into the fields to fight and leave the helpless behind to die. It was "worse than a crime, it was a blunder," for it failed in its original purpose, the insurgents proving able to find what food they required, and having little need of the shelter of the burned huts. The order failed to distress those against whom it was aimed, while it brought the deepest misery to thousands of innocent and helpless people who were crowded into the towns, without food or shelter, and under most unsanitary conditions. As a result, disease and starvation vied with each other in sweeping them away, until, in the words of Consul-General Lee, of the four hundred thousand innocents herded where they could obtain no food no less than two hundred thousand died of starvation. Small-pox, yellow fever, and other dread diseases aided hunger in this fearful work, the people being forced to live amid a filth which in that hot climate, especially in the rainy season, could not but cause pestilence to run rampant over the land.

General Weyler had issued a reconcentration decree upon his arrival in Havana. This it was not convenient to put into effect at that time, and it was deferred until he took the field in person against Maceo, when a new decree was promulgated, under date of October 21, 1896. He gave the pacificos eight days to come in to the fortified places, stating that all who remained in the country after that interval should be treated as enemies, —that is, should be killed wherever found. Zones of cultivation were marked off, adjoining the towns and villages, which the pacificos were to have permission to cultivate; but this part of the decree seems never to have been carried out, or so imperfectly as to be useless. Such is the statement of travellers, who also state that low-lying and swampy ground was selected for the reconcentrados,—the most insalubrious situations that could well be chosen.

In Jaruco, as described by Richard Harding Davis, the filth lay ankle-deep in streets and plaza, and made its way into a church which was occupied as a barrack. The pacificos occupied closely-built rows of huts, holding from four to six persons each, while ten feet away were cavalry-barracks, occupied by sixty men with their horses, and left in a state of dangerous uncleanliness. No one was vaccinated, and small-pox swept like a consuming fire through huts and barracks alike. Decency of any kind was out of the question. Utter, hopeless dejection was the aspect of the pacificos, most of whom were incapable from weakness of cultivating the ground and waiting for the slow return in food. Gaunt, hollow-eyed, half-clad in rags, they sat listless and hopeless, too dejected even to lift their eyes when money or food was handed them. At Cardenas he saw "babies with the skin drawn so tightly over their little bodies that the bones showed through as plainly as the rings under a glove. They were covered with sores, and they protested as loudly as they could against the treatment that the world was giving them, clinching their fists and sobbing with pain when the sore places came in contact with their mothers' arms."

As time went on the horrors of the situation increased. President McKinley, in his message of April 11, 1898, states that a year earlier reconcentration had been extended over all but the two eastern provinces, more than three hundred thousand of the country-people being herded in the vicinity of the towns, without shelter or means of support, poorly clad, and under most unsanitary conditions.

"As the scarcity of food increased with the devastation of the depopulated areas of production," he continues, "destitution and want became misery and starvation. Month by month the death-rate increased in alarming ratio. By March, 1897, according to conservative estimates from official Spanish sources, the mortality among the reconcentrados from starvation and the diseases thereto incident exceeded fifty per cent. of their total number. No practical relief was accorded to the destitute. The overburdened towns, already suffering from the general dearth, could give no aid. So-called zones of cultivation that were established within the immediate area of effective military control about the cities and fortified camps proved illusory as a remedy for the suffering. The unfortunates, being for the most part women and children, or aged and helpless men enfeebled by disease and hunger, could not have tilled the soil without tools, seed, or shelter, to provide for their own support or for the supply of the cities. Reconcentration worked its predestined result. As I said in my message of last December, it was not a civilized warfare, it was extermination. The only peace it could beget was that of the wilderness and the grave."

In March, 1898, a party of Congressmen visited Cuba with a partly official purpose, that of seeing for themselves and reporting to the government the actual condition of affairs in the island. Among them were Senators Proctor of Vermont, Gallinger of New Hampshire, and Thurston of Nebraska. What they saw and described in eloquent language to Congress was of a soul-harrowing character. Their description of the hopeless, unspeakable misery of the famishing reconcentrados and the frightfully-desolated condition of one of the most fertile islands under the sun roused the American people as they had rarely been aroused before, awakening a pity and indignation which rendered speedy intervention inevitable. So great, to one of sympathetic nature, was the shock of the suffering observed, that the wife of Senator Thurston, who was in delicate health, received her death-stroke from the dreadful scenes witnessed by her on this journey.

The result of it all was, that while General Weyler was living in the utmost luxury at Havana, and boasting of being surrounded by conditions of wealth and ease unequalled in the land (we quote from an interview reported by Mrs. Masterson), nearly or quite a quarter of a million of human beings were perishing of starvation and disease, the result of his brutal order, and under conditions of misery too horrible to contemplate.

This was not the only barbarity practised. That meted out to the "suspects" was quite as brutal. The mass of these were disposed of summarily by the aid of the rifle-shot or the machete. But many were thrown into prison, and kept there under maddening conditions, being held *incomunicado* ("without communication") in dark little cells, where for days and months they were not permitted to hear a human voice, have book or paper to read, or any alleviation of their suffering. Among them were a considerable number of American citizens, men of Cuban birth who had become naturalized in this country, and some of them of American ancestry. Among these were the Competitor prisoners, a number of men captured on the filibustering vessel of that name, who had been taken May 8, 1896, tried by a Spanish court organized to convict, and sentenced to death on the testimony of the captain of the Spanish gunboat that had made the capture. The execution of this unjust sentence was prevented by the intervention of the United States, but the prisoners were kept in a state of painful imprisonment until the end of Weyler's term of office.

Consul-General Lee earnestly and vigorously protested against the detention of American citizens under such circumstances as a violation of the treaty between the United States and Spain, which, he stated, limited imprisonment *incomunicado* to seventy-two hours. Weyler replied that his declaration of martial law superseded the treaty; a claim which Lee strenuously denied. Americans, he stated, had been arrested without any declared charges and without the knowledge of their friends and relatives, and put in little eight-by-ten cells, dark and with floors of stone, where they were kept for days, seeing none but their jailers and speaking to no one. Lee protested that every man was by law considered innocent until he had been proved guilty, but he found it difficult to penetrate Weyler's thick moral cuticle with the arguments usually effective among civilized people.

A final case came when Dr. Ruiz, an American dentist

of Guanabacoa, a town about four miles from Havana, was arrested, with others of the place, in consequence of an insurgent attack on a railroad train. It was charged that the rebels had received information from these prisoners. Dr. Ruiz could easily have disproved this, but he was given no opportunity to do so, being thrown into prison and kept there for three hundred and sixty hours. He was an athletic man, in perfect health, but the horrors of the *incomunicado* prison-cell crazed him. While calling pitifully for his wife and children, he was struck on the head with the baton of a brutal jailer, and died in consequence.

This cruel act, which could not be concealed, caused widespread indignation, and General Lee determined that such treatment of United States citizens should cease. Finding that another American, named Scott, was in prison under similar conditions, he demanded his release in words whose import there was no mistaking. Weyler complied; and from that time forward every American arrested was turned over to General Lee, who sent all such to the United States.

This respite applied only to Americans. Cuban suspects had no alleviation of their sufferings except the final one that came from the fusillade of the firing-party. Of those who escaped execution, many suffered exile under aggravating circumstances. A letter from Señor Carpio says of the Cuban exiles who, disembarking at Cadiz, were sent on foot to the distant castle of Figueras: "The unfortunate exiles pass here barefooted and bleeding, almost naked and freezing. At every town, far from finding rest from their fatigue, they are received with all sorts of insults; they are scoffed and provoked. I have two sons who are fighting against the Cuban insurgents, but this does not prevent me from denouncing those who ill-treat their prisoners. I have witnessed such outrages upon the unfortunate exiles that I do not hesitate to say that nothing like it has ever occurred in Africa."

The act of barbarity of the Spanish authorities that excited most interest in the United States was the imprisonment of Evangelina Cisneros, a beautiful and cultured girl related to the venerable president of the Cuban republic. The interest in her fate was largely increased by the romance attending her escape. She was arrested upon some slight suspicion, incarcerated for months among prisoners of the criminal and degraded class, and subjected to such indignities as to arouse a world-wide demand for her release or a mitigation of her sufferings. The queen-regent of Spain was applied to, but declined to interfere. Finally, the publisher of the New York *Journal*, who had been one of the most active advocates for her release, decided upon more radical measures. He sent Mr. Carl Decker, a reporter of his staff, to Havana to aid her in escaping. Mr. Decker was successful in this perilous enterprise. On the night of October 6, 1897, Miss Cisneros escaped with his aid through the broken bars of her cell window, and soon after, disguised as a boy, passed the Spanish officials unsuspected to the deck of an American vessel. In this she was conveyed to the United States, where she was received with a decided ovation.

We have not completed the story of Spanish barbarity. General Lee says that it is "difficult to comprehend the cruelties and enormities of Spanish rule, especially during the last few years," and this remark is well borne out by the facts. The Turkish barbarities in Bulgaria, which called for Russian intervention and brought on a war that almost swept the Turkish empire from the map of Europe, and the later barbarities in Crete, which resulted in European intervention between the combatants, were in no sense worse than those which forced the government of the United States to intervene between the combatants in Cuba. Despite the accusation made in Europe that selfish interest was at the basis of the American intervention, it could easily be shown that the provocation here was quite as great as in similar cases in Europe, and the cruelties as marked as those in Armenia, which the selfish fears of European statesmen permitted to go on unchecked.

We have already, perhaps, said sufficient concerning the massacres of Cubans by the Spanish soldiery under the guise of war. In evidence of this, *Leslie's Illustrated Weekly* published in December, 1896, a picture showing the corpses of six Cuban pacificos, firmly bound, their bodies mutilated by machetes, and their faces hacked out of all human aspect. The portrait was also given of their murderer, Benito Cerreros, who had found them working in a field near Sagua, had murdered them, and then brought their bodies to town and had them photographed. His claim was that he had killed them in battle; but he had been stupid enough to forget to remove from their arms and legs the ropes that told the truth of the story.

The people of Sagua celebrated by a public dinner another victory of this worthy. A colonel in the insurgent army who was dying of consumption had captured a Spanish spy, whom he had set free on condition of bringing him some medicine from Sagua. An American was with him in the hut in which he lay concealed. The spy proved a traitor, and revealed the hiding-place of the Cuban to Cerreros, who sought the hut with abundant care for his own safety, as he took with him no less than forty-four men. These shot the two inmates through the windows, and then hacked their bodies with machetes. It was in recognition of this gallant exploit that the Spanish sympathizers of Sagua tendered the victor a dinner.

These will serve as examples of barbarities of which there seem, unfortunately, to have been far too many instances in Cuba. While these cruelties to the people were in progress, those to the land continued night and day, the smoke of its torment being forever in the air. Both parties were active in this work of desolation; the result being that the smoke of burning buildings and cane-fields hung heavily everywhere. In railroading through the country the heat of burning districts would at times render the journey intolerable, sparks and cinders coming through every open car-window, while in the distance the flames of burning buildings could be seen ascending redly towards the sky.

The Spaniards burned the dwellings of the pacificos and the Cubans the cane and tobacco crops and the sugar-mills, and between them they turned a fertile country into a desert of ashes. The grinding of cane was not prevented by the Cubans alone, since Weyler seems to have secretly aided them in this. Suspecting that the planters were playing a double game, and assisting the insurgents in secret while professing to be strongly in favor of Spain in public, he took covert steps to prevent grinding. Consistency would not let him forbid it openly, but it was easy to stop it by arresting the laborers as suspects, seizing the draught oxen for army use, and by other methods,—the result being that the planters who were seemingly under Spanish protection were placed in as serious straits as those exposed to the operations of the insurgents.

Nothing more seems necessary to say in depicting what President McKinley truthfully designated as an "intolerable situation," and in showing the need of intervention of some strong party to prevent the combatants from destroying one another by the cruelest of means, and utterly ruining the fair island on which they were conducting a strife that they sadly miscalled "war." And as the United States stood guarantee for Spain that no other nation should set hostile foot on her island colony, the task of suppression remained for this country to take in hand, in the sacred name of humanity.

CHAPTER VI.

EVENTS LEADING TO INTERVENTION.

THE cruelty with which the war between Spain and the Cuban insurgents was conducted was viewed with intense indignation in the United States, while Spain's seeming inability to suppress the insurrection led to many demands for intervention by the press and people of this country. The inhumanity of the combatants, and particularly of the Spaniards, increased as the war went on, and the government of the United States was strongly urged to interfere. It was variously suggested that the insurgents should be treated as belligerents, that their republic should be recognized, and that Spain should be asked to sell Cuba. But nothing beyond suggestion came of all this; the time was not ripe for action.

Meanwhile the government of this country was kept busy in efforts to enforce its neutrality laws. The revolutionary Cuban Junta in New York was actively at work collecting funds and equipping relief-expeditions, and a considerable number of vessels became engaged in efforts to land men and munitions of war on the shores of Cuba. Both the United States and Spain endeavored to prevent this, but met with indifferent success. Many of the expeditions from American ports succeeded in eluding the vigilance of the authorities and getting away with their contraband cargoes. Many others were stopped, but in very few instances could satisfactory evidence of an intention to break the law be obtained. Only two of the captains of filibustering vessels were convicted, Captain J. H. Wiborg, of the Horsa, and Captain John H. Hart, of the Laurada. The latter, sentenced for a term of imprisonment, was pardoned by President McKinley after the war with Spain began.

In January, 1896, General Calixto Garcia sought to take a large quantity of military supplies and three hundred men to Cuba. His vessel, the Hawkins, foundered off Long Island, fortunately losing only five of its men. He made a second attempt on March 15 with the Bermuda, and this time succeeded in reaching Cuba and landing part of his supplies. He was at once given a prominent command in the Cuban army of independence.

Spain, which had the highest interest in checking these expeditions, was singularly unsuccessful in doing so. Of the many vessels which reached the Cuban coast the Spanish patrol-fleet succeeded in capturing only one, the Competitor, which left Key West April 23, 1896, and was taken near Esperanza, on the northern coast. The supplies had been landed before the Spanish patrol-boat appeared; but the bulk of them were abandoned, the men escaping into the interior with the exception of seven, who were taken prisoners. These were Alfred Laborde, captain of the vessel; William Gildea, its sailing-master; Ona Melton, a newspaper correspondent; Dr. Vezia, the physician of the expedition; a Cuban named Moza, and two sailors. None of them except the sailors sought to escape, they not fancying that they had committed any serious crime. The Spanish authorities thought otherwise. All of them except Moza, who volunteered evidence for the crown, were sentenced to death, and would have been summarily executed but for the intervention of Consul-General Lee. They were rigorously imprisoned under *incomunicado* conditions for eighteen months, being finally released by General Blanco.

In December, 1896, the war being then nearly two years old, and having seemingly fallen into a state of hopeless decrepitude, while the Weylerian cruelty and incapability had become strikingly evidenced, the first open declaration of the United States government was made in President Cleveland's annual message to Congress. In this he reviewed the situation at considerable length, stating the various propositions which had been made for recognition of Cuban belligerency or independence, or, all other methods failing, of intervention, even at the cost of a war with Spain. The President did not think that any of these measures was yet demanded by the situation, and stated that this government had intimated to Spain that if a satisfactory system of home rule were offered the islanders the United States would guarantee its execution, since nothing less would overcome the distrust of the insurgents. This offer Spain had failed to accept.

"It should be added," he continued, "that it cannot be reasonably assumed that the hitherto expectant attitude of the United States will be indefinitely maintained. . . . By the course of events we may be driven into such an unusual and unprecedented condition as will fix a limit to our patient waiting for Spain to win the contest, either alone and in her own way or by our friendly co-operation." He remarked further that if nothing remained but useless sacrifice of human life and utter desolation of the subject-matter of the conflict, "a situation will be presented in which our obligations to the sovereignty of Spain will be superseded by higher obligations, which we can hardly hesitate to recognize and discharge."

The scarcely veiled threat under these diplomatic utterances proved anything but palatable to Spain, and Prime-Minister Canovas quickly put himself on record by declaring that Spain would under no circumstances grant Cuba a system of autonomy similar to that of Canada. "No concession of any kind," he said, "will be made until the insurrection in Cuba is put under control. Spain is strong enough to carry on the campaign in Cuba and the Philippine Islands until peace is restored, no matter how long the struggle may last."

This declaration put an end to all hope of an accommodation. Spain, or at least her representatives in Cuba, had shown a marked incapability of doing anything of the kind promised, and the gates of a peaceful settlement were deliberately closed by the hands of the over-confident Spanish premier. The insurrectionary war was left to drift on in its old inconsequential way, with but a single end in view, that of final forced intervention on the part of the United States, since there seemed no hope that Spain would retire of herself from the futile contest.

Previous to the date of Cleveland's message he had sent General Fitzhugh Lee to Havana as United States consul-general, largely with the purpose of observing and reporting upon the state of affairs. A resolution recognizing the Cubans as belligerents had passed Congress, and at that time lay before the President. It was his doubt what action to take in this contingency that induced him to despatch Lee upon his errand. A week's observation enabled the quick-sighted Virginian to decide that there was no immediate prospect of either party's winning, and that meanwhile the island was being reduced to an ash-heap, property widely destroyed, commerce extinguished, and life taken on both sides under circumstances of great aggravation. The injury to commerce was causing great loss to American mercantile interests and to the people of the United States.

He found in the state of the country and the people much to provoke the Cubans and little evidence that judicious measures were being taken for their subjugation. While less than half a century before Cubans had owned most of the property and wealth of the country, now the Spaniards were the wealthy class,—doubtless in consequence of the supremacy given them by the government. Public enterprise was sadly lacking. There were no highways, scarcely any country roads, no canals, and no telegraphs except along some of the railroads. Of the latter none had been built by Spanish enterprise. The soldiers were as ill fitted for effective operations as the country was ill adapted to military movements. They were poorly drilled, disciplined, and organized; their pay was small and often failed to reach them; their clothing was poor; their officers exposed them heedlessly to all conditions of temperature and weather. As a result they had become feeble, listless, liable to disease, and unfit for active campaigning. Such was the state of affairs which gave its tone to President Cleveland's message.

Early in his administration President McKinley took similar steps to ascertain the state of affairs on the island, special reports being ordered from the consuls at the several cities. These confirmed the unofficial advices of the terrible lack of sanitary conditions under which the reconcentrados dwelt and the misery and starvation to which they were exposed, and the absence of effort on the part of Governor-General Weyler for their relief. Among the sufferers were many naturalized citizens of the United States, for whose relief the President sent a special message to Congress, asking for an appropriation of $50,000 to provide them with food and medicine or to transport them to this country. Fewer American citizens were found than had been reported, and the food provided did not reach them without difficulty, as Spanish jealousy threw obstacles in the way of its distribution.

On June 16, 1897, General Stewart L. Woodford was appointed United States minister to Spain, with instructions from the executive to inform that country that, in the opinion of the United States, the war ought to have ended, and asking it to name a date before the month of December, 1897, when it would end. The reply of the Spanish cabinet was that no such date could be named, but that they would spare no efforts to bring the war to a speedy termination. They said further, that it would have ended long before but for aid given by filibusters from the United States. This statement, with its implication of disregard of neutral obligations, created considerable irritation in American official circles, in view of the fact that this country had spent some $2,000,000 in the effort to check Cuban expeditions, and had in no sense failed in its duty.

The coming of General Blanco with his scheme of reform created a temporary hope that peace might result, a hope which vanished when the insurgents utterly refused to accept autonomy or amnesty from Spain and shot the tempters who came to them bribe in hand. The scheme of autonomy did not propose to abolish the autocratic office of governor-general, under which no true liberty could exist, and it would have left Cuba saddled with a war-debt far beyond her power to sustain. The rebels in arms refused to have anything to do with so feeble and colorless a system of home government, and the autonomous administration attempted by Blanco proved a weak and futile expedient, its officials being mere puppets, with no influence outside of Spanish garrisons. The effort, indeed, to establish a democracy under the shadow of an autocracy must have proved useless under any circumstances, and the Cubans had no intention of trusting a second time to the good faith of Spain.

In his message to Congress of December, 1897, President McKinley stated in impressive words the record of our relations with Cuba, spoke of the horrors of the war then raging in the island, and indicated that the time might come when we would be obliged to interfere. That time was much nearer at hand than he dreamed of. In truth, matters on the island were not improving, and the weakness of the ruling powers was becoming daily more declared. General Blanco had withdrawn Weyler's concentration order, but his action came too late. The evil was past remedy. In the words of General Lee, "In the first place, these people have no place to go to; their houses have been burned down; there is nothing but the bare land left, and it would take them two months before they could raise the first crop. In the next place, they are afraid to go out from the lines of the towns, because the roving bands of Spanish guerrillas, as they are called, would kill them. So they stick right in the edges of the town, just like they did, with nothing to eat except what they can get from charity."

This condition of affairs gave rise to President McKinley's next action, which was an intervention in the form of charity. He proposed now to extend aid to all the sufferers, not to limit it to American citizens, as before. On December 24, 1897, he issued an appeal to the American people, inviting contributions for the succor of the starving sufferers, and on the 8th of January, 1898, announced the formation of a Central Cuban Relief Committee under the auspices of the American National Red Cross Society. Clara Barton, president of this society, just returned from her relief-work in Armenia, made her way to Cuba to control this new duty of benevolence, and a vast quantity of supplies was sent to relieve the needs of the sufferers. Goods and money to the value of more than $200,000 were donated, and the relief, at first confined to Havana and the other large cities, gradually extended to all the towns where suffering existed. Thousands of lives were saved by this late but welcome charitable aid.

Spain, however, in her usual manner, threw difficulties in the way, objecting to the fact that some of the smaller war-vessels of the United States were employed in carrying relief-supplies, and rendering it necessary to employ other vessels for that purpose. She also showed her animus by requesting that Consul-General Lee, whose plain truth-telling had given offence, should be recalled. To this the United States government declined to accede, and Spain withdrew the request.

The activity of the Americans in their work of mercy had its effect upon the dulled moral consciousness of Spain. All American citizens in prison were released, and mercy was granted to certain Cuban prisoners who lay under sentence of death. Blanco had been authorized to sign a credit of $100,000 for the relief of the suffering. An equal sum was granted at a later date, and pacificos were sent to rebuild the small towns that had been destroyed. But the suffering people seem to have derived little benefit from the tardy benevolence of Spain.

Meanwhile the Spanish home government was as energetic as ever in its efforts to end the war,—and as unsuccessful. Money was borrowed freely from any one who would lend, until the country reached the verge of bankruptcy and the money-lords of Europe closed their purses against appeals from Spain. In addition to her funded debt of $1,200,000,000, one-third of which was due to foreign capitalists, she had a floating debt of $200,000,000, and a Cuban guarantee debt of $350,-000,000, bearing interest at five and six per cent., yet very greatly depreciated in value. These $550,000,-000 had been spent in the Cuban war, and the weight of this debt would have been laid upon Cuba in the event of subjugation. It would have constituted an overwhelming burden.

Spain was not only bankrupt in money, but was becoming so in men. The youth of the land had been sent, sorely against their will, across the ocean to feed the army in Cuba until exhaustion in this direction was at hand. And the discouraging feature of it all was that this proved to be largely waste effort. The degree of activity under Campos and Weyler, falsely directed as it had been, vanished under Blanco, who suffered the war to lag in his efforts to induce the insurgents to accept his measures of autonomy and amnesty.

The positive rejection of these by the insurgents left Spain in a hopeless state. Of the great army which she had sent to Cuba, many thousands had been swept away by the dread scourge of yellow fever, and thousands more were in a condition of unfitness for service. Of those who had escaped the hospital and the grave fully one-half were distributed among the multitudes of little forts that covered the island, and were useless for any effective operation. Of the remainder, many were needed for duties that rendered them unavailable for field operations,—such as guarding the railroads and the sugar-plantations. On the other hand, the insurgents seemed capable of continuing the war indefinitely. They needed no money, and the swift-growing roots supplied them with food. Arms and ammunition were their most pressing needs.

"Whatever may be said about old General Gomez," remarked General Lee, "he is, in my humble opinion, fighting the war in the only way it can be fought,—scattering his troops out; because to concentrate would be to starve, having no commissary-train and no way to get supplies. They come in sometimes for the purpose of making some little raid where he thinks it will do something; but he has given orders, so I have always been informed, not to fight in masses, not to lose their cartridges; and sometimes, when he gets into a fight, each man is ordered not to fire more than two cartridges. The way the insurgents do is this: they have little patches of sweet potatoes—everything grows there abundantly in a short time—and Irish potatoes and fruits. They drive their pigs and cattle into the valleys and hill-sides, and they use those and scatter out. The insurgents plant crops in many parts of the island."

Their system of warfare was to keep out of the reach of Spanish bullets and to save their own, so far as was consistent with their policy of incessantly annoying the enemy. This method, in common with the destruction of the resources of the island, must in the end have forced Spain to give up the fight through utter exhaustion. The trocha and the fort had failed. Reconcentration had done far more harm than good. The horrors of the firing-party and the military fusillade had no effect on the enemy in arms. The power of Spain had been frittered away in piecemeal operations, and, as there was no indication of the adoption of more effective methods, the strife in Cuba in the beginning of the year 1898 seemed in a stage of absolute hopelessness so far as Spain was concerned.

Meanwhile the irritation between Spain and the United States was daily increasing. The two governments seemed on the surface in accord, but the very evident sympathy for the insurgents among the people of the United States aroused hot indignation in Spain, and threats of war with this country were freely uttered by the populace and the papers. This feeling extended to Cuba. There were three parties in that island,—the revolutionary separatists, who desired complete independence; the autonomists, who wished for home rule; and the Spanish party, who opposed changes in the existing condition of affairs, bitterly objected to Blanco and his reforms, and looked upon the recall of Weyler as a fatal confession of weakness by Spain.

With the incoming of 1898 affairs rapidly approached a crisis. Early in the year the Spanish government, through its minister, De Lome, intimated that it would be agreeable to Spain if the charitable people of the United States should contribute for Cuban relief, and if money and supplies were sent to the American consuls to be forwarded and distributed under their charge. But this relief proposition was not kindly received by the people of Spain, and was furiously objected to by the conservative party in Cuba, who looked upon it as the entering-wedge for American intervention. The dissatisfaction grew so great that it gave rise on January 12 to a riotous outbreak in the streets of Havana. Though this seemed chiefly directed against two newspapers that favored autonomy, Blanco deemed it necessary to send a strong body of troops to protect the American consulate. And the fidelity of these could not be greatly trusted, in view of the fact that many of the rioters wore Spanish uniforms, showing that the hostile feeling was deeply intrenched in the army.

The United States government had been previously informed by Consul-General Lee of the critical state of affairs in Havana. It was well aware, also, that Spain was covertly preparing for war, having taken steps in the latter part of 1897 to increase her naval strength by purchasing ships in other European countries. Measures of this kind, whose threatening character was apparent, were not calculated to allay the irritation existing in the United States, and the riots at Havana were quickly followed by a significant act on the part of the government, —the North Atlantic Squadron of the navy being ordered to rendezvous at Key West and the Dry Tortugas. The squadron reached Florida on the 20th, and was joined there by the battle-ship Maine, which on the 25th was ordered to Havana harbor, ostensibly on a friendly visit, but probably with a view to protection of the American residents in case of a renewal of the riots. Other steps were taken which indicated preparation for possible hostilities, orders being sent to United States vessels in foreign waters to be ready to sail for home at short notice. Commodore Dewey, in command of the squadron at Hong Kong, was advised to hold himself in readiness to sail to the Atlantic. All these measures were significant of coming war. In return for the visit of the Maine, the Spanish cruiser Vizcaya was ordered to the United States, and reached New York harbor shortly after the wrecking of the Maine. She was received there with every courtesy.

The strained relations were greatly added to by an event that took place in early February. Señor Don Enrique de Lome, Spain's representative at Washington, had written a confidential letter to Señor Canalejas, whom Sagasta had sent to Havana to make a quiet investigation of the situation. This letter failed to reach the hands for which it was intended, being stolen from the mail by a Cuban sympathizer in the Havana post-office, probably on account of its bearing the stamp of the Spanish legation on the envelope. By him it was sent to the Cuban Junta in New York, whose members, perceiving its value to their cause, had photographed copies made, which they gave to the public press. The original was sent to the State Department at Washington.

The publication of this letter raised a storm. It was bitterly insulting to President McKinley, of whom it spoke as a "low politician," who catered to the rabble. It proposed that the question of commercial relations should be agitated, "even though only for effect," and indicated that the Spanish government was insincere and playing a double part in its negotiations. The letter further acknowledged that the military operations of Spain had been failures, and seemed likely to continue so. The war dragged on tediously, it admitted, and intimated that if Spain could conquer Cuba at all she would be ruined in the effort.

This letter rendered De Lome's position in Washington untenable. He was not slow in perceiving this, and hastened to cable his resignation before Minister Woodford could have an opportunity to demand his withdrawal. De Lome lost no time in leaving the country in which he had so suddenly brought his usefulness to an end. He was succeeded in March by Señor Polo, whose father had represented Spain in Washington many years before.

The turning-point in the tide of events came on the night of the 15th of February, 1898. The battle-ship Maine then lay in all seeming security in Havana harbor, where she swung at anchor about five hundred yards from the arsenal and two hundred yards from the floating dock. About two hundred yards away lay the American Ward Line steamer City of Washington, and a little farther off the Spanish cruiser Alfonso XII. This vessel had saluted the Maine with great display of amity upon her entrance to the harbor, and had been greeted with equal courtesy, each displaying the national ensign of the other and saluting with thirteen guns.

The night of the 15th was one of intense darkness. The crew of the Maine were asleep in their quarters. Captain Sigsbee was in bed in his cabin, and the executive officer, Lieutenant-Commander Richard Wainwright, was smoking in his quarters, when, at the hour of nine-forty, the silence was broken by a terrific explosion. The great vessel was lifted as if she had been a leaf floating on the waves, and in an instant was rent and torn almost out of all semblance to a ship-of-war. As the reverberation of the explosion died away, the darkness was broken by a great flame that burst from the ruined ship and illuminated the harbor far and near. On shore the shock of the explosion had extinguished the electric-lights, thrown down many of the telegraph-poles, and shaken the whole city front.

This dreadful event was met with great coolness and courage by the officers of the Maine. Wainwright, the executive officer, was in an instant on his feet, struck a match, for darkness prevailed in his quarters, and hurried to the captain's cabin. He found him uninjured, though the explosion had hurled him from his berth to the floor. Hurrying to the deck, the captain at once gave orders to a seaman to flood the magazine, which contained some five tons of powder. The man did so, but failed to return. He had fallen a victim to the catastrophe which had slain so many of his comrades. The explosion had wrecked the forward part of the ship, immediately under the quarters of the men, most of whom were instantly killed, while that portion of the ship was frightfully shattered.

Meanwhile the whole city had been aroused, and people were running to the water-front to learn the cause of the terrible shock. It was now easy to perceive, for the darkness was effectually broken. In addition to the glare from the burning Maine, a number of search-lights were turned on the dark surface of the waters, and electric-lights glowed on shore and ships. With the utmost haste boats were lowered from the two neighboring steamers and rowed to the wreck of the Maine, where every effort to render service was made. Thirty-seven of the wounded men were rescued by the boats of the Spanish ship and twenty-four by those of the City of Washington.

Captain Sigsbee did not for a moment lose his self-possession and worked diligently to rescue the remnants of his crew. In this his officers actively aided him. Such of the boats of the Maine as had escaped destruction were filled with the wounded, who were taken to the hospitals in Havana, where every care was given them, General Blanco lending all his influence to the work of mercy. Of the ship's company of three hundred and fifty-three only forty-eight escaped without injury. Captain Sigsbee was the last man to leave the ship, going in the launch to the Alphonso XII., where he thanked the captain and officers for their active aid. He then went to the City of Washington, arriving about midnight, and meeting there Consul-General Lee and others of prominence.

At three o'clock on the morning of February 16, President McKinley was awakened to hear a message of startling import which had just been received from Captain Sigsbee. It described the frightful disaster in the most temperate language :

"SECRETARY OF THE NAVY,
    " Washington, D.C.

"Maine blown up in Havana harbor at nine-forty to-night and destroyed. Many wounded and doubtless more killed or drowned. Wounded and others on board Spanish man-of-war and Ward Line steamer. Send light-house tenders from Key West for crew and the few pieces of equipment above water. None had clothing other than that upon him. Public opinion should be suspended until further report. All officers believed to be saved. Jenkins and Merritt not yet accounted for. [These two proved to have been lost.]

Many Spanish officers, including representative of General Blanco, now with me to express sympathy."

"SIGSBEE."

The suspension of opinion asked for by Captain Sigsbee was not accorded by the people, whose indignation was extreme on learning of the terrible event. The general opinion, aided by statements concerning the appearance of the vessel as she lay in the mud of Havana harbor, was that the loss of the Maine was not due to the explosion of her own magazines, as the Spaniards maintained, but that she had been blown up by a mine beneath her hull, and that the disaster was not the result of accident, but of Spanish malignity. The fact that among the numerous expressions of sympathy from foreign powers were cabled messages from General Blanco, the Spanish cabinet, and the Queen of Spain did not suffice to change the public opinion or to allay the excitement. No one thought that any of these had anything to do with the explosion, but many believed that Spanish officials were in some way concerned in it; and this feeling grew, instead of subsiding, as time went on.

A plot of ground in the cemetery at Havana was given for the interment of the victims, nineteen of whom were buried there with the greatest show of honor and sympathy, fifty thousand people crowding the streets and paying respect to the dead. Shortly after the destruction of the Maine, the Spanish cruiser Vizcaya, as already stated, reached the harbor of New York, where she was placed under close guard by federal and city authorities to prevent any injury to her through revenge. She remained there for a brief period and then set sail for Cuba, full courtesy and consideration being shown her officers while in New York.

The Maine was the oldest battle-ship of the American navy. While second-rate in size, being of less than 7000 tons displacement, she was a fine and powerful ship, and had been built at a cost of $2,500,000, which expenditure had been greatly added to by the cost of her arms and equipments. In addition to the total destruction of the ship itself was the loss of two hundred and sixty-six lives, including those who died from their wounds and the two officers named in Captain Sigbee's message, who had hastened to their posts of duty on being aroused by the explosion and had perished in consequence. This state of affairs gave rise to a natural feeling of resentment in the minds of the American people, which quickly deepened to a thirst for revenge and a feverish impatience which could scarce await the deliberate movements of a committee of investigation. Had the general feeling been accepted, the country would have been plunged into war at once, but the government was less hasty in its decision, feeling that investigation should precede action, and that it remained to be shown whether the disaster was due to the explosion of an external mine or of the ship's own magazines. A naval Court of Inquiry was therefore appointed by the Navy Department, consisting of Captain W. T. Sampson of the Iowa, Captain F. C. Chadwick of the New York, Lieutenant-Commander W. P. Potter of the New York, and Lieutenant-Commander Adolph Marix of the Vermont.

Divers were sent with all convenient despatch to Havana harbor to examine the condition of the sunken hull and furnish evidence for the committee to act upon.

Rear-Adm. George Dewey

Rear-Adm. William T. Sampson

Rear-Adm. Winfield Scott Schley

Capt. Charles D. Sigsbee

Capt. Charles E. Clark

Capt. John W. Philip

UNITED STATES NAVAL COMMANDERS

The investigation proceeded with a deliberation that was exasperating to the mass of the people, who had formed their opinion without waiting for the evidence. A thorough examination was made of the condition of the wreck. Here, though no trace of a submarine mine could be found, there were abundant indications that some powerful explosive had been set off below the hull of the ship which had force sufficient to cause a frightful distortion of her hull and practically to break her in two.

The evidence presented before the court was very voluminous, the testimony covering twelve thousand type-written pages. Every item of evidence was thoroughly considered and sifted. A unanimous decision of the court was reached March 21, 1898, after more than four weeks of deliberation. The verdict, as summarized, was as follows: "That the loss of the Maine was not in any respect due to fault or negligence on the part of any of the officers or members of her crew; that the ship was destroyed by the explosion of a submarine mine, which caused the partial explosion of two or more of her forward magazines; and that no evidence has been obtainable fixing the responsibility for the destruction of the Maine upon any person or persons."

This decision, given to the public on March 25, was in full accord with the opinion almost universally entertained by the American people. The long-continued investigation by our divers was followed by a hasty one ordered by Spain, which took only a day or two for its completion, and resulted in, judging from its rapidity, what may have been a predetermined decision, that the cause of the explosion was wholly internal. A settlement of the question by arbitration was demanded.

This, under the aggravating circumstances of the case, the United States government was in no mood to accord. Efforts were made to recover the heavy guns and other valuable material from the wreck, but these proved in great part futile, and the shattered hulk, as a coffin for the gallant crew, was permitted to sink into the soft and deep mud of the bottom of Havana harbor.

The Maine was not to perish unavenged. The hostile feeling of the people was reflected in the government, and active preparations were made by the War and Navy Departments for possible war. Movements in this direction had been made early in the year. They were intensified by the Maine horror. The fortifications of the coast were strengthened, war-material was collected and distributed with energy, recruiting went on for all branches of the service, and the greatest activity was manifested in adding to the strength of the navy. The ship-yards engaged on government work were kept busy day and night. All vessels needing repair were hurried into the dry-docks. The old monitors at League Island were overhauled with all haste. A fleet of auxiliary cruisers was added to the regular naval force, including a number of the largest and fastest passenger-steamers. A naval officer was hurried to Europe to purchase suitable war-ships found for sale in foreign ship-yards, and large numbers of the smaller cannon and a great quantity of ammunition were bought abroad. Of the several vessels purchased only one came into important use during the war, the New Orleans (formerly the Amazonas), a fine cruiser obtained from Brazil. The Buffalo (formerly the Nictheroy), a dynamite gunboat obtained from the same source, proved of little utility. Two small cruisers were purchased in England, the Topeka and the Albany, the latter being detained, as the war had begun before she could be removed from her English port.

Anticipating the decision of the Court of Inquiry, Congress did not wait for its verdict, but on the 9th of March, at the request of the President, voted $50,000,000 as an emergency fund for the national defence. This money was at once employed in purchasing ships and war-material at home and abroad, and in adding to the strength of the army, a bill being passed for the recruiting of two regiments of artillery, to be employed in manning the heavy guns in the forts along the coast.

Captain William T. Sampson was put in command of the fleet at Key West, with the rank of acting rear-admiral, while a "Flying Squadron" was organized at Hampton Roads, under the command of Commodore Winfield Scott Schley, with the armored cruiser Brooklyn as flag-ship, the battle-ships Massachusetts and Texas, and the cruisers Columbia and Minneapolis, the fastest afloat in the navies of the world.

In addition to the ships purchased and subsidized, work on the battle-ships under contract, five in number, was hastened, and a naval bill was passed by Congress carrying an unusually large addition to the navy, embracing three battle-ships, four monitors, twelve torpedo-boats, and sixteen torpedo-boat destroyers. This provision was made without any reference to the hostile relations with Spain, but simply in response to the war sentiment abroad and the general feeling that our navy was too weak for the possible needs of the nation.

On March 17, Senator Proctor made a speech before Congress, in which he described, with the simple eloquence of facts, the terrible scenes of destitution he had witnessed in his visit to Cuba, of which we have already spoken. The horrors of the reconcentration policy were depicted by him with a clearness never before realized by the people, and his words sent a shudder of horrified feeling from end to end of the land. Senators Gallinger and Thurston added their testimony to his, arousing the deep indignation not only of the people, but of Congress, whose members had not before fully appreciated the condition of affairs in Cuba. From all sides came fervent appeals from people and press for the relief of the starving inhabitants of the desolated island. The $50,000,000 appropriation for defence had been passed by a unanimous vote. But preparation for war, not for defence, was now demanded, since, aside from the disaster to the Maine, it was felt that the barbarous policy of Spain had rendered war inevitable. The decision of the Maine Court of Inquiry, which quickly followed, and was transmitted by the President to Congress, with an accompanying message, on March 28, added fuel to the flame and roused the House to a grim determination which no advocate of the policy of peace could restrain. Speaker Reed in vain attempted to hold it back. The Senate was equally bent on war. The disaster to the Maine was but a match touched to the powder of public sentiment. War must have come without it if Spain did not change her policy, and this she showed no intention of doing. The terrible spectacle of nearly a quarter of a million of unoffending people dying of sheer starvation was more than the moral sentiment of the American people could endure. Spain would not succor the people and could not conquer the insurgents. Nothing remained but for the United States to intervene.

Meanwhile President McKinley endeavored to avert hostilities. On March 27 he submitted a proposition to Spain, asking that country to grant an amnesty to the insurgents, to continue till October 1, during which time the United States would conduct negotiations for peace. He also asked that steps should be taken for the return of the reconcentrados to their farms, promising that the United States would relieve their wants until they were able to support themselves. This communication met the usual fate of negotiations with Spain. An evasive and unsatisfactory reply was returned, deferring the immediate cessation of hostilities and proposing a scheme for "preparing peace." The offer of aid to the reconcentrados was accepted, and a proposition to arbitrate the Maine affair was added.

The President had made his final effort. Spain's policy of procrastination could no longer be endured. He now turned the matter over to Congress, preparing a special message, in which the whole question at issue was considered and the situation delineated from its various points of view. Congress was asked for legislation. This message was ready April 4, but was kept back for a week to give time for the American consuls and other citizens to leave Cuba. It was sure to cause violent excitement in the Cuban cities, and might give rise to riotous assaults on the consulates, and the safety of American residents counselled delay. On April 9 Consul-General Lee left Havana. There were no hostile demonstrations by the people, but General Blanco treated him with marked discourtesy, and the soldiers on guard at the palace were permitted to act in an insulting manner. Many other Americans left the Cuban ports, few or none remaining, and on April 11 the message of the President was sent to Congress, a final decision on the question of peace or war being left to that body. There was added to the document, in the form of a postscript, the statement that Spain had just granted the amnesty asked for,—as usual, too late.

We have already quoted from this message. A further quotation will be in place. "The efforts of Spain," it said, "added to the horrors of the strife a new and inhuman phase happily unprecedented in the modern history of civilized Christian people. The policy of devastation and concentration inaugurated on October 21, 1896, in the province of Pinar del Rio, was thence extended to embrace all of the island to which the power of the Spanish arms was able to reach by military occupation or by military operations. The peasantry, including all dwellers in the open agricultural interior, were driven into the garrisoned towns or isolated places held by troops. The raising and movement of provisions of all kinds were interdicted. The fields were laid waste, dwellings unroofed or fired, mills destroyed, and, in short, everything that could desolate the land and render it unfit for human habitation or support was commanded by one or other of the contending parties and executed by all the powers at their disposal."

The President described in thrilling language the results of this terrible policy, with the frightful destitution, misery, and starvation to which it had given rise, saying that "The only peace it could beget was that of the wilderness and the grave." There had arisen in consequence what he designated as an "intolerable situation." "The only hope of relief and repose," he said, "from a condition which can no longer be endured is the enforced pacification of Cuba. In the name of humanity, in the name of civilization, in behalf of endangered American interests, which give us the right and the duty to speak and to act, the war in Cuba must stop." In view of the facts presented, Congress was asked to authorize the President to take measures for the termination of hostilities and to secure a stable government in Cuba, "and to use the military and naval forces of the United States as may be necessary for these purposes." Evidently the President had given up all hope of peace, for these words meant war.

In addition to his message, President McKinley transmitted to Congress an extensive series of reports received from the American consuls in Cuba during the preceding year in reference to the treatment of the reconcentrados. These had been asked for by Congress on February 14, but the sinking of the Maine on the following day had put them out of sight, and they were only now transmitted to the legislative bodies. They fully confirmed all that had been stated by General Lee, Senator Proctor, and others in regard to the inhuman treatment of the unarmed people by Spain, and furnished ample confirmation of all that the President had said, and an argument for war on the highest grounds on which a resort to arms can be based, those of humanity and the preservation of the moral standard of mankind.

An impassioned debate followed the reception of the message and continued for several days. In this scarcely a voice was raised for peace. The vast majority of the members were bent upon war, the question at issue being that of the recognition or non-recognition of the republic of Cuba, on which a prolonged disagreement was developed between the Senate and the House. This question was finally shelved, and on April 19 the two bodies of Congress united upon the following joint resolution, which was approved by the President on the 20th:

"JOINT RESOLUTION for the recognition of the independence of the people of Cuba, demanding that the government of Spain relinquish its authority and government in the island of Cuba, and withdraw its land and naval forces from Cuba and Cuban waters, and directing the President of the United States to use the land and naval forces of the United States to carry these resolutions into effect.

"WHEREAS, The abhorrent conditions which have existed for more than three years in the island of Cuba, so near our own borders, have shocked the moral sense of the people of the United States, have been a disgrace to Christian civilization, culminating, as they have, in the destruction of a United States battle-ship, with two hundred and sixty-six of its officers and crew, while on a friendly visit in the harbor of Havana, and cannot longer be endured, as has been set forth by the President of the United States in his message to Congress of April 11, 1898, upon which the action of Congress was united; therefore,

"*Resolved*, By the Senate and House of Representatives of the United States of America in Congress assembled,

"1. That the people of the island of Cuba are, and of right ought to be, free and independent.

"2. That it is the duty of the United States to demand, and the government of the United States does hereby demand, that the government of Spain at once relinquish its authority and government in the island of Cuba, and withdraw its land and naval forces from Cuba and Cuban waters.

"3. That the President of the United States be, and he hereby is, directed and empowered to use the land

and naval forces of the United States and to call into the actual service of the United States the militia of the several States to such an extent as may be necessary to carry these resolutions into effect.

"4. That the United States hereby disclaims any disposition or intention to exercise sovereignty, jurisdiction, or control over said island except for the pacification thereof, and asserts its determination, when that is accomplished, to leave the government and control of the island to its people."

There could be but one outcome from these resolutions. No one dreamed for a moment that Spain would accede to the conditions offered her. In truth, she was quick to act. She was to be given until noon of the 23d for an answer, but on the 20th Señor Polo, the Spanish minister, asked for his passports and left Washington. General Woodford, the American minister at Madrid, was not given an opportunity to present the ultimatum of the United States to the government of Spain, his passports being sent him before he had time to act. Spain thus took the initiative in inaugurating the war. Woodford left Madrid on the night of the 21st, not without some efforts at violence on the part of the excited people. On April 24 Spain issued a declaration of war. On the 25th Congress passed a resolution that war between the United States and Spain "is declared to exist, and to have existed, since April 21." After a period of thirty-three years of peace and prosperity war had again come to the great republic of the West.

War was in the air long before it was declared. The verdict of the Maine Court of Inquiry, taken in connection with Spain's denial and repellant attitude, had rendered hostilities inevitable unless some radical change should take place in the demeanor of the Spanish government and in the situation in Cuba. Of such changes there was no indication. Spain was actively engaged in efforts to purchase ships and munitions of war, and in other preparations for hostilities. Nothing was being done in Cuba, other than to permit American charity to aid the suffering. In early April, 1898, the Spanish cabinet, either shamed into action by the activity of American benevolence or for effect, voted three million pesetas—more than $600,000—for the aid of the starving reconcentrados. That this succor would reach them was very questionable. The soldiers were in almost as pitiable a state as the pacificos. General Lee, questioned concerning this subject on April 12 by the Senate Committee on Foreign Relations, replied: "I do not believe $600,000 in supplies will be given to these people and the soldiers left to starve. They will divide it up here and there—a piece taken off here and a piece taken off there. The condition of the reconcentrados out in the country is just as bad as in General Weyler's day, except as it has been relieved by supplies from the United States."

Whatever effect such a belated act of charity was likely to produce, it came too late to check the tide of hostile feeling. Like all Spanish yieldings to the pressure of circumstances, it was delayed until its force was spent. In every reform proclaimed by Spain in Cuban affairs the fatal fault of procrastination appeared. *Mañana* (tomorrow) should be taken as the national motto of Spain. In no instance that can be named has a reform measure been offered except under the absolute pressure of events, and all such have been vitiated by conditions which would quickly have negatived their effect. Such was

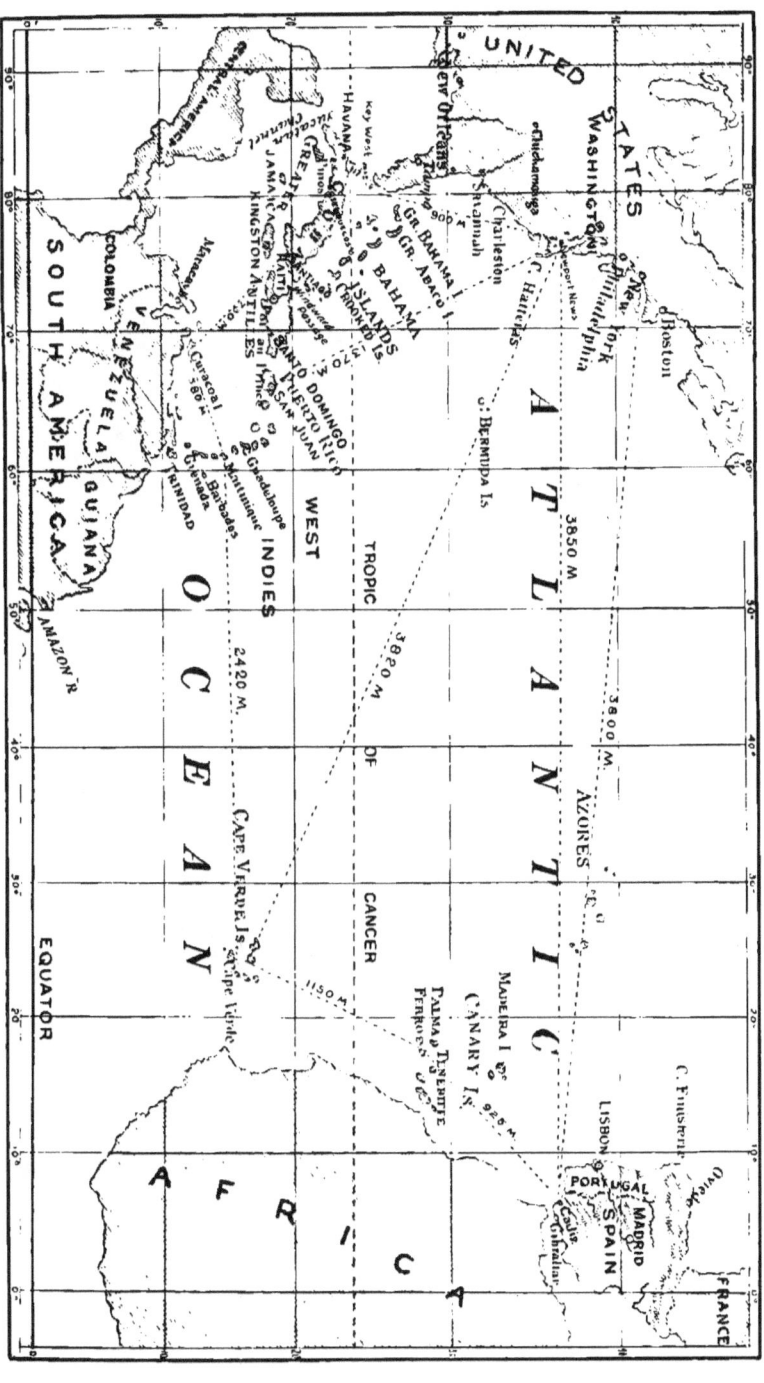

the case with the various Blanco reforms. The natives remembered too well the result of the Zanjon capitulation to accept any pacification on the same terms. The appropriation for relief was like all the other steps of reform,—it came too late. In the state of affairs then existing, it was like Dame Partington's effort to keep back the ocean with a broom.

In fact, for a month before the declaration of war such a result of the controversy had become inevitable. There was talk of friendly intervention of the nations of Europe, and the representatives of six of the great powers made an official call upon the President in the interests of peace. The courteous but decisive reply of the Executive put a final end to all efforts in this direction. Attempts to influence Spain to withdraw from her hostile attitude were also made, but without effect. The affair had gone too far to be checked without a resort to arms.

Meanwhile, preparations for hostilities went on with all activity. In addition to the movements of the fleet mentioned, the battle-ship Oregon was ordered to the Atlantic, and left San Francisco on March 19 for a long journey around the South American continent. She was accompanied in part of her course by the gunboat Marietta. The activity displayed in the navy was now paralleled in the army. Orders were issued on April 15 for the concentration of the troops at different points in the South, six regiments of cavalry and the light batteries of five regiments of artillery being ordered to rendezvous at Chickamauga, where a military camp was established. Eight regiments of infantry were set in motion for New Orleans, seven for Tampa, Florida, and seven for Mobile; making a total force of twenty thousand men. During the week ending April 18 the troops of the regular army began moving rapidly by rail towards these camps.

This movement had been under contemplation for some time, its purpose being to acclimate the troops to a climate approaching the tropical; but it had been delayed in view of the expense entailed and with the hope that an accommodation might be reached. But with the near approach of war, immediate action became necessary, and the army was set in rapid motion, converging from all points upon the new camps in the South. The whole army was under the command of Major-General Nelson A. Miles, its several divisions being under Major-General J. R. Brooke and Brigadier-Generals W. B. Shafter, J. J. Coppinger, and J. F. Wade.

While the United States was thus actively preparing for the threatened war, Spain was no less active. Her agents were abroad purchasing war-material in the other countries of Europe and seeking to obtain warships that had been built for other nations. In the latter effort she was unsuccessful, and no additions were made to her fleet. A squadron embracing some of the finest vessels in her navy was sent to the Cape Verde Islands, in preparation for a rapid run across the Atlantic should necessity demand. Thus the two nations stood at bay, while actively preparing for what seemed an inevitable strife.

The powers of Europe looked on meanwhile with much apprehension, not knowing to what complications a war might lead. Yet they had no warrant for intervention. It could not be denied that the highest interests of morality sustained the United States in its course. On the other hand, Spain was preparing to fight for its colonies, as any of these nations would have done. The loss of the Maine was an added provocation sufficient to have plunged any of these powers into war. In consequence, the European governments confined themselves to amicable efforts, which proved of no avail in preventing the appeal to arms.

CHAPTER VII.

CUBA UNDER BLOCKADE.

FOR three weary months the North Atlantic Squadron of the United States navy had lain in the waters south of Florida, lazily falling and lifting as the tide ebbed and flowed, while impatience for action on the part of the crews deepened until almost into a passion. Captain William T. Sampson, appointed acting rear-admiral, was in command, his flag-ship being the armored cruiser New York. The fleet included in addition the battle-ships Iowa and Indiana, the double-turreted monitors Puritan, Terror, Miantonomah, and Amphitrite, the cruisers Montgomery, Marblehead, Cincinnati, and Detroit, and a considerable number of gunboats, torpedo-boats, and accessory craft. On the evening of April 21, 1898, the flag-ship swung at anchor about seven miles out from Key West, flanked by the two great battle-ships, while the inner harbor presented an animated picture with its throng of monitors, cruisers, and smaller craft,—the larger vessels at anchor, the smaller ones gliding about on various errands.

Dulness and calm rested upon the ships, as it had rested for weeks past. Men and officers lounged about the decks or sought relaxation in the neighboring town. But as the night wore on a change appeared. A special boat from the flag-ship called back to their ships all those on shore, and by midnight the show of gold braid and blue jackets, which had long been familiar sights in the streets of the Gulf port, had disappeared. At the mast-heads of the New York and her consorts signal-lights flashed and flickered, their vari-colored gleams conveying significant orders to the ships in shore. From the latter flashed back replies, and during the night a conversation in points of fire was kept up through the air, telling but one thing to the interested observers, that the long wait was at an end and great events were in train.

Over the wires had come from Washington the startling words: "War is declared." With them came to the admiral of the fleet orders for an immediate blockade of the Cuban coast, and at break of day on the 22d smoke was seen to pour densely from the black-mouthed stacks, anchors were cheerily drawn from their holding-ground, the lazy swinging of the ships was exchanged for active motion, and lively hope chased despondency from the faces of the crews. At the earliest hour of dawn the final signals burned in letters of light above the ships, and some of the vessels of the fleet were already gliding out of the harbor. Shortly before six o'clock the flag-ship was seen moving slowly outward, the Iowa and Indiana following on either side. In the harbor the remaining ships were all astir, with the exception of the Puritan, the Terror, and some smaller boats, which remained behind to take on water and coal. Gradually the fleet grew smaller and less distinct, and one by one the vessels vanished in the blue distance. The time of expectation was over; that of action had begun. The ships were on their way to carry the message of war to Cuba's verdant shores. The first fruits of the new dispensation were seen when a flash broke from the side of the gunboat Nashville, and a cannonball ruffled the water in front of a passing steamer at whose mast-head flew the Spanish flag. A second shot was necessary before the Spanish captain took the hint and hove to his vessel. In a brief time she had veered and was making her way to Key West in charge of a prize crew. The vessel proved to be the merchantman Buena Ventura, laden with lumber from Texas. The captain had hoisted his flag as a salute, not knowing that war was declared.

Before nightfall the blockade of the Cuban coast had begun, and Havana, at the bottom of whose harbor lay the sunken Maine, was feeling the stress of war. On the same day President McKinley announced to the powers of the world that Havana and the neighboring ports were under blockade, and that commercial intercourse with them must be suspended. The blockade, as proclaimed, extended from Cardenas to Bahia Honda on the north coast, a distance of about one hundred and sixty miles. On the south coast it was limited to the single port of Cienfuegos.

While these events were in progress, a note of alarm came from across the seas. The great steamer of the American Line, the Paris, which had been chosen as part of our auxiliary fleet, lay at Southampton, England, with orders to sail for the United States on the 22d. Fears were entertained that this noble ship might be made a Spanish prize, and rumors were rife that cruisers from Spain were prowling about in her expected route. The anxiety did not subside until the Paris loomed up in American waters, safe from capture and without having seen a hostile sail.

In Havana, on the same day, defiance was being cast in the face of the Americans. On the night before, the public buildings and many private residences had been decorated with the national colors, and an illumination of the city followed, as though the occasion was one of festivity. The next morning the people, wearing ribbons of the Spanish colors, gathered densely in the square opposite the palace, sending a committee to the governor-general to tender their estates and their lives in aid of the national cause, for which they pledged themselves to fight to the bitter end. General Blanco thanked them in the name of the king and the governing powers, and made a speech to the people in which he assured them that he would lead them to victory.

"Otherwise I shall not live," he said. "Do you swear to follow me to the fight?"

"Yes, yes, we do!" shouted the throng.

"Do you swear to give the last drop of blood in your veins before letting a foreigner stamp his foot on the land we discovered and place his yoke on the people we civilized?"

"Yes, yes, we do!"

"The enemy's fleet is almost at Morro Castle, almost at the shores of Havana. We will throw them into the sea."

Just where the people whom Spain had civilized were to be found General Blanco, in his enthusiasm, neglected to state. But he sought to make his words good on the following day by opening fire from Morro Castle on the flag-ship of the American fleet. On the 24th Morro fired again on the American ships. It was a futile waste of powder and shot, which was not accorded the honor of a reply. The projectiles had sunk uselessly into the waves. During this fusillade the fleet was engaged in making prizes. On the 23d the New York brought to bay, after an exciting chase, the Spanish freight-steamer Pedro, the Porter captured the steamer Mathilde, and the Helena made prize of the fine steamer Miguel Jover. Four more prizes were taken on the following day, and by the end of a week the number of prizes had more than doubled, their value aggregating upwards of $3,000,000. The mail-steamer Montserrat, laden with eighteen large guns and $800,000 in silver, and having on board one thousand Spanish troops, was fortunate in discovering the lion in her path, and doubled back when near Havana, landing her cargo and troops at the distant port of Santiago de Cuba.

The Cuban insurgents were not long in receiving the glad tidings that a powerful ally was coming to their aid. For three years they had kept the field with desperate determination, but almost hopeless of help from without. Now the long-prayed-for message of hope and success was brought to their camps, a gallant American soldier risking danger and death in the perilous enterprise. Before war was declared, before the President's message had reached Congress, Lieutenant Andrew S. Rowan, of the United States army, had left Washington on a mission to the Cubans in arms. Starting from the capital on April 9, he reached Kingston, Jamaica, on the 23d, and crossed from that island to Cuba in a little sailing-boat, handled by a man whom the daring lieutenant familiarly designated his "pirate" and who was thoroughly familiar with the waters of those seas. The movements of the Spanish patrol-boats were well known to him, and he succeeded in landing Lieutenant Rowan while the coast was clear.

The danger of the enterprise was great, the coast being patrolled by land and sea, while if taken he would probably have been executed as a spy. But he was met by Cubans and escorted to the mountains in the vicinity of Santiago, making his way in a few days to General Garcia's camp, then at Bayamo, where he was greeted with the highest enthusiasm. This interior stronghold, which the Spanish troops had held against Cuban assault since the beginning of the war, had been evacuated by them on April 28. It was immediately occupied by the insurgents, who doubtless looked upon this withdrawal of their foe as the first signal of the good time coming.

Lieutenant Rowan had been charged by the President with a secret mission to General Garcia, with whom he had a long interview, laying plans for a future co-operation of the allied forces. On his return to the coast he was accompanied by General Collazo and Colonel Hernandez, of the Cuban army, as envoys to the United States. Three guides completed the party, which risked the perils of the sea in a small boat. The first morning out they came in sight of Admiral Sampson's squadron, but made no attempt to board the ships. The next day they were picked up by a sponging-sloop and carried to Nassau, New Providence, whence the adventurous party made its way to the United States. Thus ended in success the first of those daring enterprises through which Americans won reputation for boldness and courage during the war. Through it the President received valuable information concerning the numbers and condition of the Cuban army and the state of affairs in the interior. Major-General Miles gave the following tribute to Rowan's courage: "This was a most perilous undertaking, and in my judgment Lieutenant Rowan performed an act of heroism and cool daring that has rarely been excelled in the annals of warfare."

The events described at the seat of war were paralleled by as active ones at the seat of the government. An army bill was passed by Congress on April 22 providing for a temporary increase of the army, in response to which, on the following day, the President issued a proclamation calling for one hundred and twenty-five thousand volunteers to serve for two years, and to be apportioned among the States and Territories in accordance with their populations. The proclamation was enthusiastically responded to from all parts of the country, the National Guards of the several States hastening to offer their services, while there were thousands ready to fill up vacancies and to swell out the depleted columns of the regular army, so as to bring every regiment up to its full official strength. Far more offered, indeed, than the government was ready to accept, and a most rigid system of health inspection was inaugurated, in order that none but those in a state of full health and capable of enduring the hardships of campaigning in a tropical island should be enrolled. The result was to give the government one of the most physically perfect armies that had ever been put in the field.

A question of world-wide importance had meanwhile arisen, that concerning privateering. Spain had not signed the Declaration of Paris abolishing privateering, and stood free to cover the ocean with swift vessels to prey on American commerce. In such an obsolete mode of warfare, even if the United States government had met Spain by issuing letters of marque, this country would have been at a serious disadvantage, on account of the vast preponderance of American commerce over that of Spain. But it had no such purpose in view, and Spain, while formally reserving the right to send out privateers, deemed it unwise to put it in exercise, in view of the irritation such a course would have caused in the nations whose friendship she desired to preserve. Her declaration of the existence of war therefore took the following form :

"CLAUSE 1. The state of war existing between Spain and the United States annuls the treaty of peace and amity of October 17, 1795, and the protocol of January 12, 1877, and all other agreements, treaties, or conventions in force between the two countries.

"CLAUSE 2. From the publication of these presents, thirty days are granted to all vessels of the United States anchored in our harbors to take their departure free of hindrance.

"CLAUSE 3. Notwithstanding that Spain has not adhered to the Declaration of Paris, the government, respecting the principles of the law of nations, proposes to observe, and hereby orders to be observed, the following regulations of maritime law :

"*First.* Neutral flags cover the enemy's merchandise, except contraband of war.

"*Second.* Neutral merchandise, except contraband of war, is not seizable under the enemy's flag.

"*Third.* A blockade to be obligatory must be effective,—viz., it must be maintained with sufficient force to prevent access to the enemy's littoral.

"*Fourth.* The Spanish government, upholding its right to grant letters of marque, will at present confine itself to organizing, with the vessels of the mercantile marine, a force of auxiliary cruisers which will co-operate with the navy, according to the needs of the campaign, and will be under naval control.

"*Fifth.* In order to capture the enemy's ships and

confiscate the enemy's merchandise and contraband of war under whatever form, the auxiliary cruisers will exercise the right of search on the high seas and in the waters under the enemy's jurisdiction, in accordance with international law and the regulations which will be published.

"*Sixth.* [Defines what is included in contraband of war, naming weapons, ammunition, equipments, engines, and, in general, all the appliances used in war.]

"*Seventh.* To be regarded and judged as pirates, with all the rigor of the law, are captains, masters, officers, and two-thirds of the crew of vessels which, not being American, shall commit acts of war against Spain, even if provided with letters of marque issued by the United States."

Spain thus took the initiative in declaring war, this proclamation being issued on April 24, while the declaration of the United States, as already stated, was issued on the 25th. Both were merely formal declarations of the war which had existed since the 21st. On the day of the declaration, Secretary of State John Sherman retired from his post in the Cabinet, being incapacitated by age and feebleness to perform the onerous duties of the office in times of war. William R. Day, the assistant secretary, was appointed to the vacant post. The other Cabinet officers whose duties were specially affected by the declaration of war were Russell A. Alger, Secretary of War; John D. Long, Secretary of the Navy; and Lyman T. Gage, Secretary of the Treasury.

For five days the blockading fleet lay off Havana, the great ships seven or eight miles from shore, the smaller ones occasionally venturing nearer, confining themselves strictly to blockading duties, and seizing all Spanish

Copyright, 1898, by I. E. Purdy & Co., Boston
John D. Long, Secretary of the Navy

Copyright, 1896, by F. Gutekunst, Philadelphia
William McKinley, President U.S.A.

Russell A. Alger, Secretary of War

vessels that incautiously ventured within their reach. On shore the soldiers of Spain were kept busy in building and strengthening batteries, a form of activity of which Admiral Sampson did not approve, and with which he concluded to interfere. On the morning of the 27th the flag-ship steamed along the coast to Matanzas, a sea-port city some fifty miles to the east of Havana. Near the entrance to the harbor she was met by the Puritan and the Cincinnati, on blockade duty at that point. The wind blew freshly and the waves poured in sheets of green water over the low bow and stern of the monitor as she followed in the wake of the New York. Admiral Sampson stood on the bridge of the flag-ship carefully surveying the shore, where evidence appeared that the Spanish troops were actively engaged in building what seemed to be a sand battery, on which several guns had been mounted. The admiral thought that a lesson was needed. The signal call of "general quarters" was given, and with alacrity the men rushed to their guns. For more than thirty years the United States navy had not fired a hostile shot. Now a new record was to be made.

Reaching a situation about four thousand yards distant from Punta Gorda, where the new earthwork appeared, the helm of the flag-ship was put to starboard and the bugler sounded the signal, "Commence firing." Response was instant. From "Waist," the gunner's name for the eight-inch gun amidships on the port-side, came a loud roar and a shock that shook the great ship from stem to stern. The shell struck a little to the right of the earthwork, where a small cloud of dust testified to the fall of the first shot fired at an enemy from a ship of the new American navy. Two others followed, the third landing in the very centre of the earthwork, the dense cloud that rose being evidence of the perfect accuracy of the aim. These three shots were followed by a broadside from all the guns that could be brought to bear,— eight-inch and four-inch guns hurling their projectiles together upon the obtrusive work.

So far the New York had been engaged alone. But the Puritan and the Cincinnati were vigorously signalling for permission to fire. "All right; tell them to go ahead," said the admiral on learning their request. They lost no time in taking part in the work.

The bombardment had not been without a return. At Quintas de Recreo, on the east of the harbor, seven thousand yards from the New York, was a fort armed with four 8-inch guns, whose shots were coming towards the flag-ship, though falling very short. Sampson now directed his fire on this fort. The Puritan did the same, while the Cincinnati continued to attend to the earthwork. Five minutes sufficed to silence the fort, and the New York again turned her guns on the sand battery. At 1.15 P.M., nineteen minutes after the affair began, the admiral signalled to "cease firing," and the brief engagement came to an end.

About three hundred shots had been fired during this initial engagement, with few returns from the shore, no shot hitting any of the ships. The effect on shore was not apparent, other than that the forts were silenced and seemingly deserted. From Madrid came the report that the Spanish loss consisted of "one mule," a sarcastic tribute to American gunnery that elicited much mirth from our ill-wishers on the other side of the ocean. Leaving the Puritan and the Cincinnati to look after Matanzas, the New York headed for Havana. The affair had amounted to little more than useful target-practice, its chief utility being its evidence of the accuracy of American gunnery. All that need further be said about it is to note the eagerness displayed by the sailors at the opportunity to fight, four sick men springing from their cots at the first shot and rushing to their stations at the guns. It was with bitter disappointment that they returned when ordered back to the sick-bay.

While the United States navy had thus actively engaged in hostilities, that of Spain was not quite idle. In number of ships that country fairly equalled the United States. It was inferior in strength, though it had a number of vessels of good fighting capacity. Several of the best of the Spanish ships, comprising four swift armored cruisers and a number of torpedo-boat destroyers, had assembled in the days preceding the declaration of war at St. Vincent harbor, Cape Verde Islands. A second fleet, of inferior strength, lay at Manila, in the Philippines ; and a third, of considerable numerical strength, yet embracing few ships in good condition for duty, was at the port of Cadiz, Spain. It was to the Cape Verde fleet that the principal attention was paid on the American side. There was much apprehension that the powerful ships of this fleet might make a sudden dash across the Atlantic and attack some of our seaport cities, few of which were well defended, while some were in serious need of forts and guns.

To guard against this possible danger, the "Flying Squadron," under Commodore Winfield Scott Schley, was held ready at Newport News. It included the battle-ships Massachusetts and Texas, the armored cruiser Brooklyn, Commodore Schley's flag-ship, and the protected cruisers Minneapolis and Columbia. The latter were kept patrolling the coast, in which duty was also engaged a "Northern Patrol Squadron," under Admiral Howell, consisting of the subsidized passenger-steamers renamed the Yankee, Dixie, Prairie, and Yosemite. The harbor-defence ram Katahdin was included in this squadron, while the thirteen old monitors, relics of the Civil War, were being hastily refitted for harbor duty. As fast as they could be made serviceable they were sent to various harbors to aid in their defence.

The Cape Verde Islands are a Portuguese colony, and the continuance of the Spanish fleet in the harbor of St. Vincent became inadmissible after Portugal had, following most of the nations of Europe, proclaimed neutrality between the combatants. Admiral Cervera, in command of the fleet, was warned to leave, and on April 29 the squadron set sail. It consisted of the first-class armored cruisers Cristobal Colon, Almirante Oquendo, Infanta Maria Teresa, and Vizcaya, and the three torpedo-boat destroyers Furor, Terror, and Pluton. The whole comprised a formidable fleet, which, if directed against some of the less protected American sea-board cities, might cause immense damage. The activity of the patrolling ships was in consequence redoubled; mines were laid in the various harbor approaches, and guns were mounted as rapidly as possible on sea-coast defences; and apprehension of possible danger threatened to interfere seriously with the business of sea-side resorts during the coming summer.

Apprehensions of this kind, however, had no effect on the activity of the blockading fleet. On the 29th of April the batteries at Cienfuegos, on the southern Cuban coast, were bombarded by the cruiser Marblehead, and on the same day the gunboat Nashville, which had made the first prize of the war, added to her record by the capture of the Spanish steamer Argonauta, laden with troops, arms, and ammunition and seeking an open port. The prizes made up to this time consisted of vessels that had left harbor before war was declared and whose captains were unaware of the state of affairs.

On the 30th the forts at Cabanas, near Havana, were attacked and demolished by the cruiser New York, and on the same day came the welcome tidings that the Oregon and Marietta, which for weeks had been making their way along the many thousands of miles of South American coast, were in the harbor of Rio Janeiro, having progressed safely that far on their long route. Much the most dangerous stage of their journey lay before them still. Before the Oregon could reach the North Atlantic Squadron, to which she was accredited, the Cape Verde squadron might be in her track, waylaying her on the open seas or in the West India channels. The Oregon was more powerful than any one of these ships, but four against one are frightful odds, and, though she might have given a good account of herself against the whole fleet, a lively degree of uneasiness concerning her prevailed. It could not then be conjectured that the Oregon was thereafter to meet and fight this fleet under circumstances far different from those surmised.

The activity in the navy was paralleled by that in the army. A powerful force of United States regular troops began to assemble at Tampa, Florida, a point chosen for its nearness to Cuba. The purpose of this movement was believed to be an early descent upon Cuba, and expectation of stirring events in the near future was entertained. These troops, however, were illy provided with military supplies, and the hoped-for invasion was necessarily deferred; the conditions being such as are apt to arise in the hasty mobilization of an army, particularly where large deficiencies in number have to be made up by raw recruits. The difficulties were in the main the results of a sudden change from a state of peace to one of war, and the necessity of making rapid provision for the requirements of a large army. Much fault was found with the government for alleged slowness of action and neglect of the troops, and bitter comments were made on the appointment of staff-officers through seeming political influence. These complaints were not without warrant, though they were exaggerated, no allowance being made for the difficulty under which the War Department labored in the sudden necessity of obtaining and forwarding a vast quantity of supplies. In reality, no nation under similar circumstances could have made more rapid progress in preparing for war.

We have already spoken of the efforts of the powers of Europe to effect an accommodation between the United States and Spain. When war had actually begun, they quickly took sides with one or the other of the combatants. France and Germany became strong adherents of Spain, their newspapers vigorously denouncing the United States, though the governments remained passive. This attitude was supposed to be due, on the part of France, to the Spanish debt being largely owing to citizens of that country. With Germany it was ascribed to a commercial rather than a pecuniary cause, the United States tariff having aroused deep-seated hostility in the agrarian party of that country. Austria also favored Spain, though her press was less aggressive. In Italy the tide of public opinion seems to have run most strongly in favor of the United States ; while Russia was non-committal, an occasional press utterance indicating some degree of animosity to the United States.

The remaining leading power, Great Britain, from the start took strong sides with the United States, evincing an unexpected warmth of friendliness and a strong desire to ally herself with this country. It was shrewdly held by many that self-interest was at the bottom of this seemingly exaggerated show of amity ; but such was hardly the case with the people, who were strongly pro-American. The press, with very few exceptions, sustained this country, and the opposing papers in a few months veered around, probably through the influence of public opinion.

Whatever the underlying motive in the British heart, this earnest display of friendliness was of much service to the United States. It tied the hands of our enemies on the Continent, who feared that any hostile act would result in an alliance between the two great Anglo-Saxon nations. Some active efforts at interference might have been made but for this haunting fear. Great Britain stood as a buffer between us and our opponents, she refusing to co-operate in any steps of interference. The union of the English-speaking peoples was a result which none of them wished to bring about.

CHAPTER VIII.

THE SEA-FIGHT AT MANILA.

THE story of the war now leads us to a far remote locality, one, in fact, on the opposite side of the earth, that extensive archipelago lying east of Indo-China known as the Philippine Islands. These islands, probably more than fourteen hundred in number, though only a few of them are large enough to be of importance, have been in the possession of Spain almost as long as Cuba. They were discovered by Magellan in 1521, but were not made a Spanish colony until 1569. Manila, the capital, was founded two years afterwards. The natives, eight millions or more in number, were not so summarily disposed of as those of Cuba, but of late years their lot has been still more severe than that of the modern Cubans, they being oppressed in exasperating and cruel ways, and treated so badly that their hatred of the Spaniards has become quite equal to that felt by the Cubans,—it could not well be greater.

In 1896, under the incitement of news of the Cuban insurrection, the natives of the Philippines rebelled against their masters, fighting fiercely for their liberty until near the end of 1897. With this rebellion we have no direct concern. It will suffice to say that the insurgents proved very difficult to subdue, and that they were treated with revolting cruelty by the Spaniards when taken prisoners. Finally, in December, 1897, the Spanish authorities adopted the method they had em-

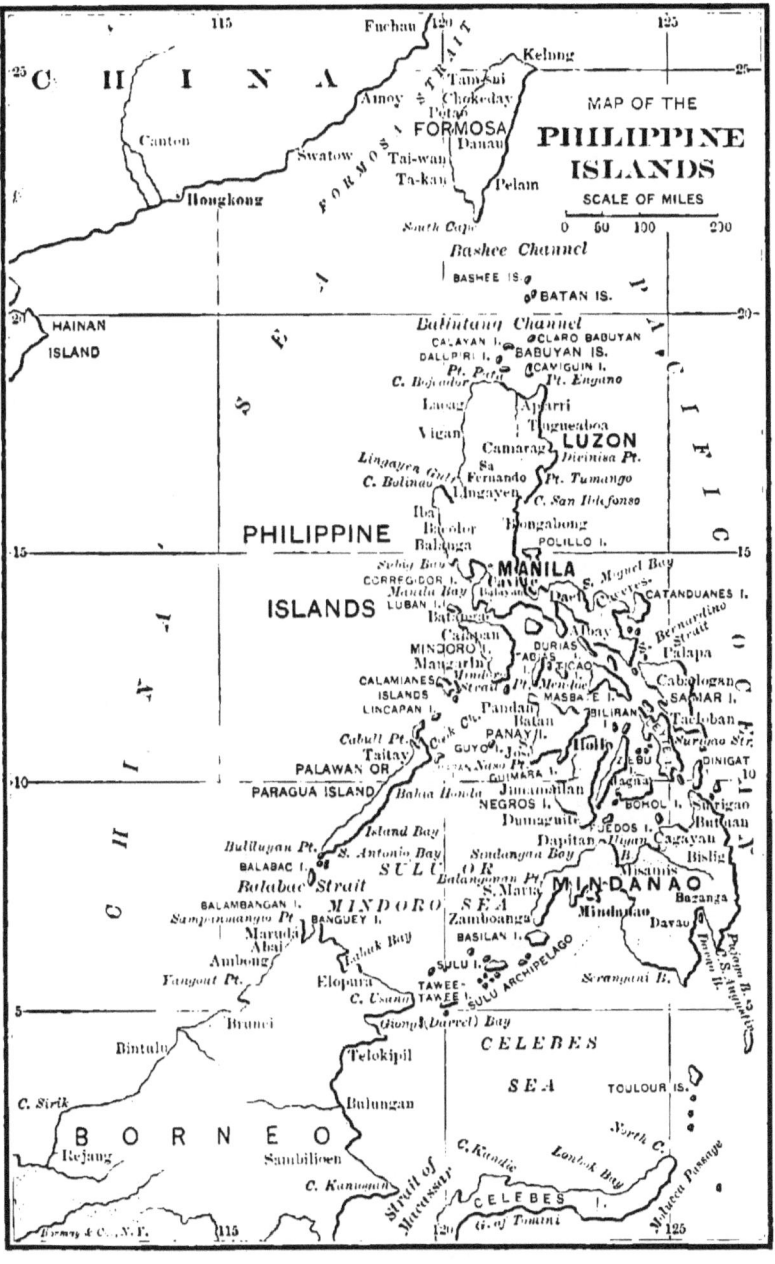

ployed in Cuba in 1878, entering into communication with General Emilio Aguinaldo, the leader in the insurrectionary movement, and promising to inaugurate an extensive system of reforms if he would bring the insurrection to an end. A large sum of money was also promised to the principal insurgents. The offer was accepted, and Aguinaldo and others retired to Hong Kong with their share of the subsidy. Spain, as usual, failed to keep her word. The remainder of the money was not paid. The leaders who, trusting in Spanish faith, had remained in the islands, were seized and executed. The promised reforms were ignored, the governor-general denying that he had pledged himself. As a result, before two months had passed the rebels were once more in arms. The country was soon again in turmoil, the anger of the insurgents being particularly directed against the priests, to whose influence they ascribed the dishonesty of the Spanish authorities. "No quarter to the priests" was the sentiment with which they went to war. They had long and bitter scores with these ecclesiastics to wipe out.

At the opening of the war little thought was given by the people of the United States to this far-off possession of Spain. But the government had it in mind. A small fleet, under the command of Commodore George Dewey, lay at Hong Kong, China, consisting of the cruisers Olympia, Baltimore, Raleigh, and Boston, the gunboats Concord and Petrel, and the despatch-boat McCullough. The declaration of war rendered the continuance of this fleet in a neutral port inadmissible under the rules of international law, and orders for its departure were given by the British authorities. It sailed on April 26, bound, not for an American port, in accordance with the instructions earlier sent it, but for the Philippine Islands, under orders from Washington to attack the Spanish fleet at Manila and "capture or destroy it." On the same day Spain made its first and only prize during the war, the American bark Saranac, taken by the gunboat El Cano at Iloilo, a Philippine port. On May 2 came, by way of Madrid, an exciting report to the effect that the United States fleet had attacked and partly destroyed the Manila fleet of Spain. The cutting of the cable put an end to further news, and for a week the American nation remained in suspense. It then was gladdened by a despatch from Commodore Dewey, saying that he had destroyed the entire Spanish fleet without the loss of a single life on his side.

Dewey's despatch, which was laconic in form but crowded with meaning, is a historical document well worthy of giving in full:

"MANILA, May 1.—Squadron arrived at Manila at daybreak this morning. Immediately engaged the enemy and destroyed the following Spanish vessels: Reina Cristina, Castilla, Don Antonio de Ulloa, Isla de Luzon, Isla de Cuba, General Lezo, Marquis de Duero, Cano, Velasco, Isla de Mindanao, a transport, and water-battery at Cavite. The squadron is uninjured and only a few men are slightly wounded. Only means of telegraphing is to American consul at Hong Kong. I shall communicate with him. DEWEY."

The story of the victory is one of the most glorious in the annals of the American navy. On April 27 the squadron left Mirs Bay, some thirty miles from Hong

Kong, to which it had sailed the day before. It was accompanied by two colliers, the Nanshan and the Zafiro, which Dewey had purchased and which were loaded with ten thousand tons of coal. The Monocacy, a corvette of the old navy, was left behind, as of no use in modern naval war, her officers and crew being distributed among the other vessels. The flag-ship was the Olympia, Captain C. V. Gridley commanding, one of the finest cruisers in the American navy, her armament consisting of four 8-inch slow-fire, ten 5-inch rapid-fire, and fourteen 6-pounder guns. The other cruisers were little behind her in power of armament and weight of projectiles.

Straight across the China Sea sailed the fleet, heavy weather forcing the war-vessels to slow up to about eight knots speed, on account of the deeply laden colliers, which plunged heavily through the waves. On the evening of the first day out the news of the declaration of war was read to the crews, followed by a proclamation of the most inflammatory character which had been issued to the people by the governor-general of Manila. This described the Americans as heretic vandals, who were coming to rob their churches and insult their women, and was full of uncomplimentary sayings about the invaders and warm appeals to the people of Manila to defend their city to the death. Its bombast elicited the derisive laughter of the men, while enthusiastic cheers for the American flag indicated their patriotic temper.

We append, as of some interest, an extract from this proclamation:

"The North American people, constituted of all the social excrescences, have exhausted our patience and provoked war with their perfidious machinations, with their acts of treachery, with their outrages against the law of nations and international conventions.

"*The struggle will be short and decisive.* The God of Victories will give us one as brilliant as the justice of our cause demands. Spain, which counts upon the sympathies of all the nations, will emerge triumphantly from the new test, humiliating and blasting the adventurers from those States that, without cohesion and without a history, offer to humanity only infamous traditions and the ungrateful spectacle of Chambers in which appear united insolence and defamation, cowardice and cynicism. . . .

"You will not allow the faith you profess to be made a mock of, impious hands to be placed on the temple of the true God, the images you adore to be thrown down by unbelief. The aggressors shall not profane the tombs of your fathers, they shall not gratify their lustful passions at the cost of your wives' and daughters' honor, or appropriate the property that your industry has accumulated as a provision for your old age. No; they shall not perpetrate any of the crimes inspired by their wickedness and covetousness, because your valor and patriotism will suffice to punish and abase the people that, claiming to be civilized and cultivated, have exterminated the natives of North America instead of bringing to them the life of civilization and of progress.

"Philippinos, prepare for the struggle, and, united under the glorious Spanish flag, which is ever covered with laurels, let us fight with the conviction that victory will crown our efforts, and to the calls of our enemies let us oppose with the decision of the Christian and the patriot the cry of 'Viva España!'

"Your General,
"BACILIO AUGUSTIN DAVILA.

"MANILA, 23d April, 1898."

The island of Luzon, the largest of the Philippines, and the one on which Manila is situated, was sighted by the fleet on the morning of Saturday, April 30, at Bolinao Cape, about one hundred and ten miles from the entrance to Manila Bay. Here the land rose green and beautiful under the morning sunlight, faint blue lines in the distance indicating the mountains of the interior. In the afternoon, when about thirty miles north of Manila Bay, the squadron approached another deep indentation in the coast, known as Subig Bay, in which it was possible that some part of the Spanish fleet might lie. The Boston and Concord led the way as this harbor was neared. They were soon followed by the Baltimore, the remainder of the fleet proceeding slowly as these pioneers dashed ahead at full speed. In the late afternoon they returned, reporting that they had explored Subig Bay, finding there only some insignificant coasting craft.

At about 5.15 P.M. the squadron came to a halt, and a council of war was held on the flag-ship, in which it was decided to enter Manila Bay during the darkness of that night. Getting under way again, the ships jogged on at a four-knot speed, in order that the harbor entrance might not be reached until the night was well advanced. Active preparations were meanwhile made for battle, all impedimenta that could be spared from the decks being thrown overboard, while mess-chests and tables, chairs, and other woodwork from between decks were also set afloat. Other steps of precaution were hastily taken, the life-boats being wrapped in canvas to prevent splinters flying, and buoyant objects placed where they would float and serve as life-rafts in case the ship went down. There were unpleasantly suggestive preparations for the care of the wounded, which brought grim looks to the faces of the men. This was no holiday excursion upon which they were bound.

As the ships moved on the battle-ports were put up, and every light was hidden except those that shone astern, a small electric-light glowing from each as a guide to the next in line. The chart-rooms were sealed and every effort was made to darken the ships. Involuntarily every one moved stealthily about the decks. Word was passed to the men that the bay of Manila would be entered during the night, and many a face grew stern with grim determination as the import of this message was understood. A half moon lit the sky, but it was hidden under masses of gray cloud. Everything favored the hope entertained of stealing in unseen past the forts that guarded Corregidor Island, in the entrance to the bay.

About 11.30 P.M. two dark headlands could be seen looming up, showing black against the shifting clouds that veiled the moon. In the intervening space lay a smaller mass, the fortified isle whose guns commanded the ship channels. The speed was increased to eight knots, and one by one the ships glided round the northern headland, and the Olympia, followed by her consorts, steered for the centre of the southern and wider channel. Soon Corregidor Island lay abeam of the leading ship. The Spanish sentinels seemed still wrapped in slumber.

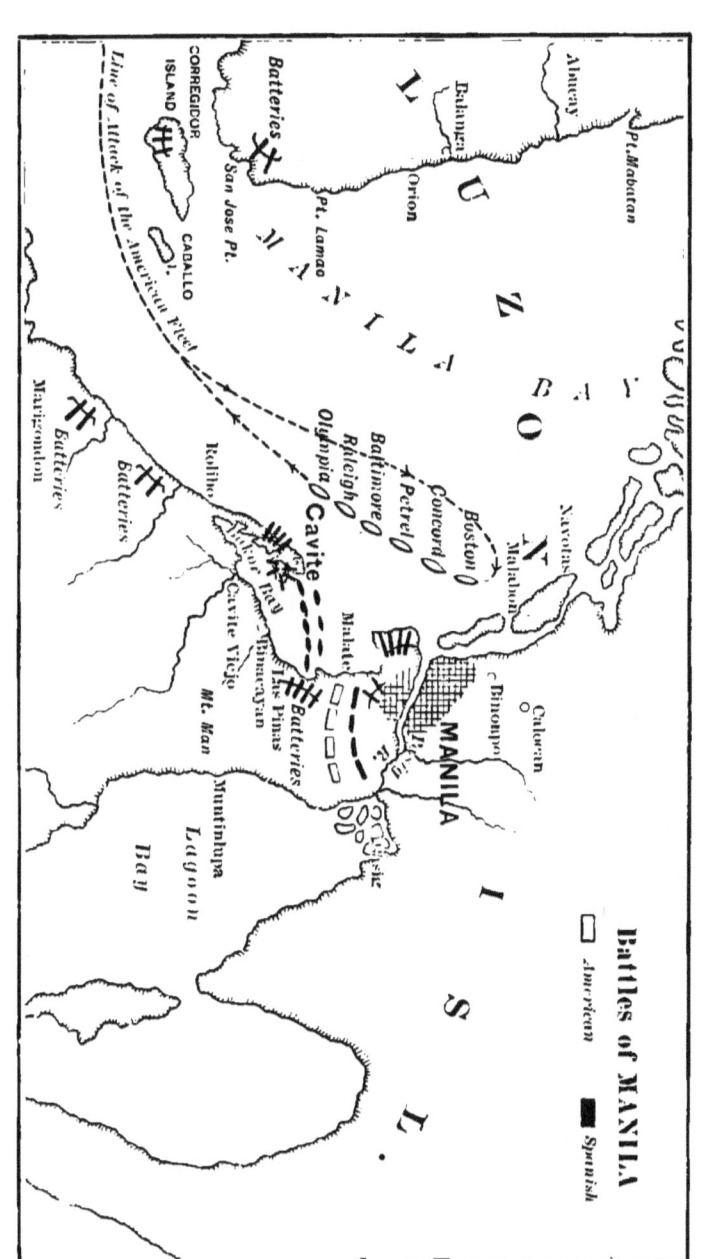

A faint light now flashed and died out on the island shore, and a rocket shot into the air. The invading fleet had been discovered. But no shot came, and the foremost ships were well past the island before a flash of flame gleamed through the darkness, followed by the boom of a heavy gun, and a shell went whistling overhead clear of the ships. The Raleigh replied with a 5-inch gun, the Boston and Concord followed, and the McCullough sent in a six-pound projectile. After a shot or two more from shore the batteries relapsed into silence, possibly from the effects of some of the shells dropped in their midst, and the fleet moved on, the colliers hugging the land close and escaping unharmed. The forts had been safely passed and the harbor-entrance won. Speed was now slowed down, and the men flung themselves on the decks beside their guns to snatch an interval of sleep. It was known that Manila would not be reached until early dawn. One casualty had occurred. Chief-Engineer Randall, of the McCullough, was overcome by a nervous shock, of probably apoplectic character, and at two o'clock he died. It was the only death on the American side during that eventful day.

As the fleet glided onward the distant lights of Manila came into view. The bay is a deep one; Cavite, the naval station of the capital, being seventeen miles from its mouth and Manila still further in. Lieutenant Calkins, the navigator of the Olympia, carried the fleet up through the dark harbor with commendable boldness and success. At four o'clock the men were roused, and a frugal meal of coffee and hardtack was served out to them, the officers joining in the repast. The first signs of dawn were visible in the sky about 4.30, when Manila was some six miles away. There lay a group of shipping, but these were made out, as the sun rose behind the city, to be merchant-ships, not the war-vessels of which the cruisers were in search. On went the fleet in close battle array, the Olympia leading, the Baltimore, Raleigh, Petrel, Concord, and Boston following in succession.

Passing to the northward of the capital and turning south, the keen eyes of Commodore Dewey caught sight of his predestined prey, the Spanish fleet, grouped in the little bay of Cavite. Here the Spaniards had a well-equipped navy-yard, known as Cavite Arsenal, protected by forts and under the command of Rear-Admiral Patricio Montojo, who was also commander-in-chief of the squadron. His flag-ship was the Reina Cristina, a 3500-ton cruiser, carrying twenty guns which ranged from 6.2-inch to 3-pounders. The others included the 3300-ton cruiser Castilla, four smaller cruisers, the Don Antonio de Ulloa, Velasco, Isla de Cuba, and Isla de Luzon, and the gunboats General Lezo, Marquis del Duero, and El Correo, with a transport, the Isla de Mindanao. Of these, the Velasco was under repair and her guns were mounted in earthworks in the harbor. There were also four torpedo-boats.

The Spanish squadron was in every respect inferior to its enemy, the ships being of less tonnage and lighter armament. In open sea they would not have had a moment's chance. But flanked by shore batteries, as they were, the conditions were far more equalized. And the Spaniards had the advantage of an exact knowledge of distances in the harbor, while the Americans were in ignorance of distance and soundings and, unable to use range-finders with effect, at a marked disadvantage in opportunities for sure marksmanship. Their principal advantage lay in the fact that the men knew how to use the guns, being trained to shoot straight and to make every shot tell. This was a training which the Spanish gunners sadly lacked, and which had a remarkable effect upon the issue of the combat.

With the flag of the American Union flying at the masthead of every ship, the squadron moved steadily on, passing the Manila forts at the distance of several miles. The great guns of the forts boomed out as they advanced, but there was no reply except a brace of shots from the Concord. The commodore had another object in view, and did not wish to hurl destruction into the crowded city behind the forts. As they advanced, the fleet of the enemy came plainly into view. Its position may be briefly described.

At Cavite a spit of land projects out into the bay, its curved shores enclosing a body of water known as Bakor Bay. Batteries occupied the extremity of the peninsula, between which and Cavite Arsenal, on the inner shore, lay extended the Spanish ships, crossing the mouth of Bakor Bay from east to west, the line ending in shoal water near the shore. Farther in, behind the arsenal boom, lay the gunboats of the fleet. Each end of the line was protected by shore batteries mounted with 6- and 8-inch guns.

Fronting this squadron, at a distance of three or four miles, the American ships swept down in the order above named. The little McCullough kept farther away, as a guard to the transports which were placed under her care. On the bridge of the Olympia Dewey stood exposed, with Flag-Captain Lamberton by his side, and maintained this position as the ship swept on through the storm of shot and shell which soon hurtled from the Spanish guns. Captain Gridley, commander of the flag-ship, took his position within the conning-tower, lest some unlucky shot should sweep away all the executive officers of the ship. This daring of Commodore Dewey is said to have been equalled by that of Admiral Montojo of the Spanish squadron. He also is credited with occupying the bridge of his ship during the fight, and, when one end of it was wrecked by a shell, taking his station on the other end.

The shore batteries began the engagement, opening on the American ships while still out of range. As the Olympia moved steadily onward, a new peril threatened her,—two submarine mines were exploded in her front. Fortunately, Spanish nervousness had set them off too soon and their force was uselessly expended on the water. How many more of these dreaded instruments of destruction might lie in their path no man could guess, but Dewey had been with Farragut in the Mississippi and was not the man to halt for the unseen.

The ships swept on until about forty-five hundred yards away, the Spanish fire growing continuous. But not a ship was struck, and they steamed onward grim and silent, with the men at the guns waiting in strained impatience for the battle-signal to be given, and disdainful of the shots that were uselessly tearing up the waters of the bay. "Remember the Maine!" came in an unpremeditated cry from the lips of one stern sea-dog, and in an instant it was taken up and ran throughout the ship. It was the war-cry of the first battle of the new American navy.

"You may fire when ready, Gridley," said the commodore at length; and in echo to his words an 8-inch shell from the forward turret of the Olympia went screaming through the air. The hour was 5.33. The guns of the Baltimore and Boston followed, and by 5.40 a continuous stream of projectiles was pouring in towards the Spanish ships. The difference in effect of the fire of the two fleets was remarkable. The Spanish shells flew high or struck the water before reaching the ships; hardly one of them touched its mark, while few from the American guns went astray. The effect was soon evident. The ships of Spain were being rent and torn and their men hurled prostrate in death, while scarcely a trace of damage was visible on an American hull.

There were narrow escapes. One fragment of a shell struck the bridge-gratings of the Olympia; another passed just under where Commodore Dewey stood, tearing a hole in the deck. Chaplain Frazier was looking out of a gun-port when a shell struck the ship's side within a yard. His head was withdrawn just in time to save it from being blown off. As the fight went on, other shots found a mark. One entered the port quarters of the Boston and burst in the state-room of Ensign Dodridge, setting it in flames. A second had similar effect on the port hammock-netting. The Baltimore was shot through and through by a shell, which fortunately struck no one in its career. Another ripped up the main deck, disabled a 6-inch gun, and exploded a box of ammunition, which wounded eight men. Strange to relate, these were the only men injured during the whole battle, and none of them was seriously hurt.

Sweeping down parallel to the Spanish line, the American fleet, on reaching the end of its course, swung round in a long ellipse and moved back over the same route, now opening fire from its starboard batteries. Six times in succession, as the hours moved on, the long line of ships moved over this course, pouring in shot and shell as they went, the boom of the great guns breaking at intervals through the continuous rattle of the rapid-fire guns, which poured out their projectiles in what seemed a continuous sheet of flame.

The Spanish ships, which had been in a measure unprepared for this assault, hastened to get up steam, and soon clouds of black smoke were pouring from their funnels. As the American squadron started upon its third course, the Spanish admiral, with a daring equal to that of his foes, headed his flag-ship, the Reina Cristina, straight for his principal opponent, steaming gallantly out, as if with the intention of running the Olympia down. It was a desperate attempt. At once the whole array of ships turned their guns on this single antagonist, tearing and rending her frightfully with shot and shell. As she came nearer, the storm of projectiles became so terrific that Admiral Montojo saw that his ship would be annihilated if he continued his perilous movement. He therefore swung her sharply round and started shoreward. Just as he did so, an 8-inch shell from the Olympia struck the Reina Cristina squarely in the stern, and drove inward through the length of the ship, rending through every obstruction, and wrecking the aft boiler and blowing open the deck in its explosion. This one shell proved the flag-ship's fate. Men lay dead throughout its course, and clouds of white smoke soon showed that the ship was in flames. For half an hour longer she kept up the fight, but the fire started in her continued to burn until she sank. It was now seven o'clock.

Early in the engagement another effort was made to destroy the Olympia. Two torpedo-boats came swiftly out and halted under the fire of the war-ships until their hoped-for prey should come within torpedo-reach. On

THE WAR WITH SPAIN. 163

came the flag-ship until but eight hundred yards distant. Then, as the daring little foes held their ground, she stopped and signalled for a concentrated fire on those dreaded terrors of the seas. In a moment they were the centre of a rain of shell, whipping the water around them until they were forced to turn and flee. As they did so a shell struck one of them fairly, and the daring craft was seen to plunge headlong under the sea. The other managed to reach cover, but was beached and deserted by her crew. Still another bold advance was made from the Spanish fleet, this time by a gunboat, which slipped out and made for the McCullough, probably hoping to destroy the transports. This effort also failed. The shot became so hot around her that she quickly drew back to her lurking-place. Meanwhile the batteries at Manila, distant as they were, were keeping up a steady fire upon the ships. No return was made by the fleet, but in the end Dewey sent a message to the governor-general that this fire must be stopped or the city would be shelled. The threat proved effectual. No more shells came from the Manila forts.

After four runs had been made at a distance of four thousand or five thousand yards, Lieutenant Calkins, the navigator of the Olympia, told the commodore that he believed it would be safe to take the ships nearer the enemy, with the lead going to test the depth of the water. Two more runs were therefore made within two thousand yards of the Spanish fleet. At this distance all the guns told, even the 6-pounders reaching their mark, and the effect on the enemy became terribly severe ; three of their ships were in full flames, their fire had slackened, and it was evident that the victory was practically won.

But the men were becoming exhausted by the strain. For two hours they had been engaged, with little more than a cup of coffee to sustain them. At 7.35, therefore, Dewey ceased firing and withdrew the squadron for breakfast. What harm had been done to his ships was not known, but when the word passed through the fleet that not a ship had been damaged or a man killed, involuntary cheers broke out. The gun-captains knew that there was a very different story to tell for the enemy, who had fought with a courage worthy of a better fate.

At 11.16, the men having had their breakfast and a few hours' rest, the ships returned to the attack, the Baltimore leading the way and the Olympia following, with Dewey occupying the perilous position on the bridge which he had maintained throughout. As they came within range, nearly the whole Spanish fleet was seen to be in flames, the flag-ship burning fiercely. Again shells were poured upon the devoted ships, the Spaniards still firing, but with less energy than before. By noon their fire had nearly ceased. At 12.30 the squadron ceased firing, the batteries being silenced and the Spanish ships sunk, burnt, and deserted. Every flag had gone down except one that floated above a small fortification in the distance. The transport Isla de Mindanao was still afloat, but a few shots through its helpless hulk soon set it in flames.

At 12.40 the squadron withdrew towards Manila, having finished its work, the little Petrel being left to complete the destruction of the gunboats which lay within the interior harbor. Lieutenant Hughes, with an armed boat's crew, set fire to these, and soon they were vying in flame with the larger vessels outside.

Copyright, 1898, by Arkell Publishing Company

Warning was sent to Governor-General Augustin, the author of the grandiloquent proclamation of a week before, that the port of Manila was under blockade, and that at a single shot from his batteries at any American ship the city would be laid in ashes.

The victory had been one without parallel in the whole history of naval warfare. For three or four hours the American ships had been exposed, within easy range, to a hot fire from the Spanish fleet and forts, and yet all that fiery storm had failed to kill a single man or to do serious injury to a single ship. On the other hand, the Spanish fleet had ceased to exist. Its burnt remnants lay on the bottom of the bay. In men the loss had been as severe as in ships. General Augustin gave their number at six hundred and eighteen. It was probably near a thousand, the Reina Cristina alone having one hundred and fifty killed, the captain among them. During the battle, Admiral Montojo had been obliged to shift his flag from the burning flag-ship to the little Isla de Cuba. This, too, was soon destroyed, the admiral being wounded, though not seriously. The forts had suffered as severely as the ships, being knocked into shapeless heaps of earth and their garrisons killed or put to flight. The remarkable difference in result was due to the skilful manœuvring of the American fleet and the accurate handling of its guns, as compared with the wretched gunnery of the Spaniards, who seemed incapable of hitting a ship in motion. A French official account spoke of the American fire as "for accuracy and for rapidity something awful."

For a week previously Manila had been on the verge of a panic. Now terror and confusion prevailed. Flight was impossible, since it would have been into the hands of the insurgents, who had been greatly emboldened by the news of the war, and swarmed in the surrounding country. It was not known but that Dewey would turn his guns on the city and batter it to the earth. General Augustin's proclamation had prepared the citizens for the wildest excesses on the part of the victorious foe, and they were in a state of pitiable dismay.

In the afternoon of May 1 Dewey's ship was boarded by the British consul, who requested the victor, in view of the many foreigners in the city, represented by the consuls of twenty-one different governments, not to bombard the place. Dewey promised on condition that the military supplies of Manila should be delivered to him, with coal for his ships and the control of the cable to Hong Kong. General Augustin, threatened by enemies on all sides, the insurgents by land, the Americans by water, telegraphed to Madrid for instructions, sending the partial report of the battle which quickly spread over the world. On May 2 the answer came. It offered defiance to the enemy. At once Dewey sent the Baltimore and the Raleigh to Corregidor Island, and summoned the colonel in command to surrender. He did so without hesitation, and the works commanding the entrance to the harbor fell into American hands. At four o'clock that afternoon communication by telegraph with Hong Kong ceased. Dewey had lifted and cut the cable, the use of which had been refused to him. The only means of communication left was by boat to Hong Kong, and thither the McCullough was despatched with news of the victory. On May 7 came by telegraph from China the message from Dewey we have quoted, and which electrified the expectant people of the United States and elicited the admiration of all Europe.

In addition to the despatch given, the McCullough brought another, dated May 4, saying :

"I have taken possession of naval station at Cavite, Philippine Islands, and destroyed the fortifications. Have destroyed fortifications at bay entrance, Corregidor Island, paroling the garrison. I control the bay completely and can take the city at any time. The squadron is in excellent health and spirits. The Spanish loss not fully known, but is very heavy. One hundred and fifty killed, including captain, on Reina Cristina alone. I am assisting in protecting Spanish sick and wounded. Two hundred and fifty sick and wounded in hospital within our lines. Much excitement at Manila. Will protect foreign residents.
"DEWEY."

The Petrel, which had been sent into the inner harbor to destroy the gunboats, found there one vessel unhurt, the transport Manila, which lay in three feet of mud near the navy-yard. She was towed off and anchored near the squadron, and proved to be a handsome steamer of about two thousand tons. She was laden with supplies and five hundred tons of coal, from which the Raleigh supplied her bunkers. The remaining prizes consisted of a number of tugs and launches, which were seized for the service of the American fleet. When the men landed from the Petrel to search the navy-yard, they were met by the doctor and a deputation of Sisters of Mercy from the hospital, who begged them not to kill the wounded or fire on the hospital. They learned with surprise and delight that American soldiers did not perform such deeds. They had been made to believe that they had ruthless savages to deal with.

The departure of the Spanish soldiers, who fled in haste to Manila after the battle, left Cavite at the mercy of the insurgents, who swarmed into the place and looted it to their hearts' content, carrying off many boat-loads of plunder over the bay. At the request of the officers and surgeons of the naval hospital, which was filled with wounded from the fleet and threatened with attack by the natives, a force of marines was sent to guard it. The work of plundering, however, went on with activity in the town of St. Roque, near Cavite, the houses of Spaniards being mercilessly looted, while hundreds of people fled from the town, carrying their household effects in all available vehicles. Even the arsenal was robbed of many boat-loads of furniture and stores before the guard of marines was posted at its gates.

The reception of the despatch from Dewey by the President was acknowledged without delay through Secretary Long, who sent the following message to the victorious commodore:

"WASHINGTON, May 7, 1898.

"DEWEY, Manila.

"The President, in the name of the American people, thanks you and your officers and men for your splendid achievement and overwhelming victory. In recognition he has appointed you acting admiral, and will recommend a vote of thanks to you by Congress.

"LONG."

On May 9, Congress, by a rising vote in both Houses, passed a resolution of thanks to Dewey and his officers and men, and appropriated $10,000 to present him with a sword and medals to all under his command. On the 11th he was nominated and confirmed rear-admiral. He hastened to return his grateful thanks to the President and Congress for the compliment paid him and the honors conferred on him and his men.

The unexpectedly complete success of the Manila expedition was followed by steps for the reinforcement of Admiral Dewey and for taking possession of the Philippine Islands, an outcome of the war which at once became urgent. Supplies and men were made ready to send across the Pacific, under command of Major-General Wesley Merritt, who on May 12 was announced as military governor of the Philippines.

On the 18th the cruiser Charleston sailed from Mare Island for Manila, loaded with supplies and ammunition. There was considerable delay in despatching men, the first detachment of troops, numbering two thousand five hundred men, not leaving San Francisco for the Philippines until May 25. The second expedition, three thousand five hundred strong, set out on June 15. To strengthen Dewey's fleet the monitor Monterey was ordered, June 1, to join him, and on June 23 the monitor Monadnock set out from San Francisco for the same purpose. Meanwhile the victorious admiral awaited in the bay of Manila the arrival of Merritt and his men, he having decided that it would be unwise to proceed against the city until amply able to hold it and restrain the insurgent forces. The two monitors sent were deemed sufficient to enable him to meet any fleet which Spain could despatch against him. A third expedition, five thousand in number, left San Francisco for the Philippines June 27 to 29, and on July 15 and subsequently a fourth expedition set sail. Admiral Dewey meanwhile awaited the arrival of these reinforcements, keeping up a strict blockade, but making no effort to take possession of a city which he was too weak to hold.

CHAPTER IX.

UNDER FIRE AT CARDENAS AND CIENFUEGOS.

ON May 1, the date of Commodore Dewey's signal victory at Manila, preparations for active work were making in the Atlantic waters. The Spanish fleet at the Cape Verde Islands had been obliged to leave harbor there on April 29, in consequence of the proclamation of neutrality by Portugal. It was believed to have steamed westward, bound, so many thought, for Porto Rico, though others feared that its destination might be some point on the coast of the United States. The uncertainty as to its goal gave rise to much apprehension among the seaboard population of this country, and active measures were taken to meet it on land and water. The defence of our seaports became of prime importance, and the whole coast was put under surveillance, a system of land patrol being organized which extended along the exposed seaboard of the country, and was alert to make instant report of the approach of suspicious vessels to any part of the coast. Harbor defence was similarly provided for, submarine mines being planted in all channels leading to commercial cities, and guns mounted on coast-defence fortifications as rapidly as they could be procured. The movements of merchant-vessels entering port were put under careful supervision, that there might be no interference by anchor or keel with the mines.

At sea the same alertness was shown as on land. The

Flying Squadron at Hampton Roads was kept ready, like so many war-hounds in leash, to fly to the defence of any imperilled point. It was strengthened by the addition of other vessels, among them the fine purchased cruiser New Orleans. The swift Columbia and Minneapolis, the greyhounds of the seas, were kept on scouting duty along the northern coast, in sharp lookout for the approach of hostile craft. The Northern Patrol Squadron was similarly on the *qui vive*, and it would have been next to impossible for an enemy to enter our waters without quick discovery and as quick preparation for his approach.

The probability that Porto Rico or some Cuban port might be the destination of the Spanish fleet gave rise to equal activity in the West India waters. The larger vessels of Admiral Sampson's squadron were withdrawn to Key West to coal and otherwise prepare for a long journey in the tropical seas, leaving the duty of the blockade to the minor vessels, the gunboats, torpedo-boats, and smaller cruisers. This squadron, under the familiar designation of the "mosquito fleet," from that time forward kept up the blockade, while the larger vessels were more actively employed.

Life was not altogether monotonous on board the mosquito fleet. It had its adventures, some of them interesting and important. The Spaniards on shore were watchful and combative, and a brisk exchange of shots was no uncommon occurrence. Certain thrilling experiences were gone through by members of the fleet in the effort to perform perilous duties assigned them. The present chapter will be devoted to an account of the more striking of these events.

On May 6 the bombardment of the Matanzas forts by

Admiral Sampson on the New York was repeated by two of the smallest vessels in the navy,—the torpedo-boat Dupont and the auxiliary cruiser Hornet. On the previous day the Dupont, while cruising close to the shore, had observed a number of men raising a Spanish flag on a point near Matanzas light-house. It was suspected that a new battery was being constructed there, and on the following afternoon the Dupont, now accompanied by the Hornet, scouted close in shore. This temerity soon called forth a response. When they were not more than six hundred yards distant a storm of rifle-bullets came whizzing towards them, lashing the water sharply about the boats, but not touching a man on board. The attack came from a body of Spanish cavalry ranged in groups along the shore. The little boats lost no time in replying, pouring a stream of projectiles from their quick-firing guns into the cavalry, which sought cover with all convenient speed. Their fire was next directed against three block-houses, which were quickly destroyed. The activity of the craft now drew an 8-inch shell from one of the Matanzas batteries. It fell short and was not repeated. On the following day the boats returned and fired on the forts, but no reply was drawn from them. Though no harm was done to the men on board, there were indications that the Spanish had suffered considerable loss.

The first engagements of the war in which the Americans suffered any loss of life occurred on May 11, at Cardenas and Cienfuegos. Cardenas, a seaport town on the north coast of Cuba, lies seventy-five miles to the eastward of Havana, and about twenty miles from Matanzas. Cardenas Bay, in which one of the engagements in question took place, is a picturesque harbor, broad and shallow, the channel, scarcely two fathoms deep, winding its way tortuously inward through clusters of verdant coral keys to the city, which spreads out on the sloping hills fully seven miles from the entrance.

The blockading squadron off this port consisted of the gunboats Wilmington and Machias, the torpedo-boat Winslow, and the auxiliary tug Hudson. The Spaniards had withdrawn from the entrance to the bay, destroying the buoys and other aids to navigation as they went. On Sunday, the 8th, the Winslow, venturing into the harbor, was chased to its entrance by three small gunboats, one of which she disabled. It was to destroy these and the signal-station, and to make observations on the harbor, that Captain Todd, of the Wilmington, and Commander Merry, of the Machias, decided on Wednesday to run into the bay. In this movement the Winslow led the way, closely followed by the Hudson. The Wilmington, which draws a little over nine feet of water, was obliged to stop at eighteen hundred yards from the city, while the Machias, which draws thirteen feet, was unable to enter the shallow harbor.

The Winslow followed the eastern and the Hudson the western shore of the bay. They had drawn close together at about one thousand yards from the waterfront of the city, when, just before two P.M., a puff of smoke was observed on shore at Cardenas and a shell whistled over the daring boats. This shot was quickly followed by others, and soon shells were bursting hotly about the little Winslow, which was firing rapidly in return. The Hudson was also actively engaged, pouring projectiles from her two rapid-fire 6-pounder guns. What effect was produced could not easily be seen for the cloud of smoke; but it was perceived that the

Spanish aim improved as the battle went on, two empty barks anchored off shore being used as ranges. The garrison had evidently prepared for an attack. At about half-past two a 4-inch shell struck the Winslow on the starboard beam, wrecking her forward boiler and starboard engine, and crippling her steam steering-gear. A minute later, while the quartermaster was hooking up the hand-gear, it also was shot away, he receiving a severe wound in the breast.

Lieutenant Bernadou, finding his vessel crippled beyond control, and that it had become the target for a stream of well-directed shot, hailed the Hudson, and asked her to take him in tow. A group of sailors on the Hudson at once made ready to heave a line, Ensign Bagley, of the Winslow, hastening them with the exclamation, "Heave her! Let her come! It's getting pretty warm."

The line was flung and was grasped by the Winslow's men, who vigorously drew it in, bringing their craft foot by foot towards the Hudson. The next instant a tragic event took place. A 4-inch shell from the shore battery burst among the crew, Ensign Bagley and Fireman Daniels being almost torn asunder by its explosion. Three others were struck by fragments of the shell, and died in a few minutes. A flying piece of shrapnel struck Lieutenant Bernadou in the thigh, cutting an ugly gash. The hawser parted and the torpedo-boat was left floundering helplessly in the water at the mercy of the enemy's fire, which never relaxed.

Meanwhile, the Wilmington was hurling her 4-inch shells rapidly on shore, with an accuracy of aim that must have done deadly execution. The enemy seemed to have the exact range of the Winslow, not a shell reaching the Hudson. With all haste the men on the latter boat threw another line, which was made fast, and the torpedo-boat pulled out of the range of the Spanish guns. The Hudson then towed her consort to Piedras Cay, a little island twelve miles off, where the Machias lay. The Wilmington followed them out.

Little trace of the enemy's shot was visible on the Hudson or the Wilmington, the Winslow alone having suffered. What damage had been done to the gunboats and batteries of the enemy could not be told, though there was reason to believe that it had been considerable. After the battle, the signal-station on Diana Cay, whose destruction had been one of the purposes of the expedition, was laid in ruins by a force of marines from the Machias.

Lieutenant Bernadou had shown intrepid courage through the action, stopping the flow of blood in his wounded thigh with a tourniquet tightened by a 1-pound shell, and remaining pluckily at his post, manœuvring his little craft as well as he could by means of her screw-propeller, and replying briskly to the enemy's fire from his 1-pounder rapid-fire gun.

The dead were brought to Key West, where four of them were interred with all the honors of war, side by side with the graves of the victims of the Maine. The body of Ensign Bagley was sent to his home for interment. As the first victims of the war, the death of these five men, and particularly of Ensign Bagley, a young man of much promise, sent a thrill of sympathy throughout the land. Many now first began to appreciate what war really is, and a shudder of dread filled thousands of hearts as they looked forward into the uncertain future, with its possible harvest of sanguinary events.

On the same day with this engagement an event of equal interest, and one that also had its victims, took place on the opposite coast of Cuba, in the bay of Cienfuegos, the only post then under blockade in the south. The town of Cienfuegos, like that of Cardenas, lies some distance back from the sea, in a harbor whose channel winds and twists. It is bounded by high hills, which completely hide the town from ships at sea. Near the harbor's mouth the land is low for some distance back, then it rises into a sharp bluff covered with trees. The cable connecting Havana with Santiago de Cuba enters the water at this point, the cable-house standing on the shore close to the water's edge. Not far away, on one side of this, a light-house then stood, and opposite it an old block-house, one of the many established along the coast to intercept filibustering expeditions. There was another cable running to Batabano, and a small one extending to some local point eastward. These cables it was determined to cut.

The blockading squadron, consisting of the cruiser Marblehead, the gunboat Nashville, and the auxiliary cruiser Windom, was detailed to do the perilous work of cutting these cables; and in the early morning of Wednesday, May 11, those vessels steamed in close to the shore. It was evident that the Spanish had made preparations for such an attempt. Rifle-pits could be seen at the water's edge, rapid-fire guns were visible, and groups of cavalry and infantry were in motion upon the hill-side and the shore. Yet, in defiance of this evident preparation, the boats assigned to the task were manned and set out on their perilous duty. They consisted of two steam launches, two launches of smaller size, and half a dozen row-boats. The launches were armed with machine-guns, their purpose being to protect the small boats as they worked, and tow them back to the ships if the men should be disabled.

The boats moved steadily inward until a point about one hundred feet from the cable-house and two hundred from the rifle-pits was reached. Lieutenant Winslow, of the Marblehead, was in command. Standing fearlessly upright in his launch as the boats drew near to the shore, he at length gave the word to anchor and grapple for the cable. Without delay the oars were shipped and the grappling-hooks thrown over the side, while the launches, and, farther out, the ships, stood ready to repel an assault. The work went on with all haste, but the cable was difficult to find, and some time passed before it was drawn from the sands in which it lay embedded and lifted to the gunwales of the boats.

Until this moment the Spaniards had made no attack. Now there came a flash on shore, and a singing shot went over the heads of the men in the boats. It was the signal for a sharp fire from the shore, which was echoed in a moment by a volley from the machine-guns of the launches and by broadsides from the ships. The shells of the Marblehead, bursting in the rifle-pits, quickly put their defenders to flight. The Nashville followed, and the little Windom opened briskly with her 4-pounders. Protected by this vigorous fire, the men continued their work, hacking away at the tough steel wires of the cable with axes, chisels, and saws. Severed at length, the cable was underrun and cut at another point, one hundred and fifty feet being taken out of its length. This was done to prevent its being lifted and spliced. The cable thus cut was supposed to be the one to Batabano.

A more important one, that to Santiago de Cuba, remained, and grappling for this at once began. It was soon found and dealt with in the same manner, eighty feet being cut out of its length. The other cable mentioned, of smaller calibre, was also cut. In the opinion of the daring workers, General Blanco's last channel of communication with the outside world was severed. This, as subsequent events proved, was an error, but the valor and energy of the workers was not the less commendable.

The work of cable-lifting and cutting took considerable time, during much of which the sailors were exposed to a sharp rifle-fire from the shore, though the activity of the attack was greatly diminished by the fierce return from the launches and the ships. A shell from the Nashville tore the cable-house into fragments. One from the Marblehead tumbled the block-house into a heap of ruins. The ships were rolling in a heavy sea, yet the marksmanship was superb,—the shots searching the rifle-pits, furrowing the sand of the beach, and sweeping the hill-side. But, despite this active bombardment, the rifle-bullets found their victims, eight men falling wounded, one of whom, Patrick Regan, died on the way back to the ships. Lieutenant Winslow was struck in the hand. All the ships bore marks of the fray, being struck many times by bullets from machine-guns. But the only casualty on the ships was on the Nashville, where a bullet passed through the shoulder of an ensign and struck Captain Maynard on the chest near the heart. Fortunately, the wound was a slight one.

It had not been proposed to injure the light-house, but it was found that the Spaniards were using it as a fort, firing from its cover on the men in the boats. The guns of the Marblehead were at once trained on it, and the commander, from the bridge, gave the order to "Cut it down!" At once fire was opened on it with remarkable accuracy, considering the rolling motion of the ships, which lay at a distance of one thousand yards. In a short time the tower was a ruin and the assailants were in hasty flight for new places of shelter.

The bold enterprise had occupied more than three hours, the boats leaving the ships at seven o'clock in the morning and returning at 10.15 A.M. During all that time they had been under fire within short rifle-range, and only the incessant work of the machine- and rapid-fire guns had saved their crews from annihilation. What loss the Spanish sustained was unknown. It was probably considerable, in view of their numbers and the torrent of fire that searched out their every lurking-place. This affair and that at Cardenas were of great moral value in showing the intrepidity of American sailors and their coolness and daring under fire. Like the battle at Manila, these smaller engagements served as valuable object lessons to America and the world.

It is not necessary to mention in detail the several later attempts that were made to cut the cables connecting Cuba with the outer world. Despite the success at Cienfuegos, Blanco at Havana kept in communication with Santiago and Spain, and, though other wires were cut at later dates, in front of Santiago, at Guantanamo Bay, and at the eastern end of Cuba, the governor-general kept in touch with the government at Madrid. Not until after the capture of Santiago was he finally cut off from communication with the world without. There was still a cable from Havana to Key West, but that, for obvious reasons, he did not care to use.

CHAPTER X.

THE SEARCH FOR THE SPANISH FLEET.

THE events narrated in the last chapter were followed on the succeeding day by a more important one, the bombardment of San Juan de Porto Rico by Admiral Sampson's squadron, which, on May 3, had sailed from Key West for a destination unknown, though shrewdly suspected. It was believed that the Cape Verde Spanish squadron was bound for the West Indies and would seek to make port at San Juan. Admiral Sampson's purpose was to cut the Spanish fleet off from this port, or, if too late for that, to attack it in the harbor of San Juan, or wherever it could be found outside. His squadron consisted of the battle-ships Iowa and Indiana, the monitors Amphitrite and Terror, the cruisers New York, Montgomery, and Detroit, and the torpedo-boat Porter. It was accompanied by the coaler Niagara, the tug Wampatuck, and the Dauntless, one of the press-boats which accompanied every expedition of the fleets.

Moving along the northern coast of Cuba, which was kept steadily in sight, the squadron on May 7 reached Cape Haytien, a northern seaport of the island of Hayti. Progress had been delayed by the slow speed of the monitors, which needed to be towed during most of the course, and won from the sailors the ungallant name of "crabs." Stopping at Cape Haytien to send despatches to Washington and receive replies, the ships moved on eastward during the 10th and 11th, and during the night of the 12th appeared off the port of San Juan, the metropolis and principal seaport of the island of Porto Rico.

The city of San Juan lies on the interior of a long, narrow bay, a high headland separating it from the ocean, while in the mouth of the channel rises the lofty Cabras Island, whose summit, like that of the headland, is fortified. The city is built on the slopes of high hills which rise on the ocean side of the bay. To reach it, it is necessary to pass the Canuelo battery on Cabras Island, the Morro Castle fortifications within, and the San Carlos battery on a promontory at the east entrance to the harbor. Inland, sharply outlined against the sky, rises a range of mountains, which send down their spurs in broken hills almost to the sea. It was about three o'clock in the morning of May 12 that the fleet came near the entrance of this bay and began its preparations for battle, stripping the decks of impedimenta and getting ready the guns, ammunition, and appliances for handling the wounded. On reaching the entrance to the bay, it became evident that the Spanish fleet was not within. It had either not reached there or had departed for some new destination. But before seeking it elsewhere, Admiral Sampson determined to attack the batteries defending the port, in order to develop their positions and strength, though with no intention of bombarding or besieging the city.

Preliminary to the assault, the admiral transferred his flag to the Iowa, and issued orders that the flag-ship, followed by the Indiana, New York, Amphitrite, and Terror, should sail inward past Cabras Island, then turn and pass outward by the westward channel, repeating this evolution until signalled to stop. The smaller vessels were directed to occupy certain positions and to keep a sharp lookout for torpedo-boat destroyers. Two principal objects of attack had been in view, the batteries upon Morro and the Spanish men-of-war, if any were found in the harbor,—care being taken to avoid firing on neutral war-vessels if present, and also to avoid striking the hospitals on Cabras Island. As soon, however, as it became evident that the ships were not within the harbor, attention was confined to the forts, which were vigorously assailed.

The attack began at 5.15 A.M. and lasted for three hours. The plans of the admiral were thoroughly carried out, the ships steaming majestically into the harbor and three times making the circuit outlined in the general order. A ten-knot easterly breeze was blowing, lifting the waters into a long, heavy swell as the great ships moved gracefully on. As they entered the harbor's mouth, no evidence of a lookout by the enemy was observed. Alike in town and forts the Spaniards seemed asleep, and only the roar of the mighty guns appeared to waken them from their slumbers. Four broadsides were fired from the ships before the Spanish gunners were thoroughly aroused to the exigencies of the situation and began to reply from their elevated positions to the projectiles of the great 12- and 13-inch guns. Inward swept the Iowa, delivering the fire from her turrets as she went. Behind her came the Indiana and then the graceful New York, while the low-lying monitors glided inward in the rear. When the Iowa turned to go back in the circuit laid down, the whole line had become engaged, the Detroit and Montgomery firing rapidly from their smaller guns on the Cabras and Morro batteries.

The squadron had completed one round and was returning on the second before the Spanish gunners became fully warmed up to their work. Then from their elevated positions they poured a plunging fire upon the fleet, one which, had the guns been well served, might have done serious execution. Their fire was furious but aimless, the shells causing the water to spurt up all around, but only one or two during the whole conflict touching a ship. The Detroit, which preceded the Iowa into the harbor, and the Wampatuck, which kept on her beam, sounding constantly as they moved inward, occupied posts of danger, but escaped injury. The Detroit drew in close under Morro, and shells seemed to rain around her as she lay within five hundred yards of the batteries, hurling projectiles from her 4-inch rapid-fire guns; yet she made a marvellous escape from damage by shot or shell.

By the end of the third round the heat of the sun had become intense, the men working under great strain; and, as his purpose had been achieved, the admiral deemed it useless to continue the attack on the forts, and signalled to withdraw. This signal failed to be seen or, at least, to be understood by the Terror, which remained in the channel and for half an hour engaged Morro Castle alone. The scene was one of intense interest as the low-lying craft hurled the shells from her turrets up-hill at the elevated forts, while the Spanish gunners poured down their projectiles with utter uselessness, the shells splashing in the water often hundreds of feet from the Terror, and, when exploding, hurling columns of water sixty feet into the air. Finally, as if weary of the work, the monitor glided slowly outward, firing as she went, while the gunners on the hill-side blazed away until she was far out of range, not a shot touching her during the whole exciting duel. The

Montgomery, meanwhile, had engaged and silenced Fort Canuelo, on Cabras Island, while the Porter, lying close under the cliff east of the Detroit, was prepared to torpedo any Spanish cruiser that sought to escape from the harbor.

It was eight o'clock when the engagement closed. The escape of the fleet from the heavy and continuous fire of the enemy's batteries, all occupying elevated positions, was something almost incredible, and could only have been due to absolute incapacity in the gunners. Of the hundreds of projectiles only two reached their mark, and only one man was killed on the fleet. A shell struck the Iowa and did some small damage on deck, where three men were slightly hurt. One that exploded on the New York was more effective, one seaman, Frank Widemark, being killed, and four wounded, while two search-lights were shattered and other slight injuries done. In addition to the man killed on the New York, a gunner's mate on the Amphitrite died from the effect of the stifling heat. Of the wounded men only two were seriously enough hurt to be transferred to the hospital-ship Solace, which subsequently joined the fleet. During the engagement the admiral occupied a position on the lee of the conning-tower, not deeming it necessary to enter that place of refuge. His experience and that of Dewey indicate that the conning-tower is little likely to be made use of unless the shots come from both sides. The commander seems as safe behind it as in it.

The results of the bombardment were the silencing of the Cabras Island battery, the damaging of the San Carlos battery, and the demolition of the north end of Morro Castle. Some damage was done to the section of the city adjoining the batteries and a panic seems to have prevailed, most of the inhabitants taking to the woods, with a natural fear that the hostile fleet might turn its death-dealing guns on the helpless city. They returned with a warm sense of relief when it was certain that the terrible ships had withdrawn.

One lesson of importance was learned from these three hours of sharp work. It was the first time that modern ships had attacked in force land fortifications, and the result was observed by the military nations of the world with deep interest. It had been an unsettled problem whether coast defence could be best provided for by war-vessels or land intrenchments. The engagement at San Juan and the subsequent naval siege of Santiago went far to settle this question. In both instances ancient forts, quite unfit to bear the fire of modern guns, sustained a hot fire for hours without being silenced or materially injured. They had, it may be said, a special advantage from their elevated situation, which rendered it difficult to plant shells effectively in their midst. On the other hand, they bore the bombardment practically without replying, for the wretched gunnery of the Spaniards was a subject of derision to the sailors, their projectiles being wasted by hundreds on the waters of the bay. Only two of the whole number reached their mark, and this perhaps more by accident than accurate aiming. Had the guns of the Morro all been of modern make and handled by well-trained gunners, the result must have been decidedly different. From their coign of vantage on the harbor hills they could have poured their shells in a devastating stream on the ships and have driven them in haste from their waters or sunk them in the channel. Such forts, well built and handled, would be impregnable to the fire of ships, and would be able to meet an attack with a deadly and destructive return.

The hospital-ship Solace, which visited the fleet after the battle on an errand of mercy, was a new departure in naval warfare,—a vessel fitted up with all requirements for aid of the sick and wounded. She was in effect an ambulance-ship, her mission being to make the suffering comfortable until they could be landed in a hospital on shore. Her white sides and the flag of the Red Cross that floated at her peak told the story of her benevolent purpose to friend and foe, while she was provided with delicacies for the sick and all the requirements for temporary hospital treatment of the wounded, having an operating-room well equipped with surgical instruments, a complete paraphernalia for treating wounds, a convalescents' room, and a full corps of surgeons and nurses. Her accommodations were sufficient for two hundred or more wounded soldiers, and her speed great enough to enable her to reach a northern port with her suffering inmates without loss of time. The wounded of the New York were the first that called for the services of this useful ship. At a later date a second vessel adapted to the same important service, the Relief, specially known as an "army hospital-ship," was added to the auxiliary vessels of the navy. Later in the war these two winged messengers of mercy proved of the highest utility.

Immediately after the end of the bombardment the squadron put to sea again, standing to the northeast until out of sight of San Juan, when the course was laid to the westward, with the view of communicating with Washington and ascertaining if anything had been learned about the movements of the Spanish fleet. At Cape Haytien the admiral received word by wire that the squadron of the enemy, under Admiral Cervera, had been heard from at the French island of Martinique. Being unable to obtain supplies there, it had made its way to the Dutch island of Curaçao, near the north coast of South America. Here entrance was forbidden to more than two vessels of the fleet at a time, the Maria Teresa and the Vizcaya being admitted to the port, where they obtained a small quantity of inferior coal and some other supplies.

As Holland and France had declared neutrality, they could not, under the rules of international law governing belligerents, permit the ships of either combatant to remain in any of their ports longer than necessity demanded, or to obtain more coal than was requisite to enable them to reach the nearest port of their respective nations. Great Britain had declared coal contraband of war. This rendered it useless for Admiral Cervera to call at any British West India port. Nothing remained for him but to make a dash for some Cuban or Porto Rican harbor, and the American fleet was on the alert to check any effort of this kind, and to meet and engage the Spanish squadron if possible.

The news of the presence of a powerful Spanish fleet in the West Indies was followed by active naval movements. On the 12th, the Flying Squadron, so long held at Hampton Roads, was released from its weary wait for a possible enemy, and sailed southward under the command of Commodore Schley. The main section of the squadron, consisting of the flag-ship Brooklyn, the battle-ships Massachusetts and Texas, and the gunboat Scorpion, put in at Key West, where coal and other supplies were taken on with all haste. The Minneapolis, leaving Hampton Roads a day later, sailed eastward and passed through the Windward Passage to the south of Cuba, where the Harvard and the St. Paul were then cruising. The Columbia was left on patrol duty off the North Atlantic States.

At Key West Schley's squadron was joined on the 18th by that of Admiral Sampson, which came dashing in at top speed, the New York far ahead of the other vessels of the squadron, which made their appearance one by one during that and the following day. They had steamed in all haste from San Juan to Key West for coal. No time was to be lost with a Spanish squadron at large in the West India seas. Orders were given to Commodore Schley to proceed south at once by the Yucatan Channel and scour the southern waters for the foe, and by the time the last of Sampson's ships had reached harbor the first of Schley's had set her forefoot towards the Cuban coast. "I congratulate you in advance. I believe you are going to meet and defeat the Spaniards," signalled Sampson from the New York as the Flying Squadron passed out to sea. The Iowa, then coaling, was ordered to follow and join it, while the North Atlantic Squadron began coaling with all rapidity, preparatory to a return voyage eastward to the Windward Channel. By the night of Saturday, the 21st, nearly all the ships had coaled and were off again. Cuba was being circumnavigated in search of the enemy.

Commodore Schley's orders were to proceed to Cienfuegos, where he would be joined by the Iowa, and could take up the Marblehead and Nashville and the two torpedo-boats then off that point. It was soon learned, however, that the blockade at Cienfuegos had been temporarily abandoned in consequence of the probable arrival of the Spanish fleet, and the Marblehead and the Nashville were soon sighted running to Key West for coal and repairs. Off Cape San Antonio, at the western extremity of Cuba, two steamers were sighted, which proved to be the cruiser Cincinnati and the dynamite boat Vesuvius. They were also running in for coal, and reported that they had seen nothing of the Spanish fleet. On Saturday, the 21st, at five P.M., the harbor of Cienfuegos came in sight. It was possible that Cervera's squadron might have taken refuge in this land-locked bay, and the commodore prepared to satisfy his mind on this important point before proceeding farther. The first evidence of activity within the bay came at an early hour on Sunday morning, when a torpedo-boat thrust its forefoot out of the harbor entrance. It quickly disappeared on seeing the group of war-vessels that lay outside. On the shore batteries the Spanish standard waved defiance, and some cavalry were visible on the hill-side, but from the position of the ships no trace could be seen of the Spanish fleet. Noon that day brought the Iowa, whose coming was greeted with cheers for its gallant commander, "Fighting Bob" Evans, whose arm had recently been crushed by the falling of a battle-hatch, but who did not let the intense pain of this accident allay his thirst for battle.

At five o'clock, Sunday afternoon, Commodore Schley made an inspection of the harbor, running close in. No ships-of-war were visible from his point of view, the only craft to be seen being a few schooners and a small gunboat. No shot was fired. "It is the Spanish squadron I am after," said the gallant commodore, "not a few of Spain's almost ruined subjects in Cuba."

If not at Cienfuegos, where was this fleet? It was all-essential to discover, and at eight o'clock that evening the Scorpion was despatched to Santiago de Cuba, three hundred miles to the east, off which port it was hoped she would find the Minneapolis or the Harvard, and perhaps gain some important information. Despatches were sent on the Scorpion to be taken by either of these swift vessels to Hayti and forwarded to the Navy Department of the United States.

On Monday, May 23, the converted yacht Hawk came in from Key West, in company with the gunboat Castine and the collier Merrimac, and bringing important news. This was that the Minneapolis, while scouting to the eastward on the 19th, had tracked the Spanish fleet to Santiago harbor, and at once hastened to Hayti and cabled the news. The Hawk had been sent with all speed to apprise Schley, who on learning the news felt much alarm for the safety of the Scorpion.

Yet the location of the Spanish fleet remained much of a mystery. It might have merely touched at Santiago and proceeded westward. The hills that bounded the winding channel of Cienfuegos harbor hid its depths from view, the city being reached through two sharp turns followed by a winding passage only wide enough for a single ship to pass. The fleet might still lie there out of sight, or might have touched at some other point along the coast. Commodore Schley deemed it wise to wait and investigate more thoroughly before leaving the way open for the enemy to make a dash to Havana. On Tuesday the Marblehead joined, with the two converted yachts Eagle and Vixen. The squadron had become large and formidable.

Meanwhile, evidence was gathering as to the actual

location and the condition of the Spanish fleet. Reports came from two captains, British and Dutch, who had seen Admiral Cervera's ships at Curaçao, and who reported them as in bad condition, the ships' bottoms being seriously fouled with barnacles and long grass. They reached there on May 14, bought all the provisions they could and a small quantity of very inferior coal, and sailed again on the evening of the 15th, seemingly in haste in consequence of a despatch received by the admiral, for much of the coal and a considerable number of cattle were left behind.

Other skippers of merchant-vessels reported having observed the Spanish fleet near Santiago, and still others claimed to have seen it enter the harbor. One of these, the captain of the British ship Adula, from Kingston, Jamaica, reported to Schley at Cienfuegos that at midnight on the 19th he had seen the lights of seven ships some seventy miles south of Santiago, and that on the following day the arrival of the Spanish fleet in that harbor had been telegraphed to Kingston. Further evidence was obtained on May 26, when the St. Paul, cruising off Santiago harbor, picked up the British steamer Restormel, which was trying to steal into the harbor with a cargo of coal, presumably for the Spanish ships. The Restormel had sailed first for San Juan. This port being deemed unsafe, she was ordered to Curaçao, and, reaching there too late, was despatched to Santiago, only to be sent on a final journey to Key West under the care of a prize crew from the St. Paul.

These various shreds of testimony, or such of them as came to Commodore Schley's ears, induced him to leave Cienfuegos for Santiago, in front of whose harbor he arrived on the night of the 27th. The result of his visit was indicated in a despatch which reached Washington May 30, and which stated that the Spanish fleet was certainly in the bay of Santiago de Cuba, since he had himself seen and recognized the vessels.

The fleet being there, the next thing was to keep it there, and the great ships of the squadron were ranged in line in front of the harbor's mouth, effectually closing it. Cervera and his fleet were safely bottled up, never again to sail the open seas under the Spanish flag.

Santiago de Cuba, which was about to become the principal seat of the war, is the second city in size on the island, and has the credit of being probably the oldest city of any importance in the western hemisphere, having been founded in 1514, twenty-two years after the discovery of America. In 1895 it had a population of 59,614. It is the metropolis of eastern Cuba, had before the war a large commerce, and is the head-quarters of three large mining plants owned by citizens of the United States. It lies near the bottom of a beautiful bay, six miles long and two miles wide, which is entered by a narrow channel, flanked by highlands, on which, to the east, stands Morro Castle,* a venerable fortification which derives its sole importance from its elevated position. Opposite the Morro were some newly-built batteries, and two others, Estrella and Catalina, on the east shore, farther in. About half a mile inward, where the channel widens out into the bay, is an islet, Cayo Smith, on

---

* The title Morro seems somewhat abundant in Spanish fortifications. There is a famous Morro Castle at Havana, and others at San Juan and Santiago. The word Morro has various significations, but as thus employed means a fort on a rounded headland, such as appears at the entrance of each of these ports.

PANORAMIC VIEW OF THE HARBOR OF SANTIAGO

Copyright, 1898, by Arkell Publishing Company

which were batteries with modern guns, while Blanco battery, near the city, was similarly armed. There was excellent reason, also, to believe that the channel was mined, and that an attempt to make a forcible entrance into the harbor would prove a very dangerous proceeding.

As regards Admiral Cervera's fleet, it was not easy to recognize it from the harbor entrance. The Reina Mercedes, a partly dismantled cruiser, not connected with the fleet, lay within easy view, and farther in were two ships, supposed to be the Almirante Oquendo and the Cristobal Colon. The remainder of the fleet could not be seen. This fleet, it is proper here to state, consisted of four armored cruisers and three torpedo-boat destroyers. Of the former, the Vizcaya, Almirante Oquendo, and Infanta Maria Teresa were similar in design and armament, being of 6890 tons displacement and of about 20 knots speed. The side armor was of ten or twelve inches thickness, while the two turrets were protected by 9-inch steel armor, and carried two 11-inch Hontorio guns, one in each turret. The main battery contained also ten 5.5-inch guns, and the secondary battery eight 6-pounders, ten 1-pounders, ten machine-guns, and eight torpedo-tubes. The Cristobal Colon was a 6840-ton cruiser, armored with a complete belt of 6-inch nickel steel. She carried two 10-inch guns in barbettes, ten 6-inch and six 4.7-inch guns, and a considerable number of small guns. The Terror, Furor, and Pluton were torpedo-boat destroyers of recent British build, and formidable examples of this type of modern war-vessels.

Of the latter craft, the Terror was not now with the fleet, having been left at Fort-de-France, Martinique.

Here was the auxiliary cruiser Harvard under repair, and apprehension was felt that the formidable little torpedo gunboat might make a prize of the large but lightly armed cruiser. The danger, however, existed more in imagination than in fact, and the Harvard sailed safely north when ready to do so.

Such was the known strength of the fleet. As regarded that of the fortifications Commodore Schley determined to satisfy himself, and on the 31st, the fourth day after his arrival, he stood close in with the Massachusetts and Iowa and the cruiser New Orleans, which had joined his squadron. At 1.15 P.M. the ships reached a point about seven thousand yards from the shore, and then headed due west, the Massachusetts in the lead, the Iowa bringing up the rear. The two battle-ships opened with their heavy guns on the Cristobal Colon, which lay about a mile inside the Morro, while the New Orleans sought to draw the fire of the forts. The narrowness of the harbor entrance permitted only a few shots to be fired at the Colon before the speed of the ships shut her out from view. All the forts, some six in number, opened fire, some of the guns being fairly well aimed, but none of them doing any damage to the ships. The round completed, a second one was made, somewhat farther in, Schley standing unconcernedly near the forward turret of the Massachusetts and watching the effect of the enemy's fire. Having accomplished his mission, he withdrew. It was evident that a heavy bombardment would be necessary to disable the Spanish batteries. A second purpose of the movement was indicated in Schley's despatch to the Navy Department: "Reconnoissance developed satisfactorily the presence of the Spanish squadron lying behind the island near the upper fort, as they fired over the hill at random. Quite satisfied the Spanish fleet is here."

About midnight the two torpedo-boats slipped out of the harbor, gliding under the shadow of the hills towards

the American fleet. They were first seen by the lookout on the Texas, whose search-light was at once turned upon them, revealing their dangerous presence. They dashed towards the Texas, which was lying farthest inshore, but were met with such a rain of shot from her rapid-fire guns that discretion appeared the better part of valor, and they turned and ran hastily back into the harbor.

On June 1, Admiral Sampson, with the New York,

Oregon, and Mayflower, arrived off Santiago and took command of the combined squadrons. He had at his disposal a total fleet of fifteen war-vessels to pit against Cervera's squadron, the escape of which was now rendered hopeless.

The presence of the Oregon calls for some further mention. For more than two months that stanch battle-ship had been sailing along the American coast, having left San Francisco on March 19 with a journey of thirteen thousand miles before her, equal to more than half the circumference of the globe. Rio Janeiro was reached on April 30, and here came the most exciting part of the journey, since there was reason to believe that the Spanish torpedo-boat Temerario, stationed on that coast, was giving chase. But this proved to be a false alarm, and the great ship sped on, reaching Bahia on May 8. Warning was received here of a possible attempt at interception by the Spanish squadron, but Captain Clark kept steadily onward without meeting an enemy, touching at Barbadoes on the 18th, and reaching Jupiter Inlet, Florida, on the 25th. The ship had coaled four times on her trip. The remarkable feature of the great achievement was that the Oregon came into port after her stupendous run at a fifteen-knot speed, and in such excellent condition that she was ready for service without any overhauling. Hastily coaling, she at once set out for Santiago, where she joined the blockading fleet.

Another of the American war-vessels, the Columbia, was less fortunate. On May 28, while cruising off the coast in a dense fog, about eight miles southwest of Fire Island Light, she collided with the British steamship Foscolio, which had left New York with a cargo the day before. The result of the collision was fatal to the Foscolio, which gradually filled and sank, all of her crew being taken off. The Columbia had a jagged hole stove in her starboard side, abreast of the mainmast, about six feet wide and extending some five feet below the water-line. The four-inch steel of the protective deck was bent backward nearly double by the blow. Only for her heavy frame and this deck of steel the great cruiser might have been cut in two. As it was, her water-tight compartments kept her easily afloat, and a brief period in dry-dock put her in serviceable condition again.

During the month of May several attempts to land supplies for the Cubans in arms had been made. On May 11 the transport steamer Gussie left Key West laden with seven thousand rifles and a large quantity of ammunition brought from Tampa, the expedition being under the charge of Captain J. H. Dorst, of the cavalry arm, who took with him over one hundred men of the First Infantry and ten Cuban scouts. The approach of the expedition was amply heralded to the Spaniards by the newspaper correspondents, who gave minute descriptions of the purpose and cargo and the probable landing-point of the Gussie. This information was duly transmitted to Havana, and preparations were made to give the transport a warm reception.

After a rough voyage the Gussie was met off the Cuban coast by the gunboats Wasp and Manning, which escorted her in. The selected place of landing was at Cabanas, province of Pinar del Rio; but as the shore was approached, a large body of Spanish soldiers appeared and opened fire on the vessels. The gunboats replied, the men being landed under cover of their guns. The Spaniards drew back, but opened fire again from their works and from the woods, maintaining their position with such energy that the Americans found it necessary to withdraw.

The failure of this expedition had an important result. It was evidently due to the publicity which had been given to the movements of the vessel, and in consequence a rigid censorship of newspaper messages was established, no despatch being allowed to go over the wires until it had passed under the blue pencil of the censor. Anticipated movements were no longer heralded to the world, and much greater secrecy afterwards surrounded military and naval movements. Conjectures were printed freely enough : no objection was made to them if they did not touch too closely on the truth, as their effect could be but to set the enemy astray.

On May 21 another expedition set sail, this time on the steamer Florida, it being under Captain Dorst, as before. It comprised nearly four hundred men, three hundred of them being Cubans, the latter under the command of Colonel José Lacret, a dashing Cuban leader. It brought with it a pack-train of seventy-five mules and twenty-five horses ; its stores consisting of seven thousand rifles and two million rounds of ammunition for General Garcia's army. The landing was made at Point Banes without interruption, though a body of Spanish soldiers and two gunboats were known to be within a few miles. The Florida spent three days in the harbor, landing all her stores, aided by insurgents, who eagerly helped in the work. And with them came some three hundred half-starved pacificos, who earnestly lent their assistance in exchange for a little food. The rifle-cases were opened and their contents distributed among the men and loaded on pack-animals, the procession then joyfully setting out with its treasures for the mountains.

CHAPTER XI.

THE HEROES OF THE MERRIMAC.

About the hour of three in the morning of June 3, a craft that loomed large through the darkness left the side of the flag-ship of the American squadron before Santiago and sailed straight for the throat of the narrow channel leading to the beleaguered city. On board were eight men, apparently devoted to death, yet all of them eager volunteers. Below decks a series of torpedoes were ranged along the sides of the ship, prepared to blow it into an utter wreck when the proper moment came. As for the safety of the crew, that had been a secondary consideration. Death was likely to be their lot, but they offered their lives in their country's service when they went on that perilous enterprise, and were ready to do and dare all that might be demanded of them. The vessel was the collier Merrimac; her crew consisted of Richmond P. Hobson, Assistant Naval Constructor, and seven volunteer seamen; their purpose was to seal up the Spanish fleet effectually in Santiago harbor.

How best to deal with Cervera and his ships had been a matter of much concern. Commodore Schley had drawn the fire of the Spanish forts and discovered that an attempt to take his fleet into the harbor over the mines and in face of the batteries was likely to prove ruinous. There was some thought of attempting to explode the mines by the use of the dynamite projectiles of the Vesuvius, but the result of this was doubtful. The ships would have to enter single file, and the sinking of one of them would block the channel to the others. At this juncture Lieutenant Hobson suggested that it would be better to sink a useless hulk than a battle-ship. If the Spanish ships could not be reached, they might be kept where they were. With the fleet was the large collier Merrimac, bought by the government at a high price, yet practically worthless. She could be put to no better service than to block up the channel. The Spanish fleet was "bottled up" in Santiago harbor. The Merrimac could be placed as a "cork in the neck of the bottle," and Hobson volunteered to be the man for the work.

Admiral Sampson hesitated to send men to what seemed likely to be certain death, but the brave lieutenant's enthusiasm finally won his consent, and the daring enterprise was determined upon. The Merrimac was brought from the side of the Massachusetts, to which she had been delivering coal, and on the day and night of June 1 crews from the New York and Brooklyn were kept busy in preparing her for her final service. A heavy weight in coal was still on board, but that was left to aid in her speedy sinking, after her sides had been torn open by the torpedoes arranged for that purpose. The night was well advanced towards morning before the work was completed and the Merrimac ready for her task.

When the news of the intended expedition passed through the fleet, with word that volunteers were wanted for the desperate enterprise, it seemed as if half the men in service were eager to take part. The six men asked for could easily have been extended into a ship's crew.

More than two hundred men on the New York offered their services. The Iowa signalled that she had one hundred and forty volunteers. Similar responses came from the other ships. The junior officers were wildly eager to take part. There was bitter disappointment in many faces when Hobson announced his choice, consisting of Daniel Montague, chief master-at-arms of the New York; George Charette, gunner's mate of the same vessel; J. C. Murphy, a coxswain of the Iowa, and three of the crew of the Merrimac, Oscar Deignan, John P. Phillips, and John Kelly. When the expedition finally started, there was another man on board, H. Clausen, a coxswain of the New York, a stowaway for the perilous enterprise.

It was 4.30 A.M. when Admiral Sampson finally left the Merrimac, after a final inspection of the work done. Day was already dawning in the eastern sky, and to most of those within view the hour seemed too late. It certainly seemed so to the admiral; yet to the general surprise the collier was seen to be in motion, and a cry arose, "She is going in!"

At this cry, Admiral Sampson seized the megaphone, and hailed the torpedo-boat Porter, which lay near at hand. "Porter, there! Tell the Merrimac to return immediately."

The Merrimac was headed directly towards the throat of the channel. The Porter darted after her, smoke pouring from her stacks. Darkness had vanished, and all eyes watched the swift little craft as she flew in the wake of the big collier. They were both within range of the Spanish guns when the Porter darted across the bows of the Merrimac, heading her off. A sigh of relief went up; to venture under the Spanish guns in full daylight seemed fatal temerity. Yet the Porter was seen returning, while the Merrimac held her place, Hobson signalling for permission to go on. He thought he could do it. The admiral displayed a peremptory order to return, and the lumbering collier slowly came back.

The 2d of June passed wearily for the men, whose nerves were strung to high tension for the perilous task, and at about three o'clock in the morning of the 3d the devoted vessel again got under weigh, heading through the darkness for the harbor and hoping to get well in before being seen. Not a light was shown, and it needed no small skill to hit the narrow channel squarely in the gloom. Clouds covered the moon as the dark vessel stole in towards the coast, heading eastward, while in the rear followed a steam launch from the New York, manned by Cadet J. W. Powell and four men, ready to pick up any member of the Merrimac's crew who should escape.

From the deck of the New York nothing could be seen of the collier after she passed under the shadow of the hills. All eyes were anxiously peering into the gloom and all ears were alert for a sound, but for a time silence and darkness prevailed. Then the gloom was broken by a flash from Morro Castle, and the sound of a distant gun boomed across the waves. Other flashes followed from the battery opposite, and for about twenty minutes flash succeeded flash rapidly in the narrow space. The Merrimac was meeting her doom. At 6.15 A.M. Powell and the launch returned, followed by spiteful but ill-aimed shots from the Spanish guns. The brave cadet had gone directly under the batteries in the hope of picking up some of the Merrimac's men, but returned disappointed. Hobson and his brave crew had

Copyright, 1898, by Arkell Publishing Company
LIEUTENANT HOBSON ON THE MERRIMAC

gone to the depths in their sinking ship or were prisoners in Spanish hands. The launch had followed the Merrimac until it had seen her headed squarely in for the harbor, the first shot being fired when the collier was about two hundred yards from the entrance. After that the firing rapidly increased, and the smoke, which hung heavily, hid the vessel from view. Then came the explosion of the torpedoes. Powell waited till full day under the cliffs, and before leaving saw a spar of the Merrimac rising out of the water of the channel. The sinking had been a success, whatever the fate of the men.

For the rest of the story we must turn to Lieutenant Hobson's narrative, given a month later. His purpose had been to take the Merrimac into the channel past the Estrella battery and sink her in the narrowest part of the passage, dropping the anchor and handling the rudder so as to turn her athwart the stream. She was longer 'than the channel's breadth, and it was hoped to close it up completely. When the proper point was reached, Hobson proposed to stop the engines, drop the anchors, put the helm hard aport, open the sea connections, and touch off the torpedoes, of which ten lay on the port-side of the ship, each containing eighty-two pounds of gunpowder, and the whole so connected that they could be fired in train. Two men were below, one to reverse the engines, the other to break open the sea connections with a sledge-hammer. The men on deck were to drop the anchor and set the helm. Then Hobson would touch the button setting off the torpedoes, and all were to leap overboard and swim to the dingy that was towed astern, and in which they hoped to escape.

This plan worked fairly well, and would have been completely successful but for one or two contingencies which seriously affected the result. The narrow channel was entered at about the hour of three, the Merrimac steaming in under the guns of the Morro through a dense darkness and a stillness like that of death. Silently onward she moved, but the Spanish were on the alert. The stillness was broken by the wash of a small picket-boat that approached from the shore and ran under the Merrimac's stern, firing several shots at the suspicious craft. One of these carried away the rudder, and put an end to the project of steering the ship athwart the channel. Another perhaps wrecked the dingy in tow.

The remainder of the adventure was highly exciting. The picket-boat hastened to give the alarm, and in a brief time the guns of the shore batteries, followed by those of the ships in the harbor, were pouring their fire upon the dark hulk. The Spaniards thought that an American battle-ship was trying to force its way into the port, and did not know but that the whole fleet was following in its train. The Merrimac drove onward at her full speed, trembling violently as a submarine mine went off harmlessly in her wake. The deep gloom and her rapid motion saved her from destruction.

At length the desired position was reached. At Hobson's signal the engines were reversed, the anchor was dropped, and the helm set. To his disappointment, the ship refused to answer her helm. Only then did he learn that the rudder had been lost. The plan of setting her lengthwise across the channel had failed and the final task remained. Hobson touched the electric button connected with the torpedoes, and, as a sullen roar broke out beneath them and the ship heavily lurched and rolled, the men, who had stripped to their underclothing to facilitate swimming, leaped over the side. Some of them were thrown over the rail by the shock and the lurching of the ship. Down she went with a surge at the bow, loud cheers from the forts and ships greeting her as she sank. The defenders thought they had sent to the depths one of the American ships-of-war.

The dingy being wrecked, the only resource of the fugitives was an old catamaran which at the last moment had been placed on the collier's deck. This float lay on the roof of the midship house, and, that it should not be lost in the suction made by the sinking ship, it had been tied to the taffrail, giving it slack line enough to let it float loose after the ship had sunk into her resting-place.

In continuation of our narrative, we cannot do better than quote from Lieutenant Hobson, giving his graphic account of the thrilling experiences of himself and men after their plunge into the waters of the channel:

"I swam away from the ship as soon as I struck the water, but I could feel the eddies drawing me backward in spite of all I could do. That did not last very long, however, and, as soon as I felt the tugging cease, I turned and struck out for the float, which I could see dimly bobbing up and down over the sunken hull.

"The Merrimac's masts were plainly visible, and I could see the heads of my seven men as they followed my example and made for the float also. We had expected, of course, that the Spaniards would investigate the wreck, but we had no idea that they would be at it as quickly as they were. Before we could get to the float, several row-boats and launches came around the bluff from inside the harbor. They had officers on board and armed marines as well, and they searched that passage, rowing backward and forward, until the next morning. It was only by good luck that we got to the float at all, for they were upon us so quickly that we had barely concealed ourselves when a boat with quite a large party on board was right beside us.

"Unfortunately, we thought then, but it turned out afterwards that nothing more fortunate than that could have happened to us, the rope with which we had secured the float to the ship was too short to allow it to swing free, and when we reached it we found that one of the pontoons was entirely out of the water and the other one was submerged. Had the raft lain flat on the water we could not have got under it, and would have had to climb up on it, to be an excellent target for the first party of marines that arrived. As it was, we could get under the raft, and, by putting our hands through the crevices between the slats which formed its deck, we could hold our heads out of water and still be unseen. That is what we did, and all night long we stayed there with our noses and mouths barely out of the water.

"None of us expected to get out of the affair alive, but luckily the Spaniards did not think of the apparently damaged, half-sunken raft floating about beside the wreck. They came to within a cable's length of us at intervals of only a few minutes all night. We could hear their words distinctly, and even in the darkness could distinguish an occasional glint of light on the riflebarrels of the marines and on the lace of the officers' uniforms. We were afraid to speak above a whisper, and for a good while, in fact whenever they were near us, we breathed as easily as we could. I ordered my men not to speak unless to address me, and with one exception they obeyed.

"After we had been there an hour or two the water, which we found rather warm at first, began to get cold, and my fingers ached where the wood was pressing into them. The clouds, which were running before a pretty stiff breeze when we went in, blew over, and then by the starlight we could see the boats when they came out of the shadows of the cliffs on either side, and even when we could not see them we knew that they were still near, because we could hear very plainly the splash of the oars and the grinding of the oarlocks.

"Our teeth began to chatter before very long, and I was in constant fear that the Spaniards would hear us when they came close. It was so still that the chattering sound seemed to us as loud as a hammer, but the Spaniards' ears were not sharp enough to hear it. We could hear sounds from the shore almost as distinctly as if we had been there, we were so close to the surface of the water, which is an excellent conductor, and the voices of the men in the boats sounded as clear as a bell. My men tried to keep their teeth still, but it was hard work, and not attended with any great success at the best.

"We all knew that we would be shot if discovered by an ordinary seaman or a marine, and I ordered my men not to stir, as the boats having officers on board kept well in the distance. One of my men disobeyed orders and started to swim ashore, and I had to call him back. He obeyed at once, but my voice seemed to create some commotion among the boats, and several of them appeared close beside us before the disturbance in the water made by the man swimming had disappeared.

We thought it was all up with us then, but the boats went away into the shadows again.

"There was much speculation among the Spaniards as to what the ship was and what we intended to do next. I could understand many of the words, and gathered from what I heard that the officers had taken in the situation at once, but were astounded at the audacity of the thing. The boats, I also learned, were from the fleet, and I felt better, because I had more faith in a Spanish sailor than I had in a Spanish soldier.

"When daylight came a steam launch full of officers and marines came out from behind the cliff that hid the fleet and harbor and advanced towards us. All the men on board were looking curiously in our direction. They did not see us. Knowing that some one of rank must be on board, I waited until the launch was quite close and hailed her.

"My voice produced the utmost consternation on board. Every one sprang up, the marines crowded to the bow, and the launch's engines were reversed. She not only stopped, but she backed off until nearly a quarter of a mile away, where she stayed. The marines stood ready to fire at the word of command when we clambered out from under the float. There were ten of the marines, and they would have fired in a minute had they not been restrained.

"I swam towards the launch and then she started towards me. I called out in Spanish: 'Is there an officer on board?' An officer answered in the affirmative, and then I shouted in Spanish again: 'I have seven men to surrender.' I continued swimming, and was seized and pulled out of the water.

"As I looked up when they were dragging me into

the launch, I saw that it was Admiral Cervera himself who had hold of me. He looked at me rather dubiously at first, because I had been down in the engine-room of the Merrimac, where I got covered with oil, and that, with the soot and coal-dust, made my appearance most disreputable. I had put on my officer's belt before sinking the Merrimac, as a means of identification, no matter what happened to me, and when I pointed to it in the launch the admiral understood and seemed satisfied. The first words he said to me when he learned who I was were 'Bienvenido sea usted,' which means 'You are welcome.' My treatment by the naval officers and that of my men also was courteous all the time that I was a prisoner. They heard my story, as much of it as I could tell, but sought to learn nothing more.

"Sharks? No, we did not have time to think of them that night," said Lieutenant Hobson in reply to a question. "We saw a great many things, though, and went through a great many experiences. When we started out from the fleet I tied to my belt a flask of medicated water, supplied to me by my ship's surgeon. The frequency with which we all felt thirsty on the short run into the passage and the dryness of my mouth and lips made me believe that I was frightened. The men felt the same, and all the way the flask went from hand to hand. Once I felt my pulse to see if I was frightened, but to my surprise I found it normal. Later we forgot all about it, and when we got into the water there was no need for the flask."

The prisoners were taken ashore and placed in a cell in Morro Castle, the solid doors of the cell being kept closed for an hour or two, but afterwards left open by order of the admiral. This gave them a view of the harbor, the city, and the Spanish fleet, while from the windows they could see and hear the shells during the bombardment that took place some days afterwards. Hobson's description of the sounds made by these shells is well worth quoting.

"The windows in the side of our cell," he says, "opened west across the harbor entrance, and we could hear and see the shells as they struck. We knew that we would not be fired upon, as word had gone out as to where we were, so we sat at the windows and watched the shells. Each one sang a different tune as it went by. The smaller shells moaned or screeched as they passed, but the 13-inch shells left a sound behind them like that of the sudden and continued smashing of a huge pane of glass. The crackling was sharp and metallic, something like sharp thunder without the roar, and the sound continued, but decreased, after the shell had gone. In many instances the shells struck projecting points of rock, and, ricocheting, spun end over end across the hills. The sound they made as they struck again and again was like the short, sharp puffs of a locomotive starting with a heavy train."

Meanwhile, on board the fleet the escape of the adventurers was unknown, and dread of their destruction prevailed. This feeling of depression was put an end to by the chivalry of Admiral Cervera, who sent Captain Ovideo, his chief of staff, to the fleet under a flag of truce to acquaint the American admiral with their safety and to make an offer for their exchange. Captain Ovideo was received by Admiral Sampson on the New York, and, after salutes had been exchanged, delivered the following message:

"Admiral Cervera, the commander of the Spanish

fleet, is most profoundly impressed with the brilliant courage shown by the men who sank the steamer Merrimac in our harbor, and in admiration of their courage he has directed me to say to their countrymen that they are alive, and, with the exception of two of the men who were slightly hurt, they are uninjured. They are now prisoners of war, and are being well cared for, and will be treated with every consideration."

The captain was given a courteous reception in the cabin of the New York, and, after an interview on the subject of exchanging the prisoners, returned with money and clothing sent them by Admiral Sampson. The courtesy of the Spanish admiral sent a thrill of admiration throughout the fleet, and throughout the country when it became known, and insured the gallant Spaniard a kind reception if the fortune of war should deliver him into American hands.

The brave Cervera estimated the boldness of the exploit at its full value, and treated the captives with great consideration while they remained in his hands. For some time the fleet desisted from firing on the Morro, fearing that the prisoners might be injured. They were kept there, however, but four days, when Cervera turned them over to General Linares, commander of the Spanish forces in the city, who was much less favorably disposed towards them.

In regard to the estimation in the navy of this most daring deed, we may quote from a remark of Commodore Schley to a correspondent of the Associated Press. Pointing towards the gray walls of Morro Castle, where Lieutenant Hobson and his brave men were said to be incarcerated, the commodore spoke as follows: "History does not record an act of finer heroism than that of the gallant men who are prisoners over there. I watched the Merrimac as she made her way to the entrance of the harbor, and my heart sank as I saw the perfect hell of fire that fell on the devoted men. I did not think it was possible one of them could have gone through it alive. They went into the jaws of death. It was Balaklava over again without the means of defence which the Light Brigade had. Hobson led a forlorn hope, without the power to cut his way out. But fortune once more favored the brave, and I hope he will have the recognition and promotion he deserves. His name will live as long as the heroes of the world are remembered."

This feeling of the people was shared by the government, and steps were at once taken to reward the gallant lieutenant and his men by promotion. Efforts were made for their speedy release and to learn what treatment they were receiving. Anxiety on this last point was set at rest by a telegram from Mr. W. F. Ramsden, the British consul at Santiago, dated June 10, in reply to one from the New York *Herald*. It said:

"Replying to your telegram, Hobson and men well cared for by authorities. Have myself just seen him.
"RAMSDEN."

Mr. Ramsden, in fact, was very kind to the prisoners, visiting them on several occasions and supplying them with food of a superior kind to that provided by the authorities. Cervera also visited them, and, aside from the discomfort of being held as prisoners in a half-starved city, they received very considerate treatment.

The story of their release comes later in point of time. It may, however, be properly given here as a close to the narrative of their adventure. Cervera's promise of a speedy exchange was not concurred in by the Spanish authorities; difficulties were thrown in the way, and it was not until after July 1, when the situation had materially changed at Santiago, that a consent to the exchange was given. A Spanish lieutenant and fourteen privates were offered on the American side in exchange for Hobson and his seven men.

On July 7 the exchange took place. At that date Santiago was beleaguered by an American army and Admiral Cervera a prisoner on the American fleet, his proud squadron being laid in ruin on the Cuban coast. Leaving the Reina Mercedes hospital, on the outskirts of Santiago, where they had been confined, in charge of Major Irles, a Spanish staff-officer, the captives were conducted to a meeting-place between the lines, Hobson on horseback, his men, in new uniforms, following on foot. Colonel John Jacob Astor and Lieutenant Miloy conducted the Spanish prisoners. The choice of two lieutenants was offered, and Adolfo Aries, of the aristocratic First Provisional Regiment of Barcelona, was chosen in exchange for Lieutenant Hobson.

As the gallant eight came up the trail leading to the American lines through an avenue of palms that arched from the high banks across the road, the soldiers stood in reverent silence, baring their heads as the hero approached, while the band struck up "The Star-Spangled Banner." Then came a cry for cheers and a welcoming roar from all the men in sight, the Rough Riders breaking into a cowboy yell. The men were past restraint, and as Hobson rode slowly through the lines, the ranks were everywhere broken, and men rushed eagerly to grasp him and his men by the hand.

It was the same all the way to Siboney,—men shouting, cheering, rushing to shake hands, fairly wild with excitement. A short distance from the shore lay the New York, waiting to take them on board. There the enthusiasm was equally great, the men growing delirious with delight when Hobson set foot on deck. Captain Chadwick had escorted him to his vessel, and there Admiral Sampson was one of the first to welcome him, almost embracing him in the warmth of his greeting, while the officers of the ship were no less earnest and ardent in their reception of their gallant comrade.

The returning hero seemed astonished at this tumultuous applause. Locked in a Spanish prison, he knew nothing of how his fellow-countrymen regarded his exploit, which, as he modestly remarked, "was not much of a feat." In this he did not find many to agree with him. People thought it very much of a feat, and days passed before Hobson was allowed to sink quietly back into the duties of his office, his heroic deed having passed into history.

CHAPTER XII.

THE FIRST FIGHT ON CUBAN SOIL.

CAREFULLY as Lieutenant Hobson's enterprise had been managed, and cool as he had been in carrying out its every detail, it proved practically a failure. The loss of the rudder had rendered it impossible to handle the vessel, and she had sunk along instead of across the channel, leaving space for a war-ship to pass by her side. Thus the services of the fleet were still necessary to hold the Spanish ships in check, and none could be spared from the blockade. The necessity of alertness was to be demonstrated before many weeks by a startling event. It was still a matter of doubt, however, whether the whole of Admiral Cervera's squadron lay within. Not all the ships had been seen, and it was not sure but that some of them might still be in the open seas, prowling for prey in the West India or North Atlantic waters. It was known that the torpedo-boat destroyer Terror was still at large, and it was just possible that others might be outside of Santiago harbor. This question it was important to settle definitely.

For this purpose, Commodore Schley, after his bombardment of the Santiago forts, opened communication with the insurgents at a point on the coast about eighteen miles east of the city. They were asked to send scouts to the vicinity of the city and try to learn the number and names of the vessels then in the harbor. On Friday, June 3, Lieutenant Sharp, of the Vixen, visited the place of rendezvous and received from the insurgents a map of the harbor, showing the entire Cape Verde fleet, with the exception of one of the torpedo-boats. They lay at the upper extremity of the harbor, under the guns of Blanco battery.

This information, definite as it appeared, was not fully satisfactory to Admiral Sampson, who seems to have preferred American to Cuban eyes as means of accurate observation. He therefore despatched Lieutenant Blue, a daring young officer of the fleet, on an enterprise only second in peril to that performed by Lieutenant Hobson. Leaving shipboard, the lieutenant made a detour of seventy miles around the harbor of Santiago, counting and inspecting the ships that lay there from commanding points of observation on the high hills surrounding, and satisfying himself beyond doubt that all the ships of the squadron, with the exception of the Terror, were there. This tour of observation in a hostile country was one that demanded no small degree of courage and resolution. In military law he would, if taken, have been adjudged a spy, and in all probability would have been hanged as one. It was simply another instance of that intrepidity which seems so common a trait of the American sailor and soldier.

The fact of the presence of the Spanish fleet being definitely established, the blockade went on, its monotony broken by occasional stirring incidents. On the night of June 3 a second attempt to use their torpedoes against the blockading ships was made by the Spaniards. It was defeated by the sharp lookout kept up on the American fleet. Shortly after ten o'clock a flash of colored lights on the deck of the New Orleans gave warning that an enemy was in sight. A second signal indicated that a torpedo-boat had been seen. Immediately night signals flashed around the six or seven miles' circuit of the blockading squadron, while shots came from the rapid-fire battery of the New Orleans. The New York sought the locality at full speed, hoping to shut off the daring stranger from the harbor.

"A torpedo-boat one point forward on the port-beam, sir; headed this way," reported Ensign Mustin to Captain Chadwick, and for some minutes the guns of the flag-ship boomed out through the night. The Oregon, coming up to the eastward, followed with two shots from her big guns. Then the signal "Cease firing" was given. The search-lights showed no signs of an enemy. The prowling craft had escaped. That it had not been a false alarm was proved the next morning, when the torpedo-boat Porter found two loaded torpedoes floating off shore. They had evidently been discharged at the ships, but had missed their mark. One of them was taken on board the Porter, the other sank as they were seeking to lift it. The one recovered was a 14-inch Whitehead torpedo, worth about $3500, in perfect condition, and calculated to have sunk any ship against which it struck. The result added another to the numerous failures in the attempted use of torpedo-boats.

A second bombardment of the forts at Santiago was made on June 7, the large vessels of the American fleet pouring in a steady and effective fire from 7.45 until nearly 11 A.M. The fleet formed in double column, six miles off Morro Castle, and steamed slowly along three thousand yards off shore, the Brooklyn leading one column, followed by the Marblehead, Texas, and Massachusetts, and moving westward. In the second column, headed eastward, the New York led, the New Orleans, Yankee, Iowa, and Oregon following. A sharp fire was directed against all the forts with the exception of the Morro, which was saved from attack by the supposed presence of Lieutenant Hobson and his men.

The bombardment appeared to be very effective, the Spanish fire weakening until it ceased entirely. The Estrella and Catalina batteries seemed to have particularly suffered, while considerable injury was done to the Reina Mercedes, the only Spanish ship within reach. Throughout the engagement not an American ship was hit and no American was injured. The Spaniards fired with their usual lack of aim, wasting their projectiles idly upon the waters of the harbor. The attack was specially directed against Aguadores, a small town on the coast a little to the east of the harbor entrance. A fort recently constructed there was completely wrecked, and a party of marines were landed at Baiquiri, some distance east of Aguadores, and near a station on the railroad running to Santiago. They were attacked by Spanish infantry and cavalry, but held their ground, being aided by a neighboring force of Cuban insurgents. The purpose of this landing was probably to hold the point as a landing-place for the expected troops; but the position was not maintained.

On the same day a similar movement was made near the mouth of the fine harbor of Guantanamo, which lies some forty-five miles along the coast east of Santiago harbor. This bay is a very fine one, the harbor being capacious and with forty feet depth of water. The town lies some six miles inland from the mouth of the bay. The Marblehead and the Yankee, under orders from Admiral Sampson, entered the lower bay on the date mentioned, drove a Spanish gunboat into the interior harbor, and silenced the batteries after a few minutes' bombardment. On Friday, the 10th, a landing was effected, forty marines from the Oregon going ashore and occupying the western entrance to the bay. Soon after the troop-ship Panther, with six hundred marines, arrived, and these were landed without opposition, the Spanish having been driven back by the fire of the Marblehead the day before. The marines found evidence that the Spaniards had left in panic haste,—watches, hammocks, and ammunition being left scattered about their works. The landing-party, under command of Lieutenant-Colonel R. W. Huntington, made its way up the rocky hill-side to the deserted earthworks on top, and soon the American flag was flying from the flagstaff of the captured Spanish camp.

The position of this force on the crest of the hill to which it had climbed was an exposed one. It occupied a bare spot surrounded on all sides by heavy brush, the ground descending inward into a ravine, whose chaparral offered close cover to the Spanish bush-fighters, while the American camp, outlined on the bare crest against the sky, seemed as if intended as a target for rifle-fire from below. Only for the aimless character of Spanish marksmanship, the marines must have suffered severely for their incautious temerity.

The guerillas had gathered thickly in the brush, and at five o'clock on Saturday afternoon, the day after the landing, a brisk fire told of the presence of an unseen foe. It was answered sharply from the camp, the men sheltering themselves as best they could and firing at random into the bushes. The exact position of the enemy could not be discovered on account of their use of smokeless powder. This firing was kept up all night long, ending only at six o'clock on Sunday morning, when reinforcements from the Marblehead joined the beleaguered troops. The loss on the American side was small, considering the advantage in position of the enemy, being but three men killed and one wounded. Among the killed was Surgeon John Blair Gibbs, son of Major Gibbs, one of the victims of the Custer massacre. The loss of the Spaniards was unknown. Fears were entertained that the advance pickets, under Lieutenants Neville and Shaw, had been cut off by the foe; but during the morning these officers appeared in camp with their thirty men, much exhausted by their long term of picket duty and all-night fight with the enemy, but otherwise none the worse for this arduous service. During most of the time they had been surrounded by a superior force, but had firmly held their ground, inflicting considerable damage and receiving none.

Shortly after midnight a fierce assault was made upon the camp, the Spanish charging boldly up the southwest slope. They were met by rapid volleys from the marines who encircled the inner side of the crest, and broke before they were one-third of the way to the top. Some of them came farther up, and at points there was almost a hand-to-hand struggle. It was during this charge that Surgeon Gibbs fell. As a rule, however, the Spaniards fought under cover, creeping up as close as they dared to the American line and delivering their fire from the brush. It was a mode of warfare in which they displayed an Indian-like skill, and which they had long practised in their contest with the Cubans.

On Sunday morning Colonel Huntington decided to change the position of his camp, the tents being removed from the crest and pitched on the side of the hill facing the harbor, where they were under the protection of the guns of the war-ships. The crest was given up to batteries and rifle-pits, two 3-inch guns being drawn up the hill and mounted on the works in expectation of a second attack on Sunday night. Other guns of smaller caliber and two Colt machine-guns were also mounted. The looked-for attack began shortly after dark and was kept up all night, the firing being incessant, but not very effective. Two of the marines were killed and three injured. During the night the Spaniards made an assault on the camp on the hill-side, and the Marblehead, under the mistaken idea that the Americans had been driven out, threw several shells into the place, fortunately without harm. The attack was easily repulsed by the few marines in camp.

The night battle was a picturesque and striking spectacle, tongues of fire darting from every bush encircling the camp, while the search-lights of the ships swept back and forth over the hills, revealing the lurking enemy to the marines on the crest. These gleams of light were accompanied by a strange variety of sounds, including the crack of the Mauser rifles, the twitter of the long steel bullets overhead, the rattle of the machine-guns, the crash of the field-guns as they drove their canister into the thicket, the sharp reports of the rapid-fire 1-pounders in the ship launches below, and an occasional screech from the large guns of the Marblehead.

Lieutenant Neville was again sent out on scout duty, and attacked a small stone fort, from which the Spaniards were driven with loss, fifteen dead bodies being found within. On Monday the marines received an important reinforcement, being joined by about sixty Cuban allies, whose acquaintance with the country and with the Spanish method of fighting made them of great value. General Garcia had sent General Rabi, his chief of staff, with about one thousand men, to occupy Ascerraderos, a village on the coast to the west of Santiago, following up this movement with the main body of his forces, and sending a detachment to reinforce the marines.

During Monday the works on Crest Hill were strengthened, and a body of Cubans and marines was sent to establish strong outposts a mile in advance. This gave the battalion a rest during Monday night, and the next day an attack was made on the Spanish camp, which scouts had located at a point about four miles inland, near the only well to be found for miles around. A force of marines under Captain Elliott and of Cubans under Colonel Thomas left the camp on Tuesday morning, and about eleven o'clock caught sight from a hill-top of the Spanish quarters on a brush-covered ridge below. Orders for an immediate attack were given, and a spirited charge was made, the troops coming close up before they were discovered by the foe. A sharp engagement followed, the Spaniards resisting for some twenty minutes the onset of the marines. Then they broke for a thicket in the rear, the American bullets pouring into the fleeing line with deadly effect. Resistance was continued until about 3.30 P.M., by which time the rout was complete, when the assailants returned, burned the camp buildings, and destroyed the well by filling it up with earth and stones. No other drinking water was to be had nearer than Guantanamo, several miles away. An attempt was made by Captain Elliott to cut off the enemy's retreat by climbing through cactus and brush a high hill in the rear, but the misdirected fire of the

Dolphin checked this movement and gave the Spaniards an opportunity to escape.

The bodies of about forty dead Spaniards were found in the vicinity of the block-house and eighteen prisoners were taken. The Cubans had two men killed and four wounded, and the marines two wounded, while twenty-three were overcome by the intense heat. In truth, the heat seemed more deadly than Spanish bullets, which were fired without regard to aim. This affair ended the conflict, the Spanish having been too severely punished to make any new assault on the camp of the marines.

The experience of the marines taught some useful lessons. It showed that the Spaniards were shrewd and daring bush-fighters, and that American camps needed to be carefully protected against night attacks. It also proved that bullets from magazine rifles might be wasted at an extraordinary rate without execution under the shades of night. In the daylight attacks the Spaniards had concealed themselves in the brush by wearing plantain leaves on their foreheads in place of hats. They also, wearing bark-colored trousers and tying green branches round their waists, had shown themselves able to move slowly across open spaces without being detected. Another trick was to make a moving screen of two or three large palm leaves, which formed an excellent disguise in the chaparral, from which stunted palms everywhere rose.

The Cuban allies far surpassed the marines in detecting these tricks, with which they were thoroughly familiar, having often practised them against the Spaniards. These men, mostly negroes, were keen-eyed woodsmen, well versed in bush-fighting, in which they displayed a daring that called forth American admiration. But they were wildly reckless in handling the magazine rifles with which they had been supplied, and as wretched in marksmanship as the Spanish troops.

The final engagement in the bay of Guantanamo was the shelling, on June 16, of the fort and earthworks at Caimanera, a town on the west side of the bay some distance inward from the camp of the marines. These works were demolished, and all resistance was brought to an end. On the same day the fleet made a third bombardment of the forts at the mouth of Santiago harbor, with the exception of the Morro, where Lieutenant Hobson was supposed to be confined. The affair continued for about an hour, the Spaniards replying briskly but wildly, while in the end most of their guns were abandoned. Not a ship was struck nor a man hurt on the American side. On the other hand, the batteries showed signs of being seriously injured, and many of their guns appeared to be dismounted.

The interesting feature of this affair, however, was the work of the dynamite boat Vesuvius. The dynamite guns carried by this vessel had been tried with good effect on land, but they had never been tested at sea, and the dread that the gun-cotton cartridges might explode within the tubes and blow the vessel to fragments made naval officers fearful of them. In consequence, the Vesuvius had been used as a despatch-boat, and only on this occasion was permission given for a trial of her guns. At midnight of the day preceding the bombardment she drew cautiously in and fired three of her 250-pound projectiles with perfect safety to the vessel. From two of these no report came. The third exploded with terrific violence on Cayo Smith, a frightful fiery gleam illuminating the harbor. From the ships the next morning a deep crater appeared on the side of the island, though subsequent observation indicated that no great harm had been done. On June 24 the Vesuvius performed a service of a different character, entering the harbor at night and passing unobserved around the wreck of the Merrimac. The result of the reconnoissance was to prove that the channel had not been closed, and that a battle-ship could pass in safety on either side of the sunken collier.

On the 20th occurred the first landing of officers of the regular army on Cuban soil. This was at Ascerraderos, twelve miles west of Santiago, where General Garcia had established his camp. General Shafter, commander of the army of invasion, with his staff, landed for a conference with the Cuban general, accompanied by Admiral Sampson and his chief of staff. No soldiers or sailors were landed, the escort of ragged Cuban soldiers sufficing. The meeting took place in a very picturesque location, on the summit of a high cliff that overlooked a valley green with the royal palm, while beyond the white breakers at the beach stretched far away the calm blue sea, dotted thickly with transports and ships-of-war.

The three commanders took their seats under the palm-leaf roof of an open hut on which the sun's rays fell hotly. Outside stood five half-naked negro sentries, and beyond were grouped hundreds of Cubans, officers and men commingled, conversing as well as they could with the staff-officers from the fleet.

Plans for the coming attack on Santiago were discussed and arrangements for the co-operation of the allied forces settled, a map of the surrounding country being frequently consulted. This done, the conference ended, the three principal actors in the drama about to be played bade one another adieu, and the Americans returned to their boats, leaving their Cuban allies to seek again their lurking-places in the brush.

CHAPTER XIII.

THE ARMY OF INVASION.

ON the 23d of April President McKinley, as already stated, called forth a volunteer force of 125,000 men for two years' service, apportioning them among the States and Territories in accordance with population. These were recruited from the existing National Guard organizations, vacancies being filled under a very careful system of health inspection. On May 23 a second call was issued, for 75,000 men, under similar conditions, though without restriction to the National Guards. The regular army was also increased by filling up the regiments to their full quotas, its limit being 62,000 men, and several special forces were called for, making the total strength of the army, when fully recruited, 278,500 men.

This force was to be made up as follows: Regular army, 62,000; volunteer, first call, 125,000, second call, 75,000; three special cavalry regiments, 3000; new engineer force, 3500; and ten regiments of volunteer infantry immune from yellow fever, 10,000. The last, composed of men who had recovered from or been exposed to this fever, were intended for use in infected districts. The first assignment of commanding officers, made public May 16, included the following major-generals: Wesley Merritt, in command of the Department of the Pacific (including the Philippines); John R. Brooke, in command of the First Corps and the Department of the Gulf; William M. Graham, of the Second Corps, Camp Alger, Falls Church, Virginia; James F. Wade, of the Third Corps, Chickamauga, Georgia; John J. Coppinger, of the Fourth Corps, Mobile, Alabama; William R. Shafter, of the Fifth Corps, Tampa, Florida; James H. Wilson, of the Sixth Corps, Chickamauga, Georgia; Fitzhugh Lee, of the Seventh Corps, Tampa, Florida; Joseph H. Wheeler, in command of the Cavalry Division, Tampa, Florida. Major-General Elwell S. Otis was made second in command to General Merritt. The whole army was under the command of Major-General Nelson A. Miles. Various subsequent appointments were made of major- and brigadier-generals and minor officers, some of which failed to win public approbation, since political influences were claimed to have controlled their selection.

This was not the only adverse criticism made. The whole management of military affairs was sharply called in question by some observers, the War Department and the "Board of Strategy" being severely taken to task for alleged neglect of the troops. These charges of the hostile press were particularly devoted to the state of affairs at Tampa, Florida, where, it was claimed, the soldiers had been grossly neglected, the men being dumped down at a railway siding like so many emigrants, and left to seek what quarters they could find in the burning sand, no preparations being made for them. It was said that they lacked suitable clothing and food, were not properly drilled, and were in every respect shamefully treated. And the reason given for this was the alleged incompetence of their officers, few of whom, it was said, had any knowledge of military affairs, while General Wheeler, a famous Confederate cavalry leader of the Civil War, was declared to be incompetent through age.

These charges were strongly denied by Richard Harding Davis, a newspaper correspondent, who quoted from General Miles, Colonel Pope, the chief surgeon of the Fifth Corps, and others, including a German military attaché, to prove that the army was in an excellent state of health, well fed and cared for, thoroughly equipped and disciplined. "I have never been so proud," said General Miles, "as I was yesterday when I rode through the camps of the Fifth Army Corps and saw the magnificent condition and physical perfection of our men. There is no army corps anywhere in the world that is better supplied with men and officers of courage, fortitude, and intelligence."

This refers in particular to the regulars. The volunteers were, necessarily, generally in charge of inexperienced officers, and for a time suffered hardships. This was in a measure unavoidable in a country without a large standing army and suddenly plunged from peace into war. "I do not believe," said General Alger, Secretary of War, "that there ever was a nation on earth that attempted to embark in a war of such magnitude while so utterly unprovided with everything necesary for a campaign. When war was declared," he further remarked, "we were unprepared, yet obstacles almost insurmountable have been overcome. I do not believe that history records an instance where so much has been done in a military campaign of this magnitude in the brief time that has elapsed since hostilities began. When the people have learned the actual condition of affairs and realize what an enormous task we have performed in the brief time allowed us by the circumstances of war, they will be entirely satisfied. The critics will be answered, and the enemies of our army will have no ground to stand on."

This was written on June 10. By July 24, three months from the beginning of the war, two hundred and sixty-one thousand men had been mustered into service, fully equipped, and prepared to take the field,—some of them having shown their discipline and fighting qualities by experience in battle. The seeming slowness in filling up the ranks was due to the severe tests applied to recruits, the physical examination being of the most searching character. This was specially the case with the regulars, not more than one in four of the applicants being accepted. The men obtained were of the best fighting material, and showed excellent aptitude for military discipline and instruction. In fact, it is doubtful if an army in better physical condition ever took the field, and the recruiting, mustering, equipping, and bringing into service of so large, carefully selected, and well trained an army within ninety days was looked upon by many as a remarkable achievement, and excited the surprise and admiration of military observers from Europe.

Of one portion of the army something further may be said, from the large place which it filled in the public estimation. This was the special cavalry corps, composed of three regiments known popularly as "Rough Riders," they being made up of cowboys and others thoroughly trained in horsemanship. Two of these regiments had been recruited in the West, and were commanded respectively by Colonel Melvin Grigsby and Colonel Jay L. Torrey, men of great influence with the cowboys, who made up the bulk of their forces. The third had been recruited by Theodore Roosevelt, who had resigned his position as assistant secretary of the navy for the purpose of taking part in the actual campaigning. This regiment was commanded by Colonel Leonard Wood, Roosevelt having voluntarily retired to the post of lieutenant-colonel as better befitting his lack of military experience. But the public persisted in speaking of the regiment as "Roosevelt's Rough Riders." It, like the others, had been principally recruited in the West, but contained about twelve per cent. of business and professional men from the Eastern cities, including college graduates and representatives of families of high social standing. These men were experts in horsemanship and physical exercises, and showed themselves the equals of their cowboy companions in the saddle.

Before they left camp the Rough Riders were drilled to charge standing in their stirrups, the horses being trained to wheel and stop short at word of command, and the men riding with a reckless abandon calculated seriously to try the nerves of foot-soldiers. Armed with machetes, rifles, and revolvers, this corps would probably have proved almost irresistible in the charge. As it proved, however, fortune put the Rough Riders into the battlefield on foot, and their record in war was made as infantry.

Early in June a large fleet of transports, thirty-five in number, gathered in Tampa Bay for the conveyance of a strong military force to Santiago de Cuba, this place having, in consequence of the presence there of the Spanish fleet, been selected as the first point of attack. The force to be sent consisted of the Fifth Army Corps, under Major-General Shafter, and four regiments of General Coppinger's corps from Mobile. Two regiments of volunteer infantry were chosen to accompany the expedition, the Seventy-first New York and the Second Massachusetts, and eight troops of volunteer cavalry selected from Roosevelt's Rough Riders. In addition, there were four batteries of light and two of heavy artillery, a battalion of engineers, signal and hospital corps, etc., the whole making a grand total of over fifteen thousand men.

The sinking of the Merrimac in the channel of Santiago harbor, with the assumed locking up of the Spanish fleet in that haven of refuge, was immediately followed by active preparations for the despatch of this army, the embarkation of troops beginning on Monday, June 6. On Wednesday afternoon, after a number of them had put to sea, came a hasty order for their recall, and the Castine was despatched to bring them back. One transport, the City of Washington, had made such progress that the coast of Cuba was sighted before the order of recall reached her. It was Saturday before she and the Castine returned.

The cause of this delay was said to be due to reports that war-vessels had left Barcelona, Spain, bound for Cuban waters, and that suspicious-looking vessels, with military tops, had been seen off Florida. That this was the actual cause, however, may well be questioned, and the delay has been claimed as due to that general lack of efficient management that afterwards declared itself. Whatever its cause, it was unfortunate for the men, who for more than a week were kept packed in the close transports, with the thermometer near 100° F., many cases of heat-prostration, even among the seasoned regulars, being the result.

The start finally took place on the 14th, the transports

being convoyed by a squadron of war-vessels, with the battle-ship Indiana in the lead. At ten o'clock A. M. came the signal for sailing, which was greeted by wild cheers from the men, who were eager to leave that stifling atmosphere, and in a few minutes the leading vessels of the fleet were gliding down the bay. On reaching the Florida Straits the transports were formed into three lines, about one thousand yards apart, the ships in each line being separated by six hundred yards. The war-vessels gathered on their flanks, on the alert by day, and at night sweeping the waters towards Cuba with their search-lights. No lights were allowed to be shown on the transports. Fortunately, the winds kept down and the sea was smooth, but the journey was a dull and tedious one, with not the show of an enemy to break its monotony, and it was with joy that the weary soldiers beheld, a week after they had set sail, the blockading fleet before Santiago. The horses and mules on the transports suffered severely during the voyage, many of them dying; but the men bore the journey well, a few cases of typhoid fever being the only serious ailments.

The news of the arrival of the troops came to Washington by direct cable message from Guantanamo Bay, *via* the wires of the French Cable Company running from Santiago to Cape Haytien. This, the first direct communication by telegraph with the seat of war, was received with the highest gratification by the government. It had been supposed that Guantanamo Bay was being held by its force of marines as a point of debarkation for the troops. But the distance to be traversed, over a hilly country, without suitable roads, rendered that locality inadvisable, and the place finally selected was the village of Baiquiri, about fifteen miles east of the mouth of Santiago harbor. From here a road led to Santiago and a railroad followed the coast to a terminus on the harbor. Midway lay Juragua, another locality considered in connection with the landing, and which was bombarded on the morning of the 22d as a feint to distract attention from the real point chosen. For the same purpose colliers were sent to the west of the harbor, the Spaniards mistaking them for transports.

During the preceding night many of the troop-ships had drawn in towards the shore, while in the thickets and mountain fastnesses on land Cuban insurgents were gathered thickly, watching, gun in hand, every road and mountain-path along which Spanish reinforcements could come. The day had not far advanced before tongues of flame and clouds of smoke rising from Baiquiri indicated that the Spaniards had fired and abandoned that place. The only evidence of Spanish occupation on the previous day had been a flag flying at the summit of a steep, rocky hill that offered excellent opportunities for defence. But with day-dawn this flag was seen to have vanished. The hill, like the village, had been abandoned.

The bombardment of Jaragua was followed by a sharp fire upon Baiquiri from the guns of the New Orleans. No response came, and in a few minutes more the waters were enlivened by a flotilla of small boats filled with troops and headed by launches, moving swiftly in towards the shore. The lighters sent with the expedition had been lost during the voyage. In a brief time more the foremost of the landing-party gladly set foot on Cuban soil, each man in full fighting trim, carrying three days' rations, a shelter-tent, a rifle, and two hundred cartridges, ready to fight or march at a moment's notice. Landing was no easy matter. There was at this point a fine pier built by the iron-mining company, but the surf broke roughly against it, and the men were obliged to fling their rifles up first and scramble up the trestle-work after them. As they reached solid ground, they at once lined up in companies and regiments and marched away, making room for their successors.

The Eighth Infantry was the first to land, followed by the First, General Shafter's old regiment. Other organizations rapidly followed, and by nightfall some six thousand soldiers were encamped in the hilly country around Baiquiri. General Lawton threw out a strong detachment to a point about six miles west, on the road to Santiago, and another to the north of the village, the remainder being quartered in the houses, few of which had been burned, and under their tents in the adjoining fields. The place was deserted when the troops arrived, but fugitive women and children soon appeared from the surrounding thickets and sought their homes. During the following two days the remainder of the troops were landed, and the occupation in force of Cuban soil was fairly inaugurated. The work of landing the siege-guns, horses, and other heavy supplies followed, but was prosecuted with difficulty on account of the lack of lighters and of landing facilities in general.

In fact, as time revealed, the whole business had been inefficiently managed, guns and other necessaries of the expedition being left at Tampa, while requisite parts of the artillery that were brought were scattered carelessly through several ships. As a result, the army was by no means in the best condition for an advance on a fortified place, and there was abundant reason for delay until all the essentials of a campaign were at hand. But delay under Cuban suns and rains was a dangerous alternative.

Yellow fever might prove a more deadly enemy than Spanish troops, and the commanding general, while doubtless deploring the position in which the haste and heedlessness of incompetent aids had placed him, seems to have felt that wisdom demanded an immediate advance. At all events, no delay was made, the troops being at once set in motion towards the enemy's lines of defence. On the day of landing a reinforcement of sixteen hundred men, comprising the Thirty-third and one battalion of the Thirty-fourth Michigan Volunteers, set sail on the Yale from Hampton Roads, and other reinforcements were rapidly preparing to follow.

The advance began on the 23d, the Cubans serving as skirmishers in front of General Shafter's army, and having several brushes with the retreating Spaniards as the latter fell back. Colonel Wagner, with fifty picked men from General Lawton's brigade, formed the skirmish line, assisted by some two hundred Cuban scouts, whose familiarity with the country and the Spanish mode of fighting rendered them of much utility. Juragua, some eight miles from the landing-place, was reached without a check, the guns of the fleet protecting the movement up to that point. The Spaniards seemed to have left the place in haste after an ineffectual attempt to burn it.

The scouting party pushed on to the west, and at a short distance came suddenly upon a party of Spanish soldiers, who exchanged shots briskly with the Cubans, two of whom were killed and eight wounded. As the skirmishers fell back, the Twenty-second regulars came up at the double quick, drawn by the firing; but the Spaniards were already in retreat and had sought the shelter of the woods. By night a junction was effected

Copyright, 1898, by W. R. Hearst

LANDING MASSACHUSETTS VOLUNTEERS AT SIBONEY

between the main divisions of the army of invasion at a point on the high ground back from the coast, and within ten miles of Morro Castle.

At nightfall of the 25th all the troops were on shore, and the Cubans of Garcia's army, some three thousand in number, had been brought by water from Ascerraderos, west of the harbor, and landed at Juragua. Most of the horses, also, were on firm land. With a single steam barge and a fleet of small boats, General Shafter had landed over fifteen thousand men, hundreds of horses and mules, and a large quantity of supplies on a difficult beach, only two men losing their lives and about fifty animals being drowned. The animals had to be pushed in the water and towed ashore. Of the supplies, hardly a package was lost.

CHAPTER XIV.

THE RAID OF THE ROUGH RIDERS.

WHILE the work of landing the army of invasion and its supplies was still in progress, the first battle had taken place on Cuban soil. The Spaniards had made a stand in force, and the vanguard of the army had received its baptism of fire. Raw as the troops were and difficult as the ground, they had behaved with conspicuous gallantry, winning victory in the face of much larger forces placed in ambush and with every advantage of position. This battle merits special attention as the first, with the exception of the minor affair at Guantanamo Bay, fought by American soldiers since the close of the Civil War, thirty-three years before. In it sons of the South and of the North fought side by side, and proved themselves worthy the reputation for courage and daring which their fathers had won on many a hard-fought field a third of a century in the past.

The men who had the honor of taking part in this initial engagement were all of the cavalry arm of the service, horsemen serving as infantry. The position was one in which horses could not have been employed had there been any to use. The force consisted of eight troops of Colonel Wood's regiment, Roosevelt's Rough Riders as they will be known in history, and four troops each of the First and the Tenth Cavalry, a total force of nine hundred and sixty-four men, constituting nearly the whole of General Wheeler's cavalry command.

On the 23d, Wheeler, under orders from the commanding general, proceeded to Siboney, to find that the enemy had withdrawn from that place towards Sevilla, skirmishing with the Cuban scouts as they retreated. He rode out to the front and found that the Spanish had halted and established themselves at a point about three miles in advance. Studying the ground with the aid of General Castillo, in command of the Cubans, Wheeler determined to make an attack on the enemy at daybreak of the 24th, a rough map of the country being drawn as an aid to the projected movement.

The country was rougher than any map that could be made of it. The theory was that it was traversed by roads; but in effect these roads were simply rude paths through a dense tropical forest, along which ox-teams could laboriously make their way in dry weather, but which in wet weather were impassable to teams and almost so to men on horseback. There were no bridges, and the rains made torrents of the streams that crossed the roads. In the subsequent movement of the army new roads had to be made before a single wagon-train could get through, and the bridges built for this purpose were repeatedly swept away. As a consequence, on several occasions the army had to depend on pack-trains, and the movement of supplies to the front became a very difficult operation. As for the siege-guns, landed with difficulty, not one got beyond Siboney.

The roads to be traversed by General Wheeler's force were of the character here described. There were two of them, one following the foot of the hill upon which the Spaniards had made their stand, the other ascending the slope. These so-called roads were little more than gullies, rough and narrow and at places almost impassable. On both sides they were lined by prickly cactus-bushes, while the underbrush was so thick that it was impossible to see ten feet on either side. The conditions were favorable for a murderous ambuscade, and this was the one mode of fighting in which the Spanish soldiers excelled.

The enemy, doubtless having good reason to look for an advance of the invaders along these roads in their movement towards Sevilla, had prepared to give them a warm reception. On the hill-slopes had been erected two block-houses, flanked by irregular intrenchments of stones and felled trees. Behind these and in the thick underbrush on both sides of the trail a large body of Spaniards had posted themselves, considerably outnumbering General Wheeler's force, and expecting to check his advance with ease. Hitherto they had fought with Cubans only, and judged their new foes from experience of their old. As the Spaniards could not be seen, their numbers could be estimated only by the weight of their fire, which was constant and heavy and much more accurate than had been expected.

There were practically two battles,—General Young leading the regulars along the road at the base of the hill, with the design of making a feint on the enemy's front, and Colonel Wood leading the Rough Riders along the ascending trail, proposing to attack them in flank. As a result, when the enemy was reached the two detachments were about a mile apart. The first part of the journey of the Rough Riders was over steep hills several hundred feet high. The men carried two hundred rounds of ammunition and heavy camp equipment. Although this was done easily in the early morning, the weather became intensely hot as the day advanced, and the sun beat down severely upon the cowboys and Eastern athletes as they toiled up the grade with their heavy packs, frequent rests becoming necessary. The trail was so narrow that for the greater part of the way the men had to proceed in single file. One by one the men, unable to endure the sweltering heat, threw away their blankets and tent-rolls and emptied their canteens, retaining only their arms and cartridges.

The first intimation that there were Spaniards in the vicinity was when they reached a point three or four miles back from the coast, when the low cuckoo calls of the Spanish soldiers were heard in the brush. It was difficult to locate the exact point from which these sounds came. The men were ordered to speak in whispers, and frequent halts were made. Finally, a place was reached, about eight o'clock, where the trail opened into a space covered with high grass on the right-hand side of the trail and the thickest kind of bramble and underbrush on the other. A barbed-wire fence also ran along the left side. The dead body of a Cuban was found on the side of the road and the heads of several Spaniards were seen in the bushes for a moment.

It was not until then that the men were permitted to load their carbines. When the order to load was given, they acted on it with a will, and displayed the greatest eagerness to make an attack. At this time the sound of firing was heard a mile or two to the right, apparently coming from the hills beyond the thicket. It was the regulars replying to the Spaniards, who had opened on them from the thicket. In addition to rapid rifle-fire the boom of Hotchkiss guns could be heard. Hardly two minutes elapsed before Mauser rifles commenced to crack in the thicket, and a hundred bullets whistled over the heads of the Rough Riders, cutting the leaves from the trees and sending chips flying from the fence-posts by the side of the men. The Spaniards had opened and were pouring in a heavy fire, which had a disastrous effect.

Sergeant Hamilton Fish was the first man to fall. He was shot through the breast and lived but twenty minutes, giving a small hunting-case watch from his belt as a souvenir to a messmate. Captain Capron and others rallied around him, firing into the bush, but they were in the thick of the Spanish fire, and the captain soon fell with a mortal wound. Dead and wounded were falling all around, but the men held their ground, seemingly without a thought of retreat. Our troops had evidently fallen into an ambush held by a much superior force, and Captain Capron's troop, in the advance, were in a hot place, the Spanish fire pouring upon them in volleys.

This was a state of affairs that called for either a retreat or a charge. Of the former no thought was entertained. Lieutenant-Colonel Roosevelt at the head of one wing, and Colonel Wood and Major Brodie leading the other, advanced in open order on the foe, Major Brodie falling wounded before the troops had advanced one hundred yards. An order for a general charge was now given, and with a yell the men sprang forward. Roosevelt, snatching a rifle and ammunition-belt from a wounded soldier, led the way at the head of his men, cheering and yelling as loudly as the best of them.

For a period the bullets were singing like a swarm of bees all around them, and at every instant men fell from the ranks. On the right wing Captain McClintock had his leg broken by a bullet from a machine-gun, while four of his men went down. At the same time

INFANTRY CAMP AT LAS GUASIMAS. ON THIS FIELD THE ROUGH RIDERS FOUGHT THEIR BATTLE.
Copyright, 1898, by W. R. Hearst

Captain Luna lost nine of his men. Then the reserves, Troops K and E, were ordered up. There was no hesitation. Colonel Wood, with the right wing, charged straight at a block-house about eight hundred yards away, and Lieutenant-Colonel Roosevelt, on the left, charged at the same time. Up the men went with their cowboy yell, never stopping to return the fire of the Spaniards, but keeping on with a grim determination to capture the block-house or die in the attempt. That charge was the last. By the time the American advance had got within six hundred yards of the block-house the Spaniards abandoned it, not having the resolution to stand that furious rush, and in the next moment were flying at their utmost speed through the brush beyond, followed by a hail of bullets from the victorious troops.

While this hot battle had been taking place on the hill, the regulars under General Young were having as lively a time below. The battle here began in much the same manner as above, and when the machine-guns poured their rain of bullets into the brush, the Spanish from their lurking-places on the hill-side sent volleys at the gunners below. A charge was now made up the hill by part of the force, while the remainder covered with their rifles every point from which the Spanish shots came. Back through the thicket, step by step, went the enemy, firing as they retreated, and finally seeking refuge in the block-house in front of Colonel Wood's command. They were dislodged with their comrades by the irresistible charge of Wood and Roosevelt and their men. In the words of General Young, the battle was one of the sharpest he had ever experienced. It was only the quick and constant fire of the troopers, whether they could see the enemy or not, that forced the Spanish so soon from their ambuscade. Reinforcements had been ordered forward from Juragua, but the march was a long one and the fight was over before they arrived.

In the two hours' fighting, during which the volunteers battled against a concealed enemy, many deeds of heroism were done. One of the men of Troop E, desperately wounded, was lying squarely between the lines of fire. Surgeon Church hurried to his side, and, with bullets pelting all around him, calmly dressed the man's wound, bandaged it, and walked unconcernedly back, soon returning with two men and a litter. The wounded man was placed on the litter and brought into our lines. Another soldier of Troop L, concealing himself as best he could behind a tree, gave up his place to a wounded companion, and in a moment or so later was himself wounded.

Sergeant Bell stood by the side of Captain Capron when the latter was mortally hit. He had seen that he was fighting against terrible odds, but he never flinched. "Give me your gun a minute," he said to the sergeant, and, kneeling down, he deliberately aimed and fired two shots in quick succession. At each a Spaniard was seen to fall. Bell, in the mean time, had seized a dead comrade's gun and knelt beside his captain and fired steadily. When Captain Capron fell he gave the sergeant a parting message to his wife and father, bade him good-by in a cheerful voice, and was then borne away dying.

A private was shot through the thigh, the bullet entering at the side and going out at the back. He made his way to the field hospital and was told nothing could be done for him. Returning to the front, he crawled along, firing with the rest.

Colonel Wood, who was at the front throughout the entire action, saw a trooper apparently skulking, fifty feet in the rear of the firing-line, and ordered him sharply to advance. The boy rose and hurried forward, limping. As he took his place and raised his carbine, he said,—

"My leg is a little stiff, sir."

Colonel Wood looked, and saw that a bullet had ploughed along the trooper's leg for twelve inches.

The ground was uneven, and the advance was impeded by vines an inch thick, trailing bushes, and cactus plants, known as Spanish bayonets, which tear the flesh and clothes. Through this the men fought their way, falling, stumbling, wet with perspiration, panting for breath, but obeying Colonel Wood's commands instantly.

The Rough Riders disproved all that had been said in criticism of them when the organization was formed. The cowboys observed perfect discipline, and the Eastern element in Troop K, from clubs and colleges, acted with the greatest coolness and intelligence.

The spirit of Mr. Marshall, a correspondent of the New York *Journal*, was as admirable as that of any soldier on the field. He was shot in the first firing-line, and though the bullet passed within an inch of his spine and threw him into frequent and terrible convulsions, he continued in his intervals of consciousness to write his account of the fight and gave it to a wounded soldier to be forwarded to his paper. This devotion to duty by a man who believed he was dying was as fine as any of the many courageous and inspiring deeds that occurred during the two hours of breathless, desperate fighting.

The result of the battle was to give the Americans possession of La Quasimas, the point of meeting of the hill-side and the valley roads. The complete exhaustion of the men, from their exertions and the great heat, prevented their continuing the pursuit, and they contented themselves with holding the ground they had gained. The total loss on the American side was sixteen killed and fifty-two wounded. That of the Spaniards could not be told, but from the number of dead found it must have been much more severe. The engagement, in the words of General Wheeler, "inspired our troops, and must have had a bad effect upon the spirits of the Spanish soldiers. It also gave our army the beautiful and well-watered country in which we established our encampments, with a full view of Santiago and the surrounding country, and enabled us to reconnoitre close up to the fortifications of that place."

An interesting commentary on this pioneer battle is contained in the words of a Spanish soldier who was in the battle and was afterwards captured by the Cubans. He said of the volunteers:

"They did not fight like other soldiers. When we fired a volley, they advanced instead of going back. The more we fired the nearer they came to us. We are not used to fighting with men who act in that way."

In other words, they were not fighting with Cuban insurgents, and the tactics used in guerilla warfare did not apply. Under the fire which the Americans faced they could without dishonor have fallen back. But, instead, they kept on in a steady, cool advance, which only ceased when they were in possession of the enemy's base and the Spaniards were in full retreat.

CHAPTER XV.

THE BATTLE OF SANTIAGO.

THE victory on the hill-side cleared the way to the vicinity of Santiago, since the enemy evacuated Sevilla—some miles in advance, where it had been expected a stand in force would be made—on the night of the 24th, and the American army occupied this post without a shot. Here the army was delayed for several days from the difficulty in getting subsistence stores to the front. It was not considered safe to move unless each man had at least three days' rations in his knapsack, and this was impossible in the wretched condition of the roads, which were converted into mud gullies by the frequent rains. Pack-trains alone could get through, and these could supply the army with food only from day to day. To make the road passable for wagon-trains, artillery, and ambulances was a task of the utmost difficulty, which seriously taxed the skill of the engineers and the endurance of officers and men. From Baiquiri the way ran through a tangle of tropical undergrowth and over treacherous swamps bordering streams for a distance of twelve miles. The engineers were kept busy levelling the track, filling pits, and bridging the streams, while a large force with axes, aided by Cubans with machetes, hacked down trees and cleared out the underbrush, widening the narrow way. All this necessarily took time, and kept the army in a waiting state.

Meanwhile, a thorough reconnoissance of the country

was being made, which, with information gained from the Cubans, who claimed exact acquaintance with it, enabled a fairly accurate map to be drawn. The daring scouts advanced to the very trenches of the enemy, near enough to hear the sentries on picket duty talking. Lieutenant Smith, of the Fourth Infantry, pushed forward as far as El Caney without meeting any Spanish troops, and Captain Wright, of General Bates's staff, followed the line of the railroad from Juragua to within two and a half miles of the city. Lieutenant Blue, of the gunboat Suwanee, repeated his exploit of a fortnight before, making a tour of some sixty miles in extent around the city and again counting the Spanish ships at anchor in the bay. He ventured close up to the enemy's batteries, and at one point in his journey reached a Cuban outpost which faced an outpost of the Spaniards only four hundred yards away. The lieutenant's account of what took place forms a sarcastic commentary upon the character of the former Cuban war.

"They popped away at one another all the time," he said; "but I do not think the Cubans hurt the Spanish very much, and I know the Spanish did not hurt the Cubans."

On June 27 the front rested on the small stream known as the Rio Guama, and extended from the crest of the Sevilla hills for a mile and a half into the interior. General Kent's men lay encamped along the railroad, their advance being not far from Morro Castle. General Lawton's division occupied the road to Santiago, the Third Brigade, which formed the centre, lying across the road and the river, the First Brigade forming the left flank, and the Second Brigade holding the opposite position on the right flank. General Wheeler, with the dismounted cavalry, lay in the rear, between the Sevilla hills and the Rio Guama. At Siboney was a brigade of reinforcements which had just landed from the Yale, and others were hourly expected on the Harvard. Drinking water for the troops was obtained from the Rio Guama, a stream fed by mountain springs and yielding excellent water. The fare, consisting of hardtack, bacon, and coffee, was hardly suited to the climate, and the men could not be kept from eating the great variety of tropical fruits—mangoes, oranges, etc.—which abounded in the woodland, though strict orders had been given to the contrary. Limes and the milk from green cocoanuts were alone considered safe to indulge in, but the attraction of the other fruits proved too great to resist.

General Shafter landed on the 27th, and rode at once to the front, in order to consult with General Wheeler and the division commanders and look over the field of operations. A few cases of sickness had appeared, due to the intense heat of midday, the dampness of the climate, and the inadequate equipment of the troops. The nights were cool, and many of the men seriously felt the need of the blankets and woollen clothing which they had thrown away in the distress of the march, and which the Cubans had hastened to pick up. The inordinate indulgence of many in the forbidden fruits of the country aided in producing sickness, and it became necessary to provide a fixed hospital. This was established at Siboney, trained nurses and the necessary conveniences being landed from the transport Iroquois. The dreaded scourge of yellow fever had not yet appeared among the troops, but some cases were reported by the Cubans, and it might at any time attack the unacclimated Americans.

Though the enemy had withdrawn from their outpost positions, there was reason to believe that a stubborn defence of their interior works would be made. Scouts reported that the top of every hill north and east of the city was occupied by block-houses, whence the movements of the invading army could be observed, while intrenchments were visible on every knoll and bit of high ground fronting the city itself. These trenches were dug to suit the conformation of the ground, overlapping where breaks in the line occurred, thus securing safe retreat to an inner line if an outer trench should be captured. Four parallel lines of rifle-pits, shoulder deep, were reported as existing, in front of which were marked ranges and several rows of barbed-wire fences. The work of defence had been carefully provided for, and to many experienced officers it appeared as if nothing could be done until more artillery was brought up, and that a regular siege might be necessary.

This was not General Shafter's opinion. The situation was a difficult one and delay was dangerous. With a large body of unacclimated men, exposed to hot suns by day and cool winds by night, under tropical rains that kept the ground constantly moist, immediate action seemed imperatively necessary. Sickness threatened, and fever might prove more difficult to combat than the Spaniards with all their rifle-pits and wire fences. And deliberation does not seem to have been General Shafter's idea of war. Whatever might have been done under a more cautious commander, we are only concerned with what was done, and that was to throw the American army upon the Spanish works within a week from the day they completed their landing on Cuban soil.

At set of sun on the closing day of June a general

order was issued commanding an advance in force at daybreak on the morrow, and before midnight every man in the army knew that a desperate struggle was at hand. The news put the men in a fever of excitement; cheering and singing banished sleep for the remainder of the night, and from end to end of the line rang the improvised strain,—

"There'll be a hot time in Santiago to-morrow."

At four o'clock in the morning of July 1, hundreds of bugles rang out the reveille; and before the sun had risen the line was complete. At the extreme left was General Duffield with the Thirty-third Michigan, his command having reached the Aguadores bridge by train. Next to the northeast was General Kent's division, a mile and a half from the sea and held as a reserve force. The centre of the line was held by a cavalry division which, until General Wheeler arrived at noon, was commanded by General Sumner. Owing to General Young's illness, Colonel Wood of the Rough Riders commanded his brigade, which consisted of the First volunteer, the First regular, the Tenth regular, and one battalion of the Ninth regular cavalry, all dismounted with the exception of two troops. On the extreme right was General Lawton's division, fully five miles from the sea.

Military balloons were in use by the signal corps for the purpose of gaining exact information of the location of the enemy and the character of their defences. One of these was sent up on the morning of the battle, rising over the tree-tops and being guided along three miles of the road towards the lines of the enemy. Photographs were taken of the fortifications as it proceeded, the

Spaniards firing at it whenever it halted for this purpose. It approached until it hung over San Juan, not more than five hundred yards from the enemy, who for five minutes vainly sought to puncture it. In the end, however, it was pierced and came down with a run, its mission ended for that day of battle.

The balloon had been of some service, but on the whole did more harm than good. The position of the advancing troops, masked by the bushes from the enemy, was revealed by this trailing globe, which served as a signal to direct the fire of the Spaniards. As a result the advancing lines suffered severely, the observation balloon being responsible for a considerable increase in dead and wounded in the American ranks. The soldiers had nothing but anathemas for this new idea in warfare.

The conflict of July 1 was mainly concentrated about two strong positions of the enemy. General Lawton's division, forming the right wing of the army, faced the picturesque old town of El Caney, a suburban place of residence for wealthy citizens of Santiago, from which it lay about four miles to the northeast. Looking down from the ridge which they occupied, Lawton's men saw in the broad valley below them this quaint old town. The valley was three miles wide. It had been a garden spot in times of peace, but now the abandoned plantations were filled with a rank tropical growth, including numbers of the formerly cultivated cocoanut- and mango-trees. Bordering it on the west rose a low ridge, on which were visible the Spanish barracks and a large red building flying the Red Cross flag. This was the Reina Mercedes Hospital, then the prison of Lieutenant Hobson and his gallant seven. Opposite, on the northern side of the valley, extended a broad plateau, accessible

Copyright, 1898, by W. R. Hearst

THE COUNTRY NEAR SANTIAGO

by a good road. This was the key to Santiago, since artillery planted there would command the city. To win it was the purpose of General Lawton's proposed move.

East of the city, in front of Colonel Wood's brigade, lay the village of San Juan, crowning a steep hill which was well fortified and defended by cannon, and which threatened, in the absence of sufficient artillery, to be very difficult to take. Barracks and other buildings occupied the crest. Nearer the coast, where the railroad crossed San Juan River, stood the village of Aguadores, garrisoned by Spanish troops.

The condition of the Americans was excellent. Despite the drenching rains and the hot sun, little sickness had shown itself, and the men were eager for the fight. In preparation for the final assault upon Santiago sixty tried men in each brigade, non-commissioned officers and privates, had been promoted to be wire-clippers, their duty being to precede the firing-line about two or three hundred yards for the purpose of cutting the barbed-wire fences that obstructed the way to the city. Their mission was a most hazardous one, as they would be exposed to the fire of their comrades as well as that of the enemy. But in the general enthusiasm there was no difficulty in obtaining volunteers for this perilous task. The use of barbed wire was a new device in defensive warfare, and could be met only by some such method as this.

The great disadvantage of the army lay in the lack of artillery. The heavy siege-guns were still at Baiquiri. It had proved impossible to convey them over the muddy roads, and General Shafter concluded not to wait for them. The only guns at the front were four batteries of light artillery, sixteen guns in all, where fully five times that many should have been in the line. Of these only eight were actually brought into use. It was a battle in which infantry did the work of artillery, and did it well and nobly, though suffering severely from the lack of guns.

At five o'clock in the morning of the 1st General Lawton's troops were put in motion, preceded by a battery of the First Artillery under Captain Allyn Capron, father of the Captain Capron who fell at La Quasimas. The plan of the battle was for Captain Capron's battery, which held a position in the centre, above General Ludlow, to shell the fort near the town; for General Chaffee to close in as soon as the artillery had reduced the fort and driven the Spaniards towards Santiago; for General Ludlow to lie in the road below the hill on which Captain Capron's battery was stationed and swing in on General Chaffee's left, and for Colonel Miles's brigade to keep close to General Ludlow's right, and by a simultaneous movement sweep the Spaniards in towards Caney. At 6.40 the battery opened fire upon the fort, the first shot falling close by, the second hitting it fairly. This accurate firing was too much for the valor of the garrison, who ran in a body down the hill towards the town. The covered way in front of the fort, however, was held by the Spanish troops, who maintained an obstinate fire upon our men as they advanced slowly through the brush and groves, firing only an occasional shot.

Captain Capron's battery opened on the enemy at once and tore up the ground with shells. A number of these were sent entirely through the fort, tearing down large sections of the walls. This fine marksmanship was of great service, the battery stopping the fire of the Spanish soldiers, who opened repeatedly from the covered-way pits. By eight o'clock General Chaffee's brigade was pressing in towards the town, and the firing at intervals was very warm. It was difficult, however, to see anything of the battle, owing to the rolling nature of the ground and the dense vegetation that obscured the view in almost every direction.

The firing continued heavy, but the Spaniards in the covered way made a most obstinate defence and refused to yield an inch. Time and again the shells from Captain Capron's battery drove them to cover, but as soon as his fire ceased they were up and at it again. In consequence, despite the hot fire of the American troops, they were able to make but little apparent progress during the morning, although eventually they steadily drew in and enclosed the town on all sides.

Up to the middle of the day the Second Massachusetts sustained the heaviest losses, although other regiments were more actively engaged. During the afternoon the conflict continued with the greatest obstinacy, the Spaniards fighting under cover and the Americans in the open. The Spaniards fought with unexpected courage and persistence, clinging to their positions with an unyielding determination that caused great loss on the American side. General Lawton's report emphasizes at once the difficulties overcome by the Americans and the valor of the Spaniards. He says,—

"It may not be out of place to call attention to the peculiar character of the battle, it having been fought against an enemy fortified and intrenched within a compact town of stone and concrete houses, some with walls several feet thick, and supported by a number of covered forts cut in solid stone, and the enemy continuing to resist until nearly every man was killed or wounded,—a desperation apparently predetermined."

At noon it became evident that the fire from the covered way could not be stopped by the artillery alone, and that no permanent advance could be made until the place was taken, and General Lawton decided to capture it by assault. Accordingly he sent a messenger to General Chaffee with instructions to take the position by a charge. General Chaffee thereupon closed in with his men rapidly from the north, while Captain Capron maintained a heavy fire on the fort, keeping the Spaniards in the covered way and making hole after hole in the stone walls. Shortly afterwards he threw a shot from the battery which tore away the flagstaff, bringing the Spanish flag to the ground. It was not raised again.

At three o'clock the advanced line of General Chaffee's skirmishers, the Seventh Infantry, began to appear on the edge of the woods below the fort, and by rapid rushes advanced up the hill towards it. No shot was fired as they swept forward, and it was evident that the covered way had been abandoned. In a few minutes the American troops were thick around the fort, which commanded the north side of the town. The Spaniards were completely surrounded. The main part of the army was between them and Santiago, and General Lawton's division was around them on the other three sides. They retreated to buildings in the town, and made a gallant defence, but from the time General Chaffee's men took the stone fort they were lost troops to Spain.

Rather than attempt to take the town by a general assault, without the aid of artillery, which must certainly result in a great loss of life, General Lawton decided to order forward artillery to shell it at close range. Although the road from the hill to the edge of the town was nearly impassable for artillery, Captain Capron made the effort, and by five o'clock had his guns in position to open upon it.

For some time General Chaffee's brigade held its position behind the stone fort, and then began the descent towards the town, firing rapid volleys as it advanced. General Ludlow and Colonel Miles pressed closely in on the other sides, and at nightfall El Caney was practically in the hands of the Americans, and a large number of prisoners had been taken.

The valley in which this battle was fought was intersected by several ridges of fifty feet or less in height. Groves of cocoanut- and mango-trees rose here and there, divided by broad fields of grass, often waist-high. It was in crossing the ridges and open spaces that the Americans suffered most severely, and this was particularly the case with Ludlow's and Miles's men, who were compelled to make their final charges across an open space through which the Spanish fire swept with deadly effect.

No finer work has ever been done by soldiers than was done by these brigades as they closed in on the town. The Spanish blazed at them with Mausers and machine-guns, but without checking their advance; nothing could stop them. They pushed in closer and closer during the afternoon, and by the time General Chaffee's men were in form Miles and Ludlow were on the skirts of the town, holding on with tenacity and preventing the Spaniards from retreating towards Santiago, while Chaffee closed in on the right.

As evidence of the opinion of American courage entertained by the Spanish, a quotation from the narrative of an officer who took part in the battle will be in place:

"The enemy's fire was incessant, and we answered with equal rapidity. I have never seen anything to equal the courage and dash of those Americans, who, stripped to the waist, offered their naked breasts to our murderous fire, and literally threw themselves on our trenches, on the very muzzles of our guns.

"Our execution must have been terrible. We had the advantage of our position and mowed them down by the hundreds, but they never retreated or fell back an inch. As one man fell shot through the heart, another would take his place, with grim determination and unflinching devotion to duty in every line of his face. Their gallantry was heroic. We wondered at these men, who fought like lions and fell like men, courting a wholesale massacre, which could well have been avoided had they only kept up their firing without storming our trenches."

On the extreme left General Duffield had begun the day's fighting by an attack on the coast village of Aguadores, in which he was aided by the fire of the war-vessels New York, Gloucester, and Suwanee, which actively shelled the fort and the rifle-pits, driving all the Spaniards from the vicinity. The railroad bridge which crossed the little San Juan River was down, and the troops were unable to occupy the town, though the Spaniards did not seem inclined to hold it.

Meanwhile, a hot engagement had been in progress at San Juan, between Aguadores and El Caney and on the main road from Siboney to Santiago. Here was, as has been said, a steep hill, strongly fortified, and likely to be very difficult to take in the absence of sufficient artillery. On the morning of July 1 Wheeler's cavalry division moved forward by the Santiago road and formed its line with its left near the road, and Kent's infantry division did the same, its right joining the left of the cavalry division. The men were all compelled to wade the San Juan River to get into line, and this they did under a very heavy infantry and artillery fire from the Spanish works on the crest of the hill, which rose before them some three hundred feet high. Men and officers fell in numbers as they emerged into the open space in full view of the enemy, and their position became a very trying one.

A charge by these troops seems not to have been contemplated, they being held in column on the road to reinforce General Lawton, if necessary, while Grimes's battery made a diversion on the left. But when the Spanish guns began to drop shells over the road which they occupied, and when word of General Lawton's success reached them, a movement of advance or retreat became necessary. Anything was better than to remain where they were. It was, as we have before said, the observation balloon, which was drawn forward by the troops as they advanced and hung in the air above them, that directed the fire of the Spanish artillerymen, whose shells reached the waiting columns in the road and caused severe loss.

Grimes's battery took a position in the little town of El Paso, from which the Spaniards had been driven by the sharp musketry fire of the cavalry division, and from here it protected the advance by pouring a steady fire into the Spanish works.

The line was no sooner formed than an advance began,

as if by a general impulse. The men simply could not stand at rest under the punishment they were receiving. "It was evident," said General Wheeler in his report, "that we were as much under fire in forming the line as we could be by an advance, and I therefore pressed the command forward from the covering under which it was formed. It emerged into open space in full view of the enemy, who occupied breastworks and batteries on the crest of the hill which overlooks Santiago, officers and men falling at every step. The troops advanced gallantly, soon reached the foot of the hill, and ascended, driving the enemy from their works and occupying them on the crest of the hill. To accomplish this required courage and determination of a high order on the part of the officers and men, and the losses were very severe."

In the charge of the Rough Riders, Colonel Roosevelt led the way, the only mounted man in the line. It was little short of a miracle that he came through that desperate charge alive. In truth, the whole line behaved with the most conspicuous gallantry, and that wild climb up a steep hill in the face of a murderous fire was one of the most courageous actions ever performed by American troops. Apparently, the Spanish, though well capable of bearing punishment when intrenched, could not stand such a charge. In the reports of the battle from Santiago the American troops were claimed to have been beaten, the Spaniards retiring only because the Americans "persisted in fighting." Evidently they belonged to the class of men who "do not know when they are whipped."

C. E. Hand, the correspondent of the London *Daily Mail*, thus graphically describes the taking of the San Juan heights, as seen by him from a distance:

"When afternoon came—I lost exact count of time—there was still a jumble of volleying over by Caney. But in front our men were away out of sight behind a ridge far ahead. Beyond there arose a long, steepish ascent, crowned by the block-house upon which artillery had opened fire in the morning.

"Suddenly, as we looked through our glasses, we saw a little black ant go scrambling quickly up this hill, and an inch or two behind him a ragged line of other little ants, and then another line of ants at another part of the hill, and then another, until it seemed as if somebody had dug a stick into a great ants' nest down in the valley, and all the ants were scrambling away up-hill. Then the volley firing began ten times more furious than before; from the right beyond the top of the ridge burst upon the ants a terrible fire of shells; from the block-house in front of them machine-guns sounded their continuous rattle. But the ants swept up the hill. They seemed to us to thin out as they went forward; but they still went forward. It was incredible, but it was grand. The boys were storming the hill. The military authorities were most surprised. They were not surprised at these splendid athletic dare-devils of ours doing it, but that a military commander should have allowed a fortified and intrenched position to be assailed by an infantry charge up the side of a long, exposed hill, swept by a terrible artillery fire, frightened them, not so much by its audacity as by its terrible cost in human life.

"As they neared the top the different lines came nearer together. One moment they went a little more slowly, then they nearly stopped, then they went on again faster than ever, and then all of us sitting there on the top of the battery cried with excitement. For the ants were scrambling all round the block-house on the ridge, and in a moment or two we saw them inside it. But then our hearts swelled up into our throats, for a fearful fire came from somewhere beyond the block-house and from somewhere to the right of it and somewhere to the left of it. Then we saw the ants come scrambling down the hill again. They had taken a position which they had not the force to hold. But a moment or two and up they scrambled again, more of

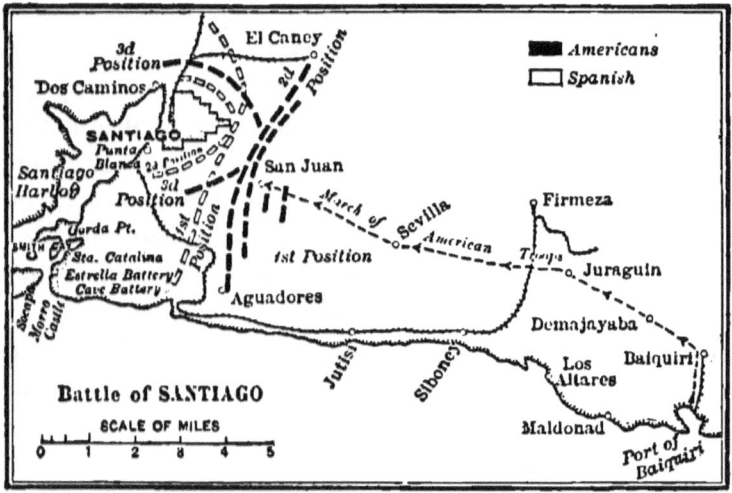

them, and more quickly than before, and up the other face of the hill to the left went other lines, and the ridge was taken, and the block-house was ours, and the trenches were full of dead Spaniards.

"It was a grand achievement,—for the soldiers who shared it,—this storming of the hill leading up from the San Juan River to the ridge before the main fort. We could tell so much at two thousand five hundred and sixty yards. But we also knew that it had cost them dear. Later on we knew only too well how heavy the cost was."

At nightfall the Americans held every point for which they had fought, and two thousand prisoners were in their hands, the fruits of the capture of El Caney. General Lawton occupied the plateau on the north, Generals Kent and Wheeler held the position at San Juan, and Aguadores had been evacuated by the enemy. The army had fought its way across two and a half miles of strongly fortified and hotly contested country, and reached a position in which its guns commanded the city of Santiago. In this work nearly the entire army had been engaged, with four thousand of Garcia's Cuban auxiliaries. But this success had not been gained without severe loss, hundreds of killed and wounded attesting the valor with which the Americans had fought and the persistency with which the Spaniards had held their ground.

The Spanish retreat from the crest of San Juan hill was precipitate, but the men were too exhausted to follow, while their shoes were soaked with water from wading the San Juan and their clothes were drenched with rain. It was afterwards asserted that had the pursuit been continued the demoralized Spaniards would have surrendered that night, but a pursuit was physically impossible. Yet, despite the exhausted condition of the men, they labored during the night in erecting breastworks, doing their best to excavate the rocky soil with shovels and picks. General Wheeler was appealed to by many officers to withdraw and take up a stronger position farther back, his lines being so thin on account of his losses during the day, and his men so worn out that it seemed doubtful if they could hold their own against an assault. He refused, however, fearing to lose prestige for the troops by a reverse movement.

At dawn on Saturday the battle began again, the Spaniards making a desperate effort on that day to regain the positions they had lost. The four batteries of artillery were placed in position, and opened fire on the San Juan quarter of the city and the works in front of the American right. One of these batteries, that of Major Diffenbach, was advanced to a position within four hundred yards of the Spanish lines, where it was exposed to so hot a fire that the men could load only while lying down, and were soon forced to withdraw. The fleet in the harbor added to the din of battle, Admiral Cervera sending in many shells which exploded close to the intrenchments. Admiral Sampson also took part in the work, his great guns at intervals sending shells which exploded within the city limits.

On this day the Americans fought mainly on the defensive, holding the earthworks which they had thrown up during the night, and from which the enemy sought in vain to dislodge them. At about ten o'clock the Spanish infantry made a vigorous charge upon the American lines, driving back the men in one or two places. But they quickly rallied, and in turn drove the enemy into their trenches, numbers of them falling before the hot rifle-fire of the American troops. The loss this day was small, as the men fought mainly under cover. The Spaniards lost heavily. One result of the morning's fight was the capture of two hundred Spanish soldiers and sixty-two officers, who were marched to the rear with the prisoners of the day before.

An element of the fight that exasperated the men was the discovery of many sharp-shooters in the trees along the trail. The courage of these guerillas cannot be overestimated, as they were absolutely cut off from their own forces, but their barbarity is beyond belief. They kept up a steady fire on a dressing-station of the field hospital, and before their hiding-places were discovered had killed and wounded many surgeons and others of the hospital corps, besides soldiers who were already wounded. A detail was sent into the woods to scout for these men, and a number of them were discovered in the branches of trees and disposed of. Their programme also included picking off officers and aides passing beneath them along the trail. For a long time their fire was supposed to be spent bullets of the enemy.

On the 3d the army rested, so far as the fire of the enemy would permit. The lack of artillery prevented any farther advance, and little reply was made to the infantry fire during the night. The situation was as follows: Santiago rises from the harbor to the crest of a long hill, three-quarters of a mile back from which rise the hills of San Juan, which were held by our army. El Caney and the commanding plateau to the north were in American possession. In these positions the troops had strongly intrenched themselves, but they were nearly exhausted from their long and severe struggle in the heat and rain, and from the lack of sleep and of food. Their position would have been a critical one had the enemy been in any condition for an assault in force. But they had suffered still more severely than the Americans, and equally needed rest and recuperation.

This battle was fought with the general in command invalided two miles in the rear. He had been overcome by the heat on the day before its opening, and lay in his tent. General Wheeler was also sick, but rose from his bed and reached the front about noon. The losses of the three days' fight, as reported by General Shafter, were 21 officers and 205 men killed, 77 officers and 1197 men wounded, 84 men missing, making a total of 1584. The Spanish loss was much heavier, as they clung to their rifle-pits until they were shot dead in windrows. General Linares, their commander-in-chief, was badly wounded, and General Vara del Rey, their second in command, was killed upon the field.

The work of the American soldiers in this desperate conflict was of the most admirable character. Not a man of them had ever faced an army in battle before. They were very largely raw troops, only about two months in service. They confronted an enemy their equal in numbers and strongly posted in intrenchments and rifle-pits, which they held with obstinate energy. They were sadly deficient in artillery, and had to trust mainly to the rifle and the bayonet. Yet, with a vim and valor which foreign observers designated as superb, they rushed upon the works of the foe, pushing forward with grim determination, never for a moment giving way, inspired apparently by the single thought that they were there to win the posts of the enemy, and must do it through blood and death, and persisting until all these posts were in their hands, their defenders dead, captive, or in flight. It was truly a remarkable instance of American courage and self-reliance, and the battle of Santiago must take its place in history among the most glorious of those in which American soldiers have fought.

CHAPTER XVI.

THE FATE OF CERVERA'S FLEET.

WHILE the army was doing such good work on shore the navy was doing as good work at sea, the final day of the land battle, July 3, being made famous by one of the most brilliant exploits in the history of the American navy. Before describing this event, however, there are some minor naval occurrences to be mentioned. It has already been stated that one of Cervera's ships, the torpedo-boat destroyer Terror, did not accompany the fleet to Santiago. It remained at Fort-de-France, Martinique, and apprehensions were entertained that its purpose there was the capture of the Harvard, then repairing in that port. Under the rules of international law, however, the Terror was not allowed to leave harbor until the Harvard had time to make a good offing, and the threatened attack did not take place.

The Terror was next heard from at San Juan, Porto Rico, where, during the last week in June, it made an attack on the auxiliary cruiser Yale. A dash was made by the destroyer for the great liner, but its assault was met by a sharp fire from the rapid-fire guns of the Yale. These were so effectively served that three shots sufficed. An officer and two men were killed and several men wounded on the Terror, which dropped back under the batteries with difficulty and was towed into the harbor in a sinking condition.

On the 28th of June President McKinley issued a

proclamation extending the blockade to the southern coast of Cuba, from Cape Francis to Cape Cruz, and also to San Juan, Porto Rico. This increased the length of blockaded coast fourfold, adding five hundred miles of coast-line to the sections already under guard. The new line lay in the great bight of the south Cuban coast, a region of shallow water with few ports, so that the fresh work laid out for the mosquito fleet was not very difficult to perform.

The only remaining event of importance was an attack by three small vessels of Admiral Sampson's fleet on the Spanish squadron at Manzanillo, during which two Spanish gunboats, a sloop, and a pontoon were sunk and a torpedo-boat and several gunboats considerably damaged. This work was done by three small craft, the Hist, the Hornet, and the Wampatuck, which unexpectedly found nine vessels in the harbor, flanked by shore batteries. The Hist, formerly a yacht, was hit eleven times, and the Hornet, also a steam yacht, was disabled by a shell that cut her main steam-pipe. No lives were lost, however, and the little boats kept pluckily to their work, with the results above mentioned, until the injury to the Hornet compelled their withdrawal, the Wampatuck towing the disabled vessel out to sea.

We have hitherto said nothing about Spain's remaining ships, the home squadron, composed of her single battle-ship, the Pelayo, an armored cruiser, the Carlos V., several torpedo-boat destroyers, and a number of other vessels likely to prove of very little service in combat. This squadron, commanded by Admiral Camara, had been kept in port at Cadiz, Spain, the government indulging in threats to use it for various purposes, but remaining apparently at a loss how to employ it to the best advantage. The first evidence that the Spanish cabinet had made up its mind came on June 22, when an English captain reported that he had seen the Cadiz squadron in the Mediterranean bound eastward. It consisted of fifteen ships, three of them being torpedo-boats, and several of them transports laden with troops. The secret was out. Manila was the goal. Admiral Dewey was to be attacked. On the 27th news came that the Spanish squadron had appeared at Port Said, at the western end of the Suez Canal.

This news called forth instant action on the part of the United States. An "Eastern Squadron" was at once formed, under Admiral Watson, including the battle-ships Iowa and Oregon and a number of cruisers and colliers, with orders to proceed to the Spanish coast, with the purpose of forcing Camara to return or of following him to the Philippine Islands. As events turned out, it was not necessary for this squadron to sail. Camara was delayed at Port Said through difficulty in obtaining coal, but finally passed through the Suez Canal into the Red Sea, only to be hastily recalled to protect the coast of Spain. Soon his squadron was lumbering back through the Mediterranean, the ships the worse for wear. A threat had sufficed to save Dewey from the proposed attack, and the sailing of Watson's fleet was deferred. Various later dates were fixed for its sailing, but subsequent events prevented its setting out at all.

Meanwhile, Sampson's fleet was diligently keeping up the blockade of Santiago, occasionally exchanging shots with the forts, but principally maintaining a vigilant watch over Cervera's ships. As to the manner in which this work was performed, we may quote from the admiral's report :

"The harbor of Santiago is naturally easy to blockade, there being but one entrance, and that a narrow one, the deep water extending close up to the shore-line, presenting no difficulties of navigation outside of the entrance. At the time of my arrival before the port, June 1, the moon was at its full, and there was sufficient light during the night to enable any movement outside of the entrance to be detected, but with the waning of the moon and the coming of dark nights there was opportunity for the enemy to escape, or for his torpedo-boats to make an attack upon the blockading vessels. It was ascertained with fair conclusiveness that the Merrimac, so gallantly taken into the channel on June 3, did not obstruct it. I therefore maintained the blockade as follows: To the battle-ships was assigned the duty, in turn, of lighting the channel. Moving up to the port, at a distance of from one to two miles from the Morro, dependent upon the condition of the atmosphere, they threw a search-light beam directly up the channel, and held it steadily there. This lightened up the entire breadth of the channel for half a mile inside of the entrance so brilliantly that the movement of small boats could be detected. Why the batteries never opened fire upon the search-light ship was always a matter of surprise to me, but they never did. Stationed close to the entrance of the port were three picket launches, and at a little distance further out three small picket vessels, usually converted yachts, and, when they were available, one or two of our torpedo-boats. With this arrangement there was at least a certainty that nothing could get out of the harbor undetected. After the arrival of the army, when the situation forced upon the Spanish admiral a decision, our vigilance increased. The night blockading distance was reduced to two miles for all vessels, and a battle-ship was placed alongside the searchlight ship, with her broadside trained upon the channel in readiness to fire the instant a Spanish ship should appear. The commanding officers merit great praise for the perfect manner in which they entered into this plan and put it into execution."

On July 1, during the battle on shore, the blockading fleet kept up a steady fire, elevating their great guns and sending shells into the water-line streets of Santiago, some six miles away. This work was continued at intervals for about nine hours on that day, and in the early morning of the 2d the work of bombardment was resumed, Morro Castle being now the main object of attack. For two or three hours shells were thrown into this venerable fortification, one shot from the Oregon bringing down the Spanish flag. The ships then withdrew to their blockading stations, and the men were given an opportunity to rest. They needed it, for terrible work awaited them during the next day.

The threatened capture of Santiago had put the Spanish admiral in an awkward position. If brought between the fire of fleet and army he might have to yield without a fight. This was not to the brave Cervera's taste nor to that of his superiors, for he received peremptory orders from Madrid to leave the harbor. Apparently, it was believed that his fleet was strong and swift enough to engage and outsail the American ships. Cervera and his captains decided to make their dash for liberty on the night of Saturday, July 2, the pilots expecting to avail themselves of the search-lights of the American ships as guides in passing the wreck of the Merrimac. Cervera's orders were to steam at full speed to the westward after clearing the harbor, and to concentrate their fire upon the Brooklyn, neglecting the other ships unless forced to attack them. He hoped by disabling the Brooklyn to dispose of the swiftest and most dreaded of his enemies, trusting to the speed of his vessels to run away from the battle-ships. Reasons satisfactory to himself, however, induced the Spanish admiral to change his purpose of a midnight flight, and to defer the hazardous enterprise till the morning of Sunday, July 3.

On that eventful morning the American fleet lacked much of its strength. The Massachusetts was at Guantanamo Bay coaling. With her were the New Orleans and the Newark. The New York was also absent, having steamed along the coast to Baiquiri to enable Admiral Sampson to confer with General Shafter. This weakening of the fleet had not escaped the eyes of the Spanish scouts, and served to confirm Admiral Cervera in his purpose. The large ships left on blockade consisted of the battle-ships Iowa, Indiana, Oregon, and Texas, and Schley's flag-ship, the Brooklyn. The Iowa lay a mile out beyond the other vessels, trying to fix her forward turret, which was out of repair, and the Indiana was engaged in similar work. The distances of the ships from the harbor's mouth varied from four thousand to six thousand yards. The Brooklyn and the yacht Vixen were the only ships west of the entrance, the others having drifted well to the east.

Several times during the morning the lookout of the Brooklyn had reported smoke in the harbor, and at about 9.30 Navigator Hodgson called to him from the bridge, "Isn't that smoke moving?" His question was answered by almost a yell from the lookout. "There's a big ship coming out of the harbor, sir!" Hodgson satisfied himself by a rapid glance of the truth of this stirring report, seized the megaphone, and shouted in vigorous tones, "After bridge, there! Tell the commodore the enemy's fleet is coming out!"

In an instant the Sunday morning calm on the deck was changed into intense excitement. "Clear the ship for action!" cried the commodore. The signal of the exciting news flew to the masthead as a warning to the other vessels, and from all parts of the ship the men rushed to their quarters. Down below the stokers hurled coal into the furnaces, in the turrets the gun crews hastily made ready their pieces, the ammunition-hoist was brought into active service, and in every section of the big ship every man was on the alert as the news spread with magical rapidity.

The signal from the Brooklyn was matched by one from the Iowa, on whose deck the trail of drifting smoke had been seen at the same instant, the bow of the leading Spanish ship quickly appearing in the narrow channel beside the sunken Merrimac. "There come the Spaniards out of the harbor!" rose in a shout. "Clear ship for action!" roared the answering command, as the Spanish vessels were seen rushing in "line ahead" around Socapa Point and heading for the open sea. The Infanta Maria Teresa, Cervera's flag-ship, led the line, followed by the Vizcaya, the Almirante Oquendo, and the Cristobal Colon. They were quickly followed by the two torpedo-boat destroyers.

"Full speed ahead! Open fire!" shouted Commodore Schley. A stunning roar answered his words, as the shells from the 8- and 5-inch port guns of the Brooklyn began to scream in their rapid flight towards the fugitives. The other ships were as alert. As the

Spaniards cleared the harbor and were observed to head to the west, the Oregon began to swing round in the same direction. The Texas was already reaching the Maria Teresa with her shells. The Iowa and the Indiana were as quick. Hardly a minute passed from the first alarm before the whistling shriek of a rapid-fire shell was heard from the Iowa's deck, and within two minutes every gun on the ship was cast loose, manned, loaded, and ready for the signal to fire.

Five minutes previously the great ships had been swinging lazily on the long rollers of the sea, the men at Sunday "quarters for inspection," none of them thinking of aught but the monotony of every-day duty. Now every ship was belching clouds of black smoke into the air, every man was at his post, his nerves strung to fighting pitch, every gun ready for action, and every ship moving with rapidly-increasing speed towards the fugitives. Not many minutes passed before a fire was concentrated upon the Spanish ships such as had hardly if ever been equalled before, and with a precision of aim that had never been surpassed. The fugitive ships were being rapidly torn and rent by a frightful shower of shells, some of them of enormous size and terrible powers of destruction.

The position of the Brooklyn, as the most westerly of the blockading fleet, rendered easy of accomplishment Cervera's purpose of concentrating his fire on this vessel, and for some ten minutes she was made the target of three of the enemy's ships at the short range of fifteen hundred yards, and of the west battery at three thousand yards distance. The fire poured upon her was terrific, but the harm done was next to nothing, owing to the unskilful handling of the Spanish guns. At the end of

Copyright, 1898, by W. R. Hearst

the interval named the other vessels, which were closing in rapidly, diverted the fire of the enemy and relieved the Brooklyn from this somewhat too close attention.

While the Spanish ships were wasting nearly all their shells upon the sea, the fire of the American gunners was remarkably accurate. "Fire deliberately, and don't waste a shot," was Schley's order to his gunners, and they worked the guns as carefully as if on practice duty. "I have never before witnessed such deadly and fatally accurate shooting as was done by the ships of your command as they closed in on the Spanish squadron," said Schley in his report to the admiral; and the outcome indicated that this statement was in no sense too strong. The results of the terrific bombardment were, indeed, momentous. In twenty-five minutes after the first Spanish vessel had been sighted only two ships of the squadron remained afloat. Two of the cruisers were on fire and beached and the torpedo-boats were sunk.

The Maria Teresa, Cervera's flag-ship, was the first to succumb. A shell from the Brooklyn exploded in the admiral's cabin, and in a minute the after part of the ship was in flames. One from the Texas pierced the side armor and exploded in the engine-room, breaking the main steam-pipe. Shells were bursting all around the bridge and riddling the hull of the ship. The engineer was signalled to start the pumps. No reply came, and it was found that every one in that part of the ship had been killed. Most of the men had been driven from the guns, the flames were increasing, and resistance had become hopeless. The captain gave orders to beach the ship and haul down the flag. As he spoke, he was struck by a shell, and his career came to an end, the second captain taking command. So fast and furious was the

American fire that the smoke of bursting shells hid the fact that the flag was down, and the fire did not cease until a white blanket was run up to the peak.

The Almirante Oquendo was receiving as frightful a baptism of fire. The Iowa, after paying her attentions to the Maria Teresa, was left in the rear by that vessel and found herself opposite the Oquendo at a distance of eleven hundred yards. Her entire battery, including the rapid-fire guns, was now opened on this vessel, and at that distance their work was terrible. Eight-inch shells were seen to explode inside the Spanish ship, two projectiles piercing her at the same moment, one forward and the other aft. For a moment her engines stopped and she lost headway, but she immediately regained her speed and drew ahead of the Iowa, only to come under the guns of the Oregon and the Texas, by which she was cruelly pounded. This punishment was more than she could endure; she was soon a mass of flames and, like the Teresa, was headed for the shore. Less than half an hour had passed when these vessels met their fate, at a point six or seven miles from the harbor's mouth. We have said nothing here of the part taken by the Indiana, but she was doing her full share in the work of destruction, filling the air with the screech of her shells and hurling her great projectiles fiercely upon the foe. Like blood-hounds in the chase, the whole squadron was hot upon the heels of the fleeing prey.

The Vizcaya as yet had not been badly hit, and her captain determined to make an effort to ram the Brooklyn, the nearest and fastest of the American ships, with the hope that the Colon and the Oquendo might get away. The flames on the Teresa showed that she was already past escape. This effort failed through the rapid circling of the Brooklyn, which in turn made an attempt to ram and force the Vizcaya towards the shore. An exchange of fire now ensued, the shells of the Vizcaya going wild, while those of the Brooklyn crashed into her side. One shell went along the entire gun-deck, killing half the men on it and wounding most of the remainder. The Oregon also got in some effective shells, the fire growing so hot that the men were driven in terror from their guns. The Vizcaya was burning when a final shell from the Oregon hit the superstructure, and Captain Eulate gave the order to haul down the flag and beach the ship. This was at Ascerraderos, twenty miles west of Santiago Bay. The hour was 10.50. The ship burned fiercely as she lay at the beach, and she blew up during the night.

Only one of the Spanish cruisers, the Cristobal Colon, the fastest of them all, remained afloat. She had as yet escaped injury, had passed all her consorts, and when the Vizcaya went ashore was about six miles ahead of the Brooklyn, the Oregon being a mile and a half and the Texas three miles farther astern. For an hour the chase continued, the Colon hugging the shore. But her spurt was finished, and the Brooklyn and the Oregon— the latter developing an unexpected speed—were gaining on her mile by mile. The Colon would have to round Cape Cruz by a long detour to escape her pursuers, and Schley put the Brooklyn on a straight course for this cape, signalling the Oregon to keep on the Colon's track.

Another hour passed; both the pursuers had gained; at 12.50, on signal from the Brooklyn, the Oregon fired one of her 13-inch guns. The huge shell struck the water not far behind the Colon, then four miles away.

Another was tried, and fell beyond her. The Brooklyn followed with her 8-inch guns, one shell going through the Colon above her armor-belt. At 1.05 both ships were pounding away at the fugitive, which returned the fire in an ineffective manner. This was kept up for some fifteen minutes; the Colon was rapidly losing ground; her hope of escape was at an end. At 1.20 she gave up the fight, hauled down her flag, and turned her prow to the shore. She touched land at Rio Torquino, after a flight for life of forty-eight miles.

Admiral Sampson's flag-ship, which had been recalled in haste and had followed the chase at her utmost speed, but too late to take part in the contest, came up while Captain Cook, of the Brooklyn, was receiving the surrender of the Colon's crew. Commodore Schley had directed that the officers should retain all their personal effects, a courtesy which the admiral confirmed. The Colon had not been injured by the firing and but little by beaching, but her sea-valves had been opened by the crew, and as she slipped off the steep beach into the sea she began to sink. To prevent her total loss she was pushed bodily on the beach by the New York, where she sank in shoal water, in a location where it was hoped she might be saved.

While this work was being done by the battle-ships and cruisers, the little Gloucester, a yacht converted into a gunboat, was attending to the torpedo-boats, which had followed their consorts from the harbor. On their appearance, the Gloucester, which, under the command of Lieutenant-Commander Wainwright, formerly of the Maine, had been in the thick of the fight with the larger vessels, dashed for them under a high head of steam, and when at short range poured in a fierce volley from her rapid-fire guns. The Indiana and others of the vessels had been firing at them from their secondary batteries, but they desisted through fear of injuring their little consort, and the Gloucester completed the work alone, riddling them with an accurate and deadly fire. Twenty minutes sufficed to end the career of the destroyers. At the close of that time the Furor and the Pluton were both sunk and two-thirds of their people were killed.

This ended the fight. The character of the result can be shown in the brief statement that the Spanish had about six hundred men killed ; the American loss was one man killed and one wounded : the Spanish ships were helpless wrecks ; the American ships were almost uninjured. The victory parallels that of Manila Bay in the utter destruction of the Spanish fleet and the marvellous immunity from injury of the Americans, both men and ships. The record of the battle is of interest in showing that the great guns had little to do with the result. Only two of the huge projectiles of the 12- or 13-inch turret guns struck a vessel, both these being put through the Maria Teresa. The 8-inch, 6-inch, 5-inch, and 6-pound projectiles did the bulk of the work and proved frightfully destructive. One of the most important lessons learned from the fight was the danger of wood-work on a war-ship. Every one of the Spanish ships was set on fire by the American shells, the crews being forced to spend their energy in fighting the fire. On the Vizcaya the water-mains were shot away, so that this was impossible. Another lesson was the difficulty of sending messages through the ships, voice-tubes being useless in the great noise and messengers too slow. Some new invention for this purpose seems called for. The conning-towers were not used, the officers seeking the bridge in preference. And the delicate range-finders, so useful in target-practice, were soon put out of order in the action, and the old system of angling on the mast-head height of the enemy had to be made use of.

The battle ended, a new state of affairs came into play. The impulse to destroy was immediately succeeded by the impulse to save, and the American sailors took as great risks in the effort to rescue their late foes as they had done in the fight. In past warfare, destruction was the one and only thing considered. In modern warfare, the sentiment of mercy quickly follows the battle rage; and this was never more fully exemplified than in the battle with Cervera's fleet. Captain Evans, of the Iowa, tells a story of his highly commendable efforts to save the crew of the Vizcaya, whose sides were just before being rent by the murderous fire of his guns. Heading for this ship, which was furiously burning fore and aft, he lowered all his boats and sent them to the assistance of the unfortunate men, who were being roasted on the decks, drowned or mutilated by sharks in the water, or fired at by Cuban insurgents on shore.

The men of the Iowa worked manfully and saved numbers of the wounded, one man clambering up the side of the Vizcaya and rescuing three at the risk of his life. In all, thirty officers and two hundred and seventy-two men of the Vizcaya were thus taken off, and were clothed, fed, and tenderly cared for by their American hosts.

The torpedo-boat Ericsson and the little Hist aided in this work, while the Harvard and the Gloucester engaged in the same errand of mercy with the Maria Teresa and the Oquendo. "This rescue of prisoners," says Admiral Sampson in his report, "including the wounded

from the burning Spanish vessels, was the occasion of some of the most daring and gallant conduct of the day. The ships were burning fore and aft, their guns and reserve ammunition were exploding, and it was not known at what moment the fire would reach the main magazines. In addition to this a heavy surf was running just inside of the Spanish ships. But no risk deterred our officers and men until their work of humanity was complete."

Of the incidents of the battle, one of the most memorable was the rebuke of Captain Philip, of the Texas, to his men, who were greeting the Spanish surrender with cheers,—

"Don't cheer, boys; the poor devils are dying."

In these words we have the true spirit of nineteenth-century war, at least as viewed from the American standpoint, and the remark of the gallant and humane captain is likely to go down in history among the epoch-making phrases of modern times.

By midnight the Harvard had nine hundred and seventy-six prisoners on board, a great number of them wounded. The Gloucester rescued Admiral Cervera, who had swam ashore from his wrecked ship with the aid of his son. He was nearly naked when rescued, and was supplied with a thin suit of flannel by Lieutenant-Commander Wainwright, of the Gloucester, who soon after delivered him to the Iowa. As the captive admiral came on board bareheaded and half-dressed, Captain Evans received him with a full admiral's guard, the crew cheering him vociferously. He was bitterly depressed, but the kindness and courtesy of his new host brought tears of gratitude to his eyes. His treatment of Lieutenant Hobson had assured him in advance a considerate reception by the officers of the fleet, and had given him a warm place in the American heart.

A few words will complete our story of the destruction of the Spanish fleet. The Reina Mercedes, a dilapidated Spanish cruiser which Cervera had found and had left in the harbor of Santiago, made her appearance just after midnight of July 4, slowly drifting out of the narrow entrance, as if with intention to escape. In a moment all the ships within reach opened upon her, pounding her with a frightful hail of shells. A few minutes sufficed. She sank to the bottom on the beach under El Morro, part of her hull and her masts and stacks being above water. She had probably been sent out with the purpose of blocking the channel against the American ships. During this brief work the shore batteries opened on the ships, and a 6-inch shell fell on the forward deck of the Indiana, exploding below in the men's sleeping-rooms. Fortunately, they were all at quarters and no one was hurt. The remarkable good fortune of the American sailors continued to the end.

Shortly afterwards an effort of a Spanish cruiser to escape from Havana harbor was made, with similar result. She was overhauled near Mariel in an attempt to run the blockade, and sent to the bottom by the hot fire of the mosquito fleet.

During the battle of the 3d an example of special gallantry was displayed on the Brooklyn, which may be given in the words of Captain Cook, commander of that ship:

"When all did their duty manfully, it is a difficult matter to select individuals for special mention. There are some, however, who deserve to be brought to notice by name for conduct that displayed in a conspicuous manner courage, intelligence, and devotion to duty. During the early part of the action a cartridge became jammed in the bore of the starboard forward 6-pounder, and in the effort to withdraw it the case became detached from the projectile, leaving the latter fast in the bore and impossible to extract from the rear.

"Corporal Robert Gray, of the port gun, asked and obtained permission to attempt to drive the shell out with the rammer. To do this it was necessary to go out on the gun, hanging over the water, and the undertaking was full of difficulties and danger, the latter due in a great measure to the blast of the 8-inch turret guns firing overhead. The gun was hot, and it was necessary to cling to the 'Jacob's ladder' with one hand while endeavoring to manipulate the long rammer with the other. After a brave effort, he was forced to give up, and was ordered in.

"Quarter-Gunner Smith then came, sent by Executive Officer Mason, and promptly placed himself in the dangerous position outside the gun-port, where he worked and failed, as the corporal had done. Neither had been able to get the rammer into the bore, and there seemed nothing left to do but dismount the gun.

"At this juncture Private MacNeal, one of the gun's crew, volunteered to go out and make a final effort. The gun was so important, the starboard battery being engaged, that, as a forlorn hope, he was permitted to make the attempt. He pushed boldly out and set to work. The guns of the forward 8-inch turret were firing, almost knocking him overboard, and the enemy's shots were coming with frequency into his immediate neighborhood. At this time the chief yeoman was killed on the other side of the deck. NacNeal never paused in his work. The rammer was finally placed in the bore and the shell ejected, and MacNeal resumed his duties as coolly as if what he had done were a matter of every-day routine."

This chapter may be fitly concluded with Commodore Schley's account of his consideration of the men below decks, and his interesting description of how the only man killed on the American side in the battle met his death. He said,—

"I took it for granted that every man on the ship was just as much interested in how the fight was going as I was, but the men behind the casements and those below decks, of course, could not see what was going on. During the battle I sent orderlies among them telling them what was happening and what effect their shots were having.

"Then, when the Vizcaya struck and only the Colon was left, I sent orderlies down to the stokeholes and engine-room, where the men were working away like heroes in the terrible temperature.

"'Now, boys,' I sent them word, 'it all depends on you. Everything is sunk except the Colon, and she is trying to get away. We don't want her to, and everything depends on you.'

"They responded nobly, and we got her."

Of the death of young Ellis, the only man killed on the Brooklyn, he said,—

"He was a bright lad, from Brooklyn, who enlisted to go before the mast; but he was a hard worker, studied navigation with the young officers of the ship, and had risen to the rank of yeoman.

"As I stood talking with Captain Cook, while we finished the Vizcaya, it seemed that our shots were

Copyright, 1898, by W. R. Hearst

THE OREGON JUST AFTER HER CHASE OF THE CRISTOBAL COLON

falling a little short. I turned to Ellis, who stood near, and asked him what the range was. He replied, 'Seventeen hundred yards.'

"I have pretty keen eyesight, and it seldom deceives me as to distances, and I told him I thought it was slightly more than that. 'I just took it, sir, but I'll try it again,' he said, and stepped off to one side about eight feet to get the range.

"He had just raised his instrument to his eye when a shell struck him full in the face and carried away all of his head above the mouth. A great deal of blood spurted around, and the men near were rattled for a moment.

"Shells are queer things," he continued, after a moment's silence. "I noticed one man standing with his hand grasping a hammock rail as a shell struck the ship, ricocheted, and burst. One piece of the metal cut the rail on one side of his hand, another on the other side, so that he was left standing with a short section of the rail still grasped in his hand. Another portion of the shell passed over his shoulder and another between his legs. He was surprised, but wasn't hurt."

CHAPTER XVII.

THE SIEGE AND FALL OF SANTIAGO.

ON July 3, at 8.30 A.M., General Shafter sent a flag of truce to the Spanish lines with a letter, in which he threatened to shell Santiago unless surrender was made, and gave until ten o'clock of the next morning for the removal of the women and children and the citizens of foreign countries. This was no empty threat, for the positions gained during the battle of the 1st and 2d had given his batteries command of the city, which lay under his guns. General José Toral, who had succeeded to the command of the Spanish forces on account of the serious wounding of General Linares, replied that he would not surrender, but would inform the consuls and people of the permission to remove. At the request of the foreign consuls, the bombardment was deferred until noon of the 5th, it being stated that fifteen thousand or more people, many of them old, would probably leave the city.

The offer to escape was gladly taken advantage of by the people of Santiago, particularly by those of foreign birth, and during the next day there was a pitiful scene as the fugitives swarmed in hosts out of the city and trudged wearily over the road to El Caney, San Luis, and other towns in the vicinity. All day long the hegira continued, the fugitives struggling painfully onward under the blazing sun, and over a road in many places ankle-deep in mud. Tottering old men and women supported by their children, mothers carrying their infants, rich and poor, white and black, cultured and ignorant, all fled in terror from the horrors of an expected bombardment that was never to come.

Most of them made their way to El Caney, in which town, with accommodations for not more than five hundred people, over five thousand slept that night, crowded into the deserted houses and camping out on the verandas and in the rain-soaked streets. At dawn of the next day hundreds who had been overtaken on the road by the darkness began to come in, and the flood continued until a multitude of fugitives, estimated at fifteen thousand, overflowed the little town. They had not been permitted to bring food, and there was none in the town, so that those with money were as destitute as those without. Pathetic sights were to be seen on all sides. Ladies of good birth, supported by frail girls, came feebly into the town, seeking to hide their faces from the vulgar gaze of the ignorant and coarse who surged about them. Despair filled all countenances, hunger threatened the miserable multitude with death, the scene being a reproduction on a minor scale of the results of General Weyler's brutal reconcentration order.

General Shafter was appealed to for the support of the miserable throng. This he was not well able to afford, but promised to give them a limited daily supply of food, the necessities of the troops and the difficulty of getting supplies to the front standing greatly in the way of his feeding this starving multitude. In this dilemma, Clara Barton and the Red Cross officials did noble work, making the most earnest efforts to feed the starving. But it was a difficult task, the tides and the surf standing greatly in the way of landing supplies, while transportation was very difficult to obtain, and the roads between the landing-place and the front were almost impassable.

The wounded in the late battle were in as deplorable a state as the refugees. The field hospitals were inadequately supplied with the simplest necessaries for the care of the sick,—medicines, beds, tents, all requisites, being greatly lacking. In many cases only the packages of "first aid for the wounded," which the soldiers carried with them, were available, while the wounded, on being taken from the operating-tables, had to be laid on the ground, often without a blanket between them and the rain-soaked soil or shelter from the scorching Cuban sun.

The result of this unfortunate state of affairs was a new hegira, many of the wounded painfully dragging themselves down the long, winding, muddy road to Siboney, where the general hospital had been established, the field hospitals being devoted to those too badly hurt to be moved. Improvised ambulances, principally composed of army-wagons, were crowded with men who could not walk, and whose ride over the rutted roads in these rough vehicles was an awful experience. But of these there was not enough, and numbers of feeble, bullet-pierced unfortunates were forced to drag themselves on foot along that dreary road, which wound for a distance of eight miles around the bases of the hills, and several miles farther for those who set out from El Caney. Nor was the weary drag of the wounded over this wheel-scarred and water-soaked trail all that had to be endured. Ruthless Spanish guerillas lay hid in the branches of trees that lined the way, and whistling bullets added to the terrors of that dreadful journey. The sharp-shooting was not very straight, but now and then a wounded soldier was killed. The vandals, however, did not do their heartless work with impunity. Some of the men had brought their rifles and fired back at the flash. One of these tells that he took the rifle of a fallen man and fired in succession from different points to give the impression that there were men in the lines able to shoot in all directions. All night long and until the middle of the next day the dreadful march kept up, many of the bleeding plodders ending their life's march on that terrible road. It formed a painful epilogue to a day of battle and blood.

A striking feature of the case was the cheerfulness with which the soldiers endured their painful journey. In evidence of this, we cannot do better than quote from a correspondent of the London *Daily Mail:*

"Besides the wagons there came along from the front men borne on hand-litters, some lying face downward, writhing at intervals in awful convulsions, others lying motionless on the flat of their backs, with their hats placed over their faces for shade. And there also came men, dozens of them, afoot, painfully limping, with one arm thrown over the shoulders of a comrade and the other arm helplessly dangling.

"'How much farther to the hospital, neighbor?' they would despairingly ask.

"'Only a quarter of a mile or so, neighbor,' I would answer; and, with a smile of hope at the thought that, after all, they would be able to achieve the journey, they would hobble along.

"But the ammunition-wagons and the few ambulance wagons did not carry them all. For hobbling down the steep bank from the hospital came bandaged men on foot. They sat down for awhile on the bank, as far as they could get from the jumble of mules and wagons in the lane, and then, setting their faces towards Siboney, they commenced—to walk it. They were the men whose injuries were too slight for wagon-room to be given them. There was not enough wagon-accommodation for the men whose wounds rendered them helplessly prostrate. So let the men who had mere arm- and shoulder-wounds, simply flesh-wounds, or only one injured leg or foot, walk it: Siboney was only eight miles away.

"True, it was a fearfully bad road, but then the plain fact was that there was not enough wagons for all, and it was better for these men to be at the base hospital, and better that they should make room at the division hospital, even if they had to make the journey on foot.

"There was one man on the road whose left foot was heavily bandaged and drawn up from the ground. He had provided himself with a sort of rough crutch made of the forked limb of a tree, which he had padded with a bundle of clothes. With the assistance of this and a short stick he was paddling briskly along when I overtook him.

"'Where did they get you, neighbor?' I asked him.

"'Oh, durn their skins!' he said, in the cheerfullest way, turning to me with a smile; 'they got me twice,—a splinter of a shell in the foot, and a bullet through the calf of the same leg when I was being carried back from the firing-line.'

"'A sharp-shooter?'

"'The fellow was up in a tree.'

"'And you're walking back to Siboney. Wasn't there room for you to ride?'

"I expected an angry outburst of indignation in reply to this question. But I was mistaken. In a plain, matter-of-fact way, he said,—

"'Guess not. They wanted all the riding-room for worst cases 'n mine. Thank God, my two wounds are both in the same leg, so I can walk quite good and spry. They told me I'd be better off down at the landing yonder; so I got these crutches and made a break.'

"'And how are you getting along?' I asked.

"'Good and well,' he said, as cheerfully as might be; 'just good and easy.' And with his one sound leg and his two sticks he went cheerfully paddling along.

"It was just the same with other walking wounded men. They were all beautifully cheerful. And not merely cheerful. They were all absolutely unconscious that they were undergoing any unnecessary hardships or sufferings. They knew now that war was no picnic, and they were not complaining at the absence of picnic fare. Some of them had lain out all the night, with the dew falling on them where the bullets had dropped them, before their turn came with the overworked field surgeons.

"'There were only sixty doctors with the outfit,' they explained, 'and, naturally, they couldn't 'tend everybody at once.'

"That seemed to them a quite sufficient explanation. It did not occur to them that there ought to have been more doctors, more ambulances. Some of them seemed to have a faint glimmering of a notion that there might perhaps have been fewer wounded; but then that was so obvious to everybody. The conditions subsequent to the battle they accepted as the conditions proper and natural to the circumstances. The cheerful fellow with the improvised crutches was so filled with thankfulness at the possession of his tree-branch that it never occurred to him that he had reason to complain of the absence of proper crutches. I happened by chance to know that packed away in the hold of one of the transports lying out in Siboney Bay there were cases full of crutches, and I was on the point of blurting out an indignant statement of the fact when I remembered that the knowledge would not make his walk easier. So I said nothing about it."

The impossibility of supplying the many thousands of refugees at El Caney with army rations soon started a new movement towards the army base at Siboney, and within a day or two thousands of these miserables were plodding along the muddy road in the trail of the wounded, women, and children, dragging wearily on, staggering and slipping under the burdens they bore, and ready to endure any privations to escape from the horrors of a bombarded city. Fortunately, nature provided one alleviation from the suffering which all endured. The woods were full of mango-trees, bountifully laden with fruit, then ripe and at its best. This fruit is of the size and shape of a pippin apple, of a deep yellow color, and rich and luscious in taste. Just then it was the most precious of nature's gifts.

The truce which had been granted in order that non-combatants might leave the city was extended for more than a week in hope that the Spaniards might by a surrender avoid the necessity of further bloodshed. There was no truce, however, in the preparations for attack and defence. Active measures for bombardment were taken on the American side, new batteries being brought up from the rear and planted in commanding positions. Three of these were posted on El Paso ridge, twenty-four

hundred yards from the city, while the batteries of Captains Capron and Grimes, which had done such good service in the battle, were placed in the rear of General Lawton's division, fifteen hundred yards north of the road. In firing they would have to shell the town over the heads of the troops; but this could be safely done from their elevated position.

Twelve mortars had been brought to the front, and were mounted in a battery ready for use. A dynamite gun which had played its part in the battle of San Juan was depended upon to do effective work in the coming bombardment, its twenty-pound charges of gun-cotton being likely to cause havoc in the Spanish trenches. The navy was also expected to play an imposing part in case hostilities were reopened, Admiral Sampson promising to drop a shell into the city every five minutes, or every two minutes if deemed necessary.

On the Spanish side similar activity was displayed, the trenches being deepened and extended and guns mounted in position for active work. Some of these guns were of much heavier caliber than any the American army had been able to get to the front, but many of them were of antiquated pattern and not likely to do serious damage. There were, however, a fair show of modern guns, capable of excellent performance, and the works of defence were very strong. The principal weakness was a deficiency of food and water. The main aqueduct leading to the city was cut by the Americans on the 11th, yielding them an abundance of excellent water of which they had deprived the enemy.

At the end of the truce the American lines extended around the city in the shape of a horseshoe, five miles in length. The side of the hills facing the city was a succession of bomb-proof rifle-pits, trenches, and redoubts, looking like the openings of so many mines, and threatening to turn the Spanish works into pits of death. General Garcia, with the Cubans, hitherto of little service, had been thrown out on the roads of approach from the west to cut off reinforcement sseeking to enter the city, which was not invested on that side, and it seemed to be but a question of hours when surrender would become inevitable.

General Toral, acting commander-in-chief, was fully aware of his desperate position, and at noon on the 9th, the hour fixed for the beginning of the bombardment, sent a flag of truce to the American lines with an important proposition. The little group of officers under the flag were met and escorted to comfortable quarters, while the letter they bore was taken to General Shafter's tent, two miles in the rear. It conveyed an offer from General Toral to surrender the city, provided his army might capitulate "with honor." This, he stated, meant that they should march from the city with colors flying and arms in hand, and go unmolested whither they would. Surrender under any other conditions, he said, was impossible and could not be considered.

This proposal Shafter unhesitatingly refused, but agreed to extend the truce until Sunday at noon, so that he might communicate with his government. During Sunday he notified General Toral that no terms but unconditional surrender could be granted. These the Spanish general declined to consider, and at four o'clock, to which hour the truce had been extended, a fire from the Spanish trenches began. It was answered from the American works, and until dark a hot fire was kept up, the fleet joining in from its position five miles away, and for an hour dropping shells at intervals of two minutes. Most of these, however, fell short and wasted their energy on the waters of the bay, the intervening cliffs, over which the shells had to be thrown, preventing the guns from doing their best work. The Spanish return to the severe American fire was so weak that fear was entertained that the enemy might have withdrawn from the city, leaving a few men in the trenches. Shafter's army, on the contrary, had been strongly reinforced during the truce, and now numbered nearly twenty-six thousand men, of whom about twenty-three thousand were available for duty.

The bombardment continued on Monday, the 11th, the army and navy joining in the work, while the reply from the Spanish guns continued very weak. Step by step the Americans advanced, entering several of the Spanish trenches, in which they found no soldiers and only dummy wooden guns. At one P.M. the booming of the guns ceased, and Shafter again sent a flag of truce into the city, once more demanding its unconditional surrender. While he awaited a reply he extended his lines on the north down to the bay, thus completing the investiture of the place and placing a barrier of American guns between the Spaniards in the city and any reinforcements which might seek to enter from the west. This line, as yet a thin one, was composed of General Lawton's division, whose flank occupied the little town of Caimenes, on the harbor's edge, the trenches vacated by Lawton's men being occupied by reinforcements from Juragua. Ten batteries of light artillery had also been landed, and were ordered to be rushed to the front.

General Toral delayed his reply to General Shafter's demand until eight o'clock on the morning of the 12th, when he sent a defiant message, saying in effect that if the Americans wanted Santiago they could come and take it. Unconditional surrender, he declared, was unreasonable and impossible, and he was ready to meet an attack whenever the invading army chose to make one. The white flag which had been flying over the city during the truce was withdrawn, and defiance was the order of the day.

General Shafter accepted this reply as final, and, while not ordering an immediate bombardment, he made rapid preparations for a severe struggle. In truth, the state of the weather was far from favorable to active operations. For two days the army had learned to the full what is meant by the rainy season in Cuba, fierce thunder-showers coming in rapid succession with an almost incessant downpour of rain. The rifle-pits and trenches were flooded, and the men who sought to sleep under their shelter-tents were drenched to the skin, the canvas proving unable to keep out the pitiless floods of rain. Cooking was impossible; not a stick of dry wood could be found. There was nothing to eat but hardtack. The trail to the front was in a frightful condition, the streams and the fords being swollen and the soft soil everywhere cut into deep ruts by the wheels of the supply-wagons. Through this violent tropical storm General Miles, commander-in-chief of the armies of the United States, who had just landed, rode to the front, his horse in many places sinking to its knees in the mud as it toiled despondently onward. Bad as conditions were in the American camp, they were still worse in that of the refugees, for whom it had become next to impossible to provide food, and most of whom were exposed without shelter to the drenching floods.

Maj.-Gen. Nelson A. Miles

Maj.-Gen. Wesley Merritt

Maj.-Gen. Joseph H. Wheeler

Maj.-Gen. William R. Shafter

Col. Theodore Roosevelt

Maj.-Gen. Fitzhugh Lee

UNITED STATES ARMY COMMANDERS

The bad conditions in the American army due to the rains were added to by the yellow fever, which had broken out in the camps, probably through infection from some of the refugees. General Miles found the buildings at Siboney so shockingly lacking in sanitary conditions that he had them set on fire as the most available means of cleaning them, several wooden buildings, including the one he had himself temporarily occupied, being reduced to ashes. The *débris* being removed, fresh, clean tents were provided, with a ditch around each to carry off the rain. To these the sick were removed. The wounded, except those who were only slightly hurt, had already been placed on hospital-ships for conveyance to the cooler climate of the north.

On reaching the front, General Miles showed no intention of superseding General Shafter in command, but, in fear of a possible epidemic of yellow fever, pressed for an immediate settlement of the surrender question. As a final attempt at a peaceable solution of the problem, an offer was made to General Toral, under sanction from the government, to send all his troops, if surrendered, back to Spain. At eight o'clock on Wednesday, the 13th, Generals Miles and Shafter, with their respective staffs, rode to the front under a flag of truce and sent a request to General Toral for a personal interview. This was acceded to, and at nine o'clock Miles, Shafter, Wheeler, and others of the American commanding officers crossed the intrenchments and rode into the valley beyond. Here they were met by General Toral and his chief of staff under a spreading mango-tree midway between the lines, and an interview of an hour's length took place.

Toral was offered the alternative of being sent home

with his army or of leaving Santiago province with his troops, but without their arms. He replied that he had no discretion. He had been granted permission by his government to evacuate Santiago, but nothing more. He could accept no other terms without permission from Madrid. He was accordingly given until noon of the 14th for a final answer.

"If he refuses," said General Shafter on his return, "I will open on him at twelve o'clock to-morrow with every gun I have, and will have the assistance of the navy, which is ready to bombard the city with 13-inch shells." Evidently the case had reached a climax.

On the previous day the wounded General Linares, the Spanish commander-in-chief, had telegraphed an urgent appeal to Madrid, showing clearly the hopelessness of the situation. They had but half forage for the horses and no food but rice for the men, he said. The works were so thinly held that even the sick had to serve in the trenches. It would be impossible, in their weakened condition, to break through the enemy's lines, and there was no hope of aid from without. He drew a pathetic picture of the condition of the men under his command, and made a moving appeal for authority to obtain what terms they could, ending with the usual rodomontade that they would all die in their tracks if ordered to do so.

This and Toral's appeal brought Madrid to its senses. The proposed bombardment did not take place, being prevented by an agreement to surrender on the terms proposed. "Santiago surrendered at three," came the significant despatch to the President at Washington, and soon the exhilarating news passed from end to end of the land. The strained situation at Santiago was at an end, and what seemed to many the decisive turning-point in the war was reached.

Shortly after midnight, on the morning of July 15, the preliminary basis for the capitulation of the Spanish forces in Eastern Cuba was agreed to and signed under a picturesque cieba-tree half-way between the lines. Efforts to obtain further delay and further consent from Madrid had been made, but the American commissioners insisted upon final action then and there, only consenting to substitute the word "capitulation" for the harsher word "surrender." As for Toral's desire to take the arms of his men back to Spain, as a concession to Spanish honor, the utmost the commissioners would do was to offer to recommend it to Washington. With this understanding the papers were signed. The conference had lasted, with intermissions, from two o'clock in the afternoon until midnight. Further delay followed, due to Toral's desire to obtain an authorization of his action from Madrid. It duly came, Sagasta, the Spanish prime minister, being fully convinced that a longer struggle in that quarter was useless and perilous, and on the morning of the 16th the following letter, couched in English "as she is wrote" in Spain, reached the American lines:

"SANTIAGO DE CUBA, July 16.

"TO HIS EXCELLENCY, Commander-in-Chief of the American forces.

"EXCELLENT SIR,—I am now authorized by my government to capitulate. I have the honor to so apprise you, and requesting that you design the hour and place where my representatives shall appear to compare with those of your excellency to effect the articles of capitulation, on the basis of what has been agreed upon to this date in due time. I wish to manifest my desire to know the resolutions of the United States government respecting the return of army, so as to note on the capitulations, also the great courtesy of your great graces and return for the great generosity and impulse for the Spanish soldiers, and allow them to return to the peninsula with the honors the American army do them the honor to acknowledge as dutifully descended.

"JOSÉ TORAL,
"*General Commanding Fourth Army Corps.*
"GENERAL SHAFTER,
"*Commanding American Forces.*"

The receipt of this letter was followed by the following despatch from Shafter to Washington:

"HEAD-QUARTERS NEAR SANTIAGO, July 16.
"ADJUTANT-GENERAL U. S. ARMY, Washington.
"The conditions of capitulation include all forces and war-material in described territory. The United States agrees, with as little delay as possible, to transport all Spanish troops in district to kingdom of Spain, the troops, as far as possible, to embark near to the garrisons they now occupy. Officers to retain their side-arms, and officers and men to retain their personal property. Spanish authorized to take military archives belonging to surrendered district. All Spanish forces known as volunteers, Moirilizadves, and guerillas who wish to remain in Cuba may do so under parole during present war, giving up their arms. Spanish forces march out of Santiago with honors of war, depositing their arms at a point mutually agreed upon, to await disposition of the United States government, it being understood United States commissioners will recommend that the Spanish

soldiers return to Spain with arms so bravely defended. This leaves the question of return of arms entirely in the hands of the government. I invite attention to the fact that several thousand surrendered, said by General Toral to be about twelve thousand, against whom a shot has not been fired. The return to Spain of the troops in this district amounts to about twenty-four thousand, according to General Toral.

"W. R. SHAFTER,
"U. S. Volunteers."

At nine o'clock in the evening a further message was made public at the White House, saying: "The surrender has been definitely settled, and the city will be turned over to-morrow morning, and the troops will be marched out as prisoners of war. The Spanish colors will be hauled down at nine o'clock and the American flag hoisted." In response, President McKinley and Secretary Alger thanked the victorious general and army in the following congratulatory words:

"To GENERAL SHAFTER, Commanding, Front, near Santiago, Playa.

"The President of the United States sends to you and your brave army the profound thanks of the American people for the brilliant achievements at Santiago, resulting in the surrender of the city and all of the Spanish troops and territory under General Toral. Your splendid command has endured not only the hardships and sacrifices incident to the campaign and battle, but in stress of heat and weather has triumphed over obstacles which would have overcome men less brave and determined. One and all have displayed the most conspicuous gallantry and earned the gratitude of the nation. The hearts of the people turn with tender sympathy to the sick and the wounded. May the Father of Mercies protect and comfort them.

"WILLIAM MCKINLEY."

"To MAJOR-GENERAL SHAFTER, Front, near Santiago, Playa.

"I cannot express in words my gratitude to you and your heroic men. Your work has been well done. God bless you all.

"R. A. ALGER,
"*Secretary of War.*"

Shafter's reply, reaching Washington on the evening of the 16th, said:

"TO THE PRESIDENT:

"I thank you, and my army thanks you, for your congratulatory telegram of to-day. I am proud to say every one in it performed his duty gallantly. Your message will be read to every regiment in the army at noon to-morrow.

"SHAFTER,
"*Major-General.*"

Shafter and the army richly deserved congratulation, for they had accomplished much more than the capture of Santiago and its garrison. The territory surrendered by General Toral included a large portion of the province of Santiago de Cuba, embracing the eastern extremity of the island. The surrendered territory lay east of a line drawn from Ascerraderos, twenty-five miles west of Santiago, northward to Dos Palmas, and thence northeastward to Sagua de Tanamo on the northern coast. This district embraced some five thousand square miles of territory and a population of more than one hundred and twenty-five thousand, and contained the four important cities of Santiago, Guantanamo, Sagua, and Baracoa. These cities and other points had their garrisons, equalling in total number those in Santiago, making the total number of prisoners included in the surrender, as estimated by Toral, twenty-two thousand seven hundred and eighty-nine. Officers and troops were at once sent, accompanied by Spanish officers, to receive the surrender of those interior garrisons. In Santiago over ten thousand rifles and about ten million rounds of ammunition were sent in to the American ordnance officer.

At exactly nine o'clock on the morning of Monday, July 18, the Spanish flag was lowered from the staff crowning the heights on which stood the venerable antiquity known as Morro Castle, which, mediæval as it was, had borne its several bombardments with the best of modern guns with little material harm. This immunity was mainly due to its elevated situation. Immediately after the lowering of the flag, Lieutenants Hobson and Palmer entered the harbor in steam launches, penetrating as far as the firing station of the submarine mines. These mines were all exploded in the afternoon, and once more Santiago harbor was open to the commerce of the world. Shortly after noon, Commodore Schley and Captain Cook, of the Brooklyn, entered the harbor and made an inspection of the condition of affairs. The main result of their reconnoissance was to discover that the batteries had borne their bombardments remarkably well, conveying the lesson that in the duel between ships and land defences the latter have largely the advantage.

The conclusion reached from a later and more complete inspection was that "over two million dollars' worth of ammunition thrown at the batteries defending Santiago harbor was absolutely harmless in its effect, so far as the reducing of the batteries was concerned, and simply bore out the well-known fact that it is a waste of time and money to bombard earthworks." And this bombardment had been done by the same men who had effectually proved their skill in gunnery on the Spanish fleet under conditions of unusual haste and excitement.

Shortly after six o'clock on Monday morning, July 18, Lieutenant Crook, of General Shafter's staff, entered the city and received a surrender of all the arms in the arsenal. At about seven o'clock General Toral sent his sword to General Shafter in evidence of his submission, and about nine o'clock Shafter and his generals, with mounted escorts of one hundred picked men of the Second Cavalry, rode over the trenches to the open ground beyond, midway to the deserted Spanish works. On the crest of the heights beyond the several regiments of the army were drawn up under arms; comprising, as they did, a total of over twenty thousand men, and extending along seven miles of intrenchments, they formed an imposing spectacle.

On reaching the selected ground, General Shafter found confronting him General Toral and his staff, all mounted and in full uniform, followed by a select detachment of Spanish troops. The scene that followed was dramatic and picturesque. General Shafter, with his generals and their staffs grouped immediately in the rear, and the troops of cavalrymen with drawn sabres on the left, advanced to meet his vanquished foe. A few words of courteous greeting passed, and then the American general returned General Toral his sword, with words of compliment which seemed to touch him deeply and drew from him a warm response of thanks. The conclusion of the ceremony was performed by the Spanish company, which in miniature represented the army, and, under Toral's command, grounded arms, wheeled, and marched across the American lines to the place selected for the prisoners' camp.

General Toral throughout the ceremony was deeply dejected. When General Shafter introduced him by name to each member of his staff, the Spanish general appeared to be a very broken man. He seemed to be about sixty years old and of frail constitution, though stern resolution was shown in every feature. The lines were strongly marked, and his face was deep drawn, as if he was in physical pain. He replied with an air of abstraction to the words addressed to him, and when he accompanied General Shafter, at the head of the escort, into the city to take formal possession of Santiago, he spoke but few words. The appealing faces of the starving refugees streaming back into the city did not move him, nor did the groups of Spanish soldiers lining the road and gazing curiously at the fair-skinned, stalwart-framed conquerors. Only once did the faint shadow of a smile lurk about the corners of his mouth. This was when the cavalcade passed through a barbed-wire entanglement. No body of infantry could ever have got through this defence alive, and General Shafter's remark about its resisting power found the first gratifying echo in the defeated general's heart.

Farther along, the desperate character of the Spanish resistance, as planned, amazed our officers. Although primitive, it was well devised. Each approach to the city was thrice barricaded and wired, and the barricades were high enough and sufficiently strong to withstand shrapnel. The slaughter among our troops would have been frightful had it ever become necessary to storm the city, General Shafter remarking that it would have cost him the lives of five thousand men to take the city by storm.

The palace was reached soon after ten o'clock, the American generals being here introduced to the municipal authorities. At noon the closing ceremony took place, the American flag rising gracefully to the peak of the staff over the palace walls, and Santiago finally changed hands. After nearly four centuries of rule it had passed from the control of Spain and become for the time being an appanage of the great republic of the West.

CHAPTER XVIII.

EVENTS AFTER THE SURRENDER.

WITH the raising of the stars and stripes over the governor's palace at Santiago, a remarkable change came upon that ancient city. Not many days before its inhabitants had been streaming outward in hopeless misery and destitution. Now they came hurrying back, many of them with smiling faces and hopeful hearts. The streets, silent and deserted on the day of the surrender, were thronged with people; the houses, many of which had been looted by the Spanish soldiers, were occupied by their former inmates; life in the deserted city had begun again. The roads were still filled with the homecoming refugees, plodding wearily but hopefully onward. In the city most of the people were gathered about the wharves, where the Red Cross steamer, the State of Texas, was unloading food for the needy. There were few signs of gloom on the faces of these people. Mercurial in disposition, they gazed with lively interest on the activity in the harbor, while smiles wreathed their faces at the prospect of getting other food than rice and salt meat. Of the better class of inhabitants, however, few had returned. Their houses were closed, and they remained at El Caney and their other places of refuge. Everywhere filth was in evidence in the streets, the odors were the reverse of salubrious, and all could see that to fit Santiago for American residence radical sanitary work needed to be done.

In addition to the Red Cross steamer, several other large steamers were unloading cargoes of supplies and provisions, numbers of vessels flying the stars and stripes lay in the harbor, small boats were plying briskly to and fro, and everywhere bustle and activity replaced the recent death-like quiet of the scene. The great sheds along the water-front were being packed with merchandise, and the large stores rented on Marina Street were steadily receiving goods. A revival of commercial activity seemed to have been suddenly inaugurated. The electric-light plant was working, the ice-factory was busy, and the water-supply pipes were being repaired. Miss Barton was rapidly distributing supplies to the hungry and destitute, and, as with the turn of a kaleidoscope, the aspect of the whole city had changed.

Between the American and Spanish soldiers the best of good feeling prevailed. A few days before they had been doing their best to kill one another; now they met and mingled on the most friendly terms, victors and vanquished alike glad that the period of strife was at an end and the horrors of the siege were things of the past. The narrow, cobble-paved streets, grilling in the fierce sunshine, were filled with groups of chatting Spanish soldiers and of laughing and rollicking Americans, while about the plaza facing the palace and in the numerous airy cafés the officers of the opposing armies lounged and fraternized. The saloons remained closed by order of the military governor, to prevent the quarrels likely to arise from drunkenness, but business of other kinds showed marked symptoms of revival. Busiest of all were the pawnshops, which were doing a rushing business, goods of all kinds being offered by the people, the officers tendering for small loans their medals, spurs, and swords, and the civil employés their gold-headed canes of office. These in turn were bought by American officers and soldiers at fancy prices. Machetes in particular were purchased in numbers as souvenirs of the war.

An amusing story is told of one way in which the needy Castilian cavalry provided themselves with American coin. Knowing that they would have to turn over their horses to the Americans as part of the spoils of victory, they contrived to do so in a profitable manner. It stood to reason that the invading soldiers would be glad of a meal of fresh meat after their diet of salt bacon and hardtack, and for a time meat was to be had in abundance at good prices at the local restaurants, until the hungry soldiers began to suspect that they were dining on horse-steaks, when the demand suddenly ceased. Then for a few days an active business went on in the sale of horses on the hoof, the chivalrous Spaniards deeming it better to sell cheap than to give up for nothing. As a result, when General Toral turned over the horses of his army on July 24, the sum total of Spanish steeds delivered was one hundred and forty-nine.

General McKibben had been appointed temporary military governor of the city. He was succeeded by Colonel Wood, of the Rough Riders, who at once began a sanitary work that was sadly needed. The narrow streets, the malodorous alleys and by-ways of the city, were encumbered with refuse of every kind to an indescribable extent, while drainage and sanitary conditions in general were absolutely lacking. The people had lived for centuries in disregard of the simplest laws of hygiene, considering yellow fever a mysterious dispensation of Providence, and the only cleaning the city ever got came in the flushing of its streets by the fierce summer rains. Hundreds of carts were soon at work carrying the filth from the streets, and orders were given that every house should at once be cleaned, inside and out, an order which produced very inadequate results. In people who have been born and reared in filth, belief in the virtues of sanitation cannot be instilled in a day.

Meanwhile, the Americans, while making the Spanish their friends, were making the Cubans their enemies. Bad blood had existed between them almost from the start, and it grew as the days went on. The Cubans, while brave enough in their own way, were not used to the open fighting of the Americans, and did not shine in the methods of regular warfare. The American soldiers soon began to look upon them with contempt, which was changed to anger when their Cuban allies refused to lend their aid in road-making and hospital labors, preferring the pleasanter task of disposing of rations, an enjoyment of which they had long been deprived. The insurgents were not as black as they were painted. The number of their wounded in the hospitals indicated that they had not feared to face the bullets of the enemy. The difficulty was perhaps largely due to ignorance of the language and misunderstanding of orders. But their evident disinclination to exert themselves in any useful way excited a scorn in the Americans which they took little pains to conceal.

This difficulty between the soldiers was followed by one between their leaders, General Garcia taking deep offence because he had not been consulted in the terms of surrender and the subsequent steps for the government of the city. General Shafter personally invited him to go with him into the city on the occasion of the

Copyright, 1893, by W. R. Hearst

surrender, but he declined, sending the message, "I cannot be your guest under the Spanish flag." His leading cause of offence, however, was that the Spanish civil officers were left in power. It was explained that these officials were retained only until it would be convenient to change them for others, but this explanation did not suffice to heal his wounded feelings.

"The trouble with General Garcia was," said General Shafter, "that he expected to be placed in command at this place; in other words, that we would turn the city over to him. I explained to him fully that we were at war with Spain, and that the question of Cuban independence could not be considered by me. Another grievance was that, finding that several thousand men marched in without opposition from General Garcia, I extended my own lines in front of him and closed up the gap, as I saw that I had to depend upon my own men for any effective investment of the place."

Shafter explained his attitude in a conciliatory letter to Garcia, but it failed to placate the offended Cuban general, who withdrew with his forces and marched inwards towards Holguin, an interior town with a considerable Spanish garrison. He proposed to resume the war of the insurrection on his own account, and cut loose from these American invaders, whom he conceived to be conducting the war for themselves. "I have the most kindly feeling for General Garcia," said Shafter, "and sincerely regret that he has found cause for complaint, and that he should feel offended because he was not permitted to be a signatory party to the Spanish surrender. It is idle, however, to argue the point, for, no matter how warmly one may sympathize with the Cubans, the proposition to install them in power immediately after the surrender of the Spanish is untenable, and lacks support among Cubans themselves."

Shafter not alone declined to place the Cubans in immediate power, but also failed to include any of them among the military guard in charge of the city, fearing evil results from their bitter hostility to the Spanish and a possible sacking of the deserted houses. This added to Garcia's injured feeling and was another inciting cause in his removal of his troops. His action was not likely to prove to the advantage of the Cubans, as it added strength to the growing belief that they were not to be trusted in control, and that the United States would have to hold the reins of military rule over the island until its people had proved themselves capable of self-rule and the amenities of modern government.

While this state of affairs ruled at Santiago, events of some interest were taking place elsewhere on the island. General Gomez, the Cuban commander-in-chief, had apparently remained dormant during the war, leaving all active operations to his subordinate; but on July 3 an expedition landed a large cargo of supplies for his army at Palo Alto, on the southern coast. It was the final expedition for the aid of the insurgents, and did not succeed in its purpose without risk and loss, Captain Nunez, brother of General Emilio Nunez, being killed in the attempt to land.

On July 21 the last important naval engagement on the Cuban coast took place, four American war-ships entering the harbor of Nipe, on the northeast coast of Santiago province, where, after a furious bombardment, they took possession of the port. The vessels engaged were the Topeka, Annapolis, Wasp, and Leyden. The place was defended by three forts and the Spanish gunboat Jorge Juan, the latter being attacked by the Topeka, which sent 4-inch shells crushing into her at such a rate that she went to the bottom within twenty minutes. The forts were as easily silenced, and the riflemen who had taken part in the engagement were quickly put to flight. The bay of Nipe, thus taken, is a large land-locked harbor, almost directly north of Santiago and about fifty miles distant. It lies two days nearer than Santiago to Key West and other American ports, has harborage for a host of vessels, and is a place which may become of much commercial importance under American control.

Meanwhile, the several garrisons included in General Toral's capitulation were one by one making their submission and marching to the camp at Santiago. Guantanamo was among the last to yield, its garrison, six thousand men in number, bringing the total of captives up to Toral's estimate of nearly twenty-three thousand men. The sending of this large body of prisoners to Spain in accordance with the terms of the capitulation was the next thing to be considered. It was not deemed safe to trust American transports within Spanish ports, and bids were asked from the shipmasters of neutral powers. An unlooked-for result followed, the lowest bid coming from Spain itself, the successful bidder being the Compania Transatlantica Española, of Barcelona. The fact that this was a Spanish company proved no hindrance; it was given the contract, and at once began preparations for conveying the Spanish soldiers home in Spanish ships. They were to be sent without their arms, the United States government holding in abeyance as yet the recommendation of the commissioners to honor them by a return of the arms which they had so bravely used.

There remained another problem to be solved. On the coast of Cuba lay the wrecks of Spain's four best ships, the armored cruisers which had gone down in their daring rush for liberty. Two of these, the Vizcaya and the Almirante Oquendo, were wrecked beyond repair, so torn by shell and ruined by flame and explosion that they were useless hulks. But the remaining two were in much better condition, and might be saved as useful additions to the navy of the United States. It was thought possible to float the Maria Teresa without serious difficulty. The Cristobal Colon was in a more critical state. Little hurt as she was by shot or shell, she had been filled by the opening of her sea-valves, and lay upon her beam ends sunk upon a very shelving beach, where she was sure to be totally lost if a hurricane should arise. The task of raising her was given to Lieutenant Hobson, of Merrimac fame, who proposed to do so by the aid of external pontoons and internal air-bags, and also by pumping the water from her watertight compartments.

In Santiago a special commission was appointed to investigate the city prison, the commissioners finding instances of gross injustice and criminal negligence which fully justified the rending of the city from the cruel hands of Spain. The prison records and the questioning of prisoners revealed shameful examples of injustice,—men and women having been thrown into cells and kept there for years without a trial for such a petty offence as speaking disrespectfully of the Spanish government. In many instances all records of the charges against untried prisoners had been lost, the witnesses had died, the existing officials were ignorant why they were held, and in some cases the prisoners themselves had forgotten. One man named José Silvera, for a petty theft, the maximum penalty for which was six months' imprisonment, had been detained for fourteen years. Other cases of crying injustice were found, and the prisoners thus foully dealt with were released. It seemed indeed full time that the colonial dominion of Spain was brought to an end and mediævalism replaced by modern civilization on Cuban soil.

While these events were taking place in and about Santiago, the army of invasion had fallen into a deplorable state. By men accustomed to the temperate climate of the north and exposed to the scorching suns and drenching rains of a Cuban summer, with little shelter from the humid atmosphere and the water-soaked soil, sickness could not well be avoided, and was likely to prove more dangerous than the bullets of the enemy. The difficulty of making the men observe sanitary precautions added to the danger, and febrile disorders of a malarial character soon began to spread among the troops. The dreaded yellow fever, a disease indigenous to the soil, was not long in making its appearance, probably through infection from the Santiago refugees, and fear of its rapid spread among the troops hastened the negotiations for the surrender of the Spanish army.

The wounded were in less peril than the sick. Fortunately for them, the Mauser rifle, used by the Spanish soldiers, makes what surgeons call a "humane wound." During the Civil War, when a man was shot through the lungs by a bullet from a Springfield rifle, he was almost sure to die in a few days or a few months from consumption, pneumonia, or other affections brought on by the wound. This is not the case with the Mauser bullet, which does not lacerate the parts, and does not crush bones so as to render amputation necessary. If not struck in a mortal spot, the wounded man is very apt to recover. Antiseptic treatment, which was practised in this war to an extent probably never before known in warfare, also had much to do with the remarkable percentage of recoveries of our men. A small package marked "first aid to the wounded" was carried in the hip-pocket of each of the soldiers, and proved a most fortunate provision in the deficiency of medical supplies. It enabled the doctors at once to apply an antiseptic dressing to the wounds, causing them to heal without the appearance of inflammation or the formation of pus. The results were remarkable, the large percentage of recoveries among the wounded being perhaps unequalled in any preceding war. The lack of medical supplies seems to have been more a misfortune than a fault of the surgical authorities. They had been brought in abundance in the transports, but in the general difficulty of landing the first attention had been given to the munitions of war, and the transports had been moved to make room for others before their medicines and surgical instruments were put on shore. The means for making wounds were given precedence; the means for healing wounds were left untouched in the holds of the ships. This was due mainly to the haste and confusion of the operations, though General Shafter did not escape blame through failure to respond satisfactorily to the appeals of the surgeons for aid in landing and transporting their stores.

It was fortunate for the wounded that an improved method of treatment was adopted, for the arrangements for their comfort were of the most wretched character. The tents provided were far too few to accommodate the suffering, and many of the wounded soldiers were obliged to lie in the open air, exposed to a scorching sun-bath during part of the day and drenched with rain during the remainder. At Siboney little better provision was made, many of the wounded being obliged to lie on the water-soaked ground. The more severely wounded, however, were soon taken north on hospital-ships, leaving only the lighter cases to be dealt with on Cuban soil.

Meanwhile, sickness was increasing with a rapidity that soon became alarming, nearly five thousand of the troops, almost a fourth part of the whole army, being down with various diseases by August 1. Three-fourths of these were cases of fever, and yellow fever had grown dangerously prevalent. When this state of affairs became known in the North, a sharp criticism of the War Department arose, this branch of the government being considered responsible for the condition of the army, which was believed to be due to lack of proper care and foresight. The trouble was not confined to Cuba, for at Camp Alger, in the immediate vicinity of Washington, typhoid fever had become epidemic, and had existed since the formation of the camp. There was excellent reason to believe that the water-supply was contaminated and that the soldiers were being unnecessarily kept in a dangerous locality.

As the unfortunate situation at the front became better known, the adverse criticism grew more stringent, Secretary of War Alger and Surgeon-General Sternberg being sharply denounced by many newspapers, while General Shafter by no means escaped. Dr. Nicholas Senn, chief of the operating staff of the army at Santiago, and a man of the highest reputation in his profession, made the following incriminating statement, under date of July 17 :

"SIBONEY, CUBA, July 17.

"In the present war with Spain every one knew that our army would be exposed to an unusual extent to disease and the debilitating effect of the tropical climate of Cuba. The invasion of the province of Santiago meant certain exposure to yellow fever infection. The commanding general must have been aware of this. It is said the seafaring men along the coast of Cuba fear Santiago more than any other port. Yellow fever reigns there more or less throughout the entire year. At Siboney and Baiquiri it is known as 'hill fever.' It appears that the precautions outlined by Colonel Greenleaf, chief surgeon of the army in the field, were entirely ignored by the commander of the invading force.

"I was more than astonished when I arrived at Siboney, on July 7, to find that thousands of refugees from infected districts were permitted to enter the camps unmolested and mingle freely with our unsuspecting soldiers. All along the road, from the base of operations to the line of intrenchments, could be seen at short intervals scenes which were sure to bring about disastrous results. Our soldiers, in a strange land and among strange people, enjoyed at first the novelty, and were free in buying the fruits of the land and exchanging coins, not knowing how dearly they would be called upon to pay for such a questionable privilege. Houses and huts in which yellow fever had raged were visited freely, and the dangerous germs of the disease were inhaled, as a matter of course. The results of such intimate association of our susceptible troops with the natives could be readily foreseen.

"It required only the usual time for the disease to make its appearance, and when it did so it was not in a single place, but all along the line from our intrenchments to Siboney.

"Dr. Guiteras, the yellow fever expert, recognized a few of the cases on the day of my arrival. He is extremely cautious, and will only make a positive diagnosis in cases in which albumen is exhibited in combination with the usual symptoms which accompany the disease. On the recommendation of Dr. Guiteras, our isolation hospital was established a mile and a half from Siboney, and in less than three days it contained more than one hundred yellow fever patients, among them General Duffield, of Michigan, and Professor Victor C. Vaughn, of the University of Michigan.

"During my first visit to the front I found two hundred fever patients near the First Division Hospital, most of them under shelter tents, others lying on the moist ground with nothing but a wet blanket to protect them.

"The appearance of yellow fever cases in such a short time, in such large numbers, and originating in so many different localities simultaneously proved a source of surprise and alarm to the medical officers. They realized the danger and the necessity for the employment of most energetic measures, but this could not be done without a hearty co-operation on the part of the general in command.

"Major Lagarde applied to General Shafter for a detail of a company of infantry to aid him in fighting the disease. His request was promptly denied, under the pretence that all of the troops available were needed more at the front than in the rear. This action left the major powerless in checking the extension of the disease.

Fortunately, Major-General Miles arrived in the nick of time, and with him Colonel Greenleaf, chief surgeon of the army in the field.

"Colonel Greenleaf made the same request of General Shafter for troops to aid him in gaining control of the disease, but it was ignored as peremptorily as that of Major Lagarde. He now turned to General Miles, who placed at his disposal not only a battalion, but a whole regiment of colored troops.

"The work of sanitation was then taken earnestly in hand. At present there are about eight hundred cases of yellow fever here. Fortunately the disease is of a mild type, the number of deaths being small. General Miles has done everything in his power to aid the medical officers in limiting and weeding out the disease."

Correspondents with the army gave similar testimony, declaring that no precautions were taken to ward off yellow fever from the troops; that ambulances and supply-wagons were used to carry sick refugees and afterwards employed, without disinfection, for the conveyance of our wounded; and that, if those in charge had specially desired to infect the regiments, they could not have adopted more effective methods. Only the fortunate circumstance mentioned by Dr. Senn, that the type of fever proved to be an extremely mild one, deaths being few and convalescence rapid, saved the army from a disaster greater than that of war.

As the days went on and the number of the sick rapidly increased, the public excitement grew, enhanced by the persistent charges that red tape and official incompetency were largely responsible for the reprehensible state of affairs. As regards this condition, further evidence was given on August 4 by the Rev. Drs. Henry C. McCook and Joseph Krauskopf, who had just returned from a visit to Santiago on behalf of the National Relief Commission. Dr. McCook gave the following account of his experiences:

"The army was in an awful condition. The medical supplies were almost exhausted, some of the most important remedies being absolutely run out. Many of the doctors were sick. Of the sick men in camp there was not one on a cot. There were no supplies, not even a change of clothing for the men that were stricken. They lay on the ground in their blankets, which the rains kept constantly in a damp or soaked condition. Once or twice a day came the torrential rains to drench them, and make them even more miserable than they would be from the sickness alone. Hundreds of men with dysentery and typhoid lay in this wretched condition. With one-quarter of the army on the sick-list and a large part of the remainder convalescent, with pestilence among them, with the sun smiting them by day, and the rains keeping them damp in spite of the sun, with nature exhausted after the long battle, with inadequacy of supplies and hospital equipments and clothing, and with lack of variety of food, the army was facing a terrible situation.

"It was but the natural result of this awful condition of affairs that, as we went among the soldiers, we heard this appeal on all sides: 'Do you know the President or the Secretary? Won't you tell him for God's sake to take us away from here? We are worn out, broken down, and we never will get well until we get a breath of other air.' They were all anxious to get away, for they felt that to stay there would mean death.

"Yet there was remarkable resolution left in the men, for all that. I believe if there had been a call to fight the troops would have been found ready. The conditions that surrounded them appalled them more than the prospect of battle could have done. They were discouraged and drooping, but if they had heard the bugle they would have gone in with a good deal of vim.

"We at once went about the work of relieving the suffering that existed. Too great credit cannot be given to Major Summers, the surgeon, who went with us on the Resolute. He simply threw red tape to the winds. No sooner had we landed than surgeons of the various commands came to the ship for medicines and other supplies. The government stores were in charge of Major Summers, but he told the surgeons to take what they wanted. He comprehended that the first thing was to relieve the distress, and he didn't stop to consider requisitions and other forms of red tape. He told the surgeons he would take their receipts the following day, and they helped themselves to what was needed."

Dr. Krauskopf gave similar testimony, stating that fearful blunders had been made, and that the medical supplies and delicacies sent by the Commission had arrived just in time to save many lives. "The troops are all weak and totally unfit for work," he said.

These converging testimonies as to the scandalous condition of affairs in the army at Santiago, and the denunciation of government officials that followed, at length aroused the War Department to action. On August 3 General Shafter called the commanding and medical officers of the army together for conference, and read them a cable message which he had just received from Secretary Alger, ordering him, on the recommendation of Surgeon-General Sternberg, to move the army to San Luis, in the interior, a higher and presumably healthier location.

This order, while apparently sufficient to meet the situation in the opinion of the officials named, proved the reverse of satisfactory to the army leaders, from whom it called forth energetic protests. Colonel Roosevelt was the first to give voice to the prevailing sentiment in the following letter to General Shafter:

"MAJOR-GENERAL SHAFTER,—Sir: In a meeting of the general and medical officers called by you at the palace this morning we were all, as you know, unanimous in our view of what should be done with the army. To keep us here, in the opinion of every officer commanding a division or brigade, will simply involve the destruction of thousands. There is no possible reason for not shipping, practically, the entire command north at once.

"Yellow fever cases are very few in the cavalry division, where I command one of the two brigades, and not one true case of yellow fever has occurred in this division, except among the men sent to the hospital at Siboney, where they have, I believe, contracted it. But in this division there have been fifteen hundred cases of malarial fever. Not a man has died from it, but the whole command is so weakened and shattered as to be ripe for dying like rotten sheep when a real yellow fever epidemic, instead of a fake epidemic like the present, strikes us, as it is bound to do if we stay here at the height of the sickness season, August and the beginning of September. Quarantine against malarial fever is much like quarantining against the toothache.

"All of us are certain, as soon as the authorities at Washington fully appreciate the conditions of the army, to be sent home. If we are kept here, it will in all human possibility mean an appalling disaster, for the surgeons here estimate that over half the army, if kept here during the sickly season, will die. This is not only terrible from the stand-point of the individual lives lost, but it means ruin from the stand-point of the military efficiency of the flower of the American army, for the great bulk of the regulars are here with you.

"The sick-list, large though it is, exceeding four thousand, affords but a faint idea of the debilitation of the army. Not ten per cent. are fit for active work. Six weeks on the north Maine coast, for instance, or elsewhere, where the yellow fever germ cannot possibly propagate, would make us all as fit as fighting cocks, able as we are eager to take a leading part in the great campaign against Havana in the fall, even if we are not allowed to try Porto Rico.

"We can be moved north, if moved at once, with absolute safety to the country, although, of course, it would have been infinitely better if we had been moved north or to Porto Rico two weeks ago. If there were any object in keeping us here, we would face yellow fever with as much indifference as we face bullets, but there is no object in it. The four immune regiments ordered here are sufficient to garrison the city and surrounding towns, and there is absolutely nothing for us to do here, and there has not been since the city surrendered. It is impossible to move into the interior. Every shifting of camp doubles the sick rate in our present weakened condition, and, anyhow, the interior is rather worse than the coast, as I have found by actual reconnoissance. Our present camps are as healthy as any camps at this end of the island can be.

"I write only because I cannot see our men who fought so bravely, and who have endured the extreme hardship and danger so uncomplainingly, go to destruction without striving, so far as lies in me, to avert a doom as fearful as it is unnecessary and undeserved.

"Yours respectfully,
"THEODORE ROOSEVELT,
"*Colonel Commanding First Brigade.*"

This energetic demand broke the ice of military etiquette. The remaining leading officers of the army were thoroughly in sympathy with Colonel Roosevelt in this view, and expressed their sentiments in an unusual and decisive manner. This took the form of a sort of "Round Robin" communication to the commanding general, signed by all the general officers, saying that the army "must be moved at once or perish," that to move it to the interior would be as bad as to leave it where it was, and that any one who stood in the way of its removal north would be responsible for its virtual destruction. It read as follows:

"We, the undersigned, officers commanding the various brigades, divisions, etc., of the army of occupation in Cuba, are of the unanimous opinion that this army should be at once taken out of the island of Cuba and sent to some point on the northern sea-coast of the United States; that it can be done without danger to the people of the United States; that yellow fever in the army at present is not epidemic; that there are only a few sporadic cases; but that the army is disabled by malarial fever to the extent that its efficiency is destroyed, and that it is in a condition to be practically entirely destroyed by an epidemic of yellow fever, which is sure to come in the near future.

"We know from the reports of competent officers and from personal observations that the army is unable to move into the interior, and that there are no facilities for such a move if attempted, and that it could not be attempted until too late. Moreover, the best medical authorities of the island say that with our present equipment we could not live in the interior during the rainy season without losses from malarial fever, which is almost as deadly as yellow fever.

"This army must be moved at once or perish. As the army can be safely moved now, the persons responsible for preventing such a move will be responsible for the unnecessary loss of many thousands of lives.

"Our opinions are the result of careful personal observation, and they are also based on the unanimous opinion of medical officers with the army, who understand the situation absolutely.

"J. FORD KENT, *Major-General Volunteers, Commanding First Division, Fifth Corps.*

"J. C. BATES, *Major-General Volunteers, Commanding Provisional Division.*

"ADNA R. CHAFFEE, *Major-General, Commanding Third Brigade, Second Division.*

"SAMUEL S. SUMNER, *Brigadier-General Volunteers, Commanding First Brigade Cavalry.*

"WILL LUDLOW, *Brigadier-General Volunteers, Commanding First Brigade, Second Division.*

"ADELBERT AMES, *Brigadier-General Volunteers, Commanding Third Brigade, First Division.*

"LEONARD WOOD, *Brigadier-General Volunteers, Commanding the City of Santiago.*

"THEODORE ROOSEVELT, *Colonel Commanding Second Cavalry Brigade.*"

Many of the critics of the War Department held that the slowness of action on the part of that branch of the government was due to a purpose of questionable character. General Miles was at that time in the island of Porto Rico at the head of a large army, which seemed more than sufficient, in view of the feeble opposition, to make a rapid conquest of the island. The War Department, nevertheless, proposed to reinforce him with General Wade's division of troops, and held back a number of transports for that purpose. The critics of the Department declared that this expedition was wholly uncalled for, and that the movement was based upon political instead of military reasons. It was spoken of as a picnic at the expense of the government for the pleasure of the soldiers, who were expected to respond with ballots instead of bullets.

The sarcastic comments of the press, in connection with a message from General Miles, saying "Do not send me any more troops," put an end to the proposed expedition, while the emphatic action of the generals at Santiago broke up the leisurely movement of departmental routine, and roused the officials to a realizing sense of the situation. The transports which had been intended for Wade's men were ordered to proceed with all haste to Santiago, and those which had been used for Miles's army were sent to the same point, the whole being held sufficient to carry from twelve thousand to fifteen thousand men. All clothing and bedding likely to be infected were ordered to be destroyed, all men who were suffering from yellow fever or other infectious diseases to be left behind, and every precaution to be taken for the safe and healthy carriage of the men to their destination.

The convalescent camp selected was at Montauk Point, Long Island, where a tract of land three miles square had been secured. It was said to possess many sanitary advantages, including excellent drinking water, a lake of considerable dimensions, and facilities for fresh-water bathing.

Adverse criticism soon found new food for comment in the way the direction to take precautions for the safe and healthy carriage of the men was carried out. The transport Concho, which reached Hampton Roads on August 1, with officers, non-commissioned officers, and nurses, was found to be in a most horrible condition, due to the lack of water, food, and medicine on the ship. There was no ice on the steamer and no water except the stale supply taken on in early June at Santiago. The only food consisted of coarse army rations utterly unfit for sick men to eat. Of medicine, there was only a scant supply of quinine, camphor, and sulphur. For thirty-eight hours the bodies of three dead men lay uncovered under the saloon, yielding a terrible stench. The health officer at Hampton Roads refused permission to bury these on shore, and the ship had to put to sea, two others dying in the meantime. "I believe if the men had had proper food and medicines all of them would have been alive to-day," said one of the staff on board. "I never saw such blundering in my life." "The food given the sick men would have sickened well men," said the doctor in charge. "Men who had just recovered from yellow fever should have had better food than hardtack and beans."

The condition of the Concho should have served as a useful object-lesson in the conveyance of the sick soldiers to Montauk Point, but those in charge do not seem to have availed themselves of the lesson. Following the Concho came the Seneca, marked by little less scandalous conditions. Other transports open to severe criticism were the Breakwater, the Santiago, the Comal, and the San Marco. It was evident not only that "some one had blundered," but also that some one kept blundering. And a new series of blunders cropped out at the Montauk Point camp, where the first soldiers who landed found no preparations for their reception, while the excellent water promised was conspicuously absent. Days passed before proper tentage was provided and the camp was supplied with palatable water, while the food supply was composed of the ordinary army rations, no delicacies suitable for the sick being provided.

The situation at Camp Alger called for as radical measures of relief as that at Santiago. Here were twenty thousand men exposed to unsanitary conditions and visited by a serious epidemic of typhoid fever. It was not until August 2 that an order for their removal to a healthier location was given, the old battle-site of Manassas being chosen for their new camp. The march was conducted in the bungling fashion which seemed to have become epidemic in the army, the officers in charge erring seriously through ignorance or carelessness. The troops were moved, but their food-supplies were not moved with them, the supply-wagons starting twelve hours after the march began, so that the men went to bed hungry and their rations failed to reach them until sunrise of the following day. The medicine-chests were similarly wanting, and in the whole movement the lack of a directing head was painfully apparent.

The soldiers at Chickamauga soon proved to be no better off. Sickness appeared and increased there until the camp was a veritable pest-hole, the water-supply, never very abundant, growing daily more and more contaminated, until it seemed, if something were not speedily done, that all the soldiers present would be prostrated with typhoid fever and other dangerous diseases. In truth, sickness had invaded and was increasing in all the camps, and immediate action for relief was imperatively necessary.

The disposition in the public press to hold the War Department responsible for all these evidences of carelessness and incompetency was perhaps unwarranted. Inexperienced and negligent subordinates have a habit of blundering in spite of the wisest and most judicious orders, and for such delinquencies as that shown in the march to Manassas only the officers in charge could justly be held responsible. The lack of suitable supplies on the transports was perhaps due to a similar cause. Yet when we consider the many and varied evidences of incompetency and neglect, we cannot but consider the general directing head in some degree culpable,—in how large a degree only a full investigation can determine.

After detailing the criticisms to which Secretary Alger was subjected, we must in justice let him speak for himself, quoting from a letter written by him on August 13, and which described the great and multifarious labors of the Department during the war:

"There is nothing young men in robust health are so

prodigal of as their health until it is gone. Men go into camp feeling that they can stand anything and everything, and cannot be made to believe to the contrary, and are stricken with disease. Every effort has been made from the beginning to furnish every camp with all appliances asked for, but of course the commanding officers in the field are the ones who have the direct charge of these men.

"For instance, one army corps commander has given orders, and enforces them, respecting sanitary affairs, and he had to-day but a fraction over two per cent. on the sick-list. Others have been less successful, and the consequence is typhoid and other fevers have been bred and spread to a considerable extent. One regiment in the Chickamauga camp has a colonel who enforces sanitary rules in his regiment, obliging the men to boil all the water they drink, keeping the camp cleanly, and the result,—less than twenty-five sick, and his camp, too, in as unfavorable a place as any in the command. Others more favorably situated have ten times that number on the sick-list. One of the regiments of the last call, not yet removed from its State, sends bitter complaints of typhoid fever.

"Concerning the Santiago campaign, when the ships left Tampa they had on board three months' provisions and an abundance of hospital supplies. They had lighters to unload with at points of debarkation. These lighters were lost in severe storms on the way. As soon as we were notified of the fact two tows of lighters were sent from Mobile and New Orleans, which were also overtaken by storm and lost. The navy supplied us with lighters, and one of these was wrecked. The army disembarked, getting off a portion of its supplies and medical stores, and immediately marched to the front to fight the Spaniards.

"The great difficulty of landing supplies subsequently was that the wind sprang up every morning at ten and made a high surf, rendering almost impossible the use of small boats, with one lighter, which was all they had left for this purpose. Of the packers who were employed, sixty per cent. soon fell sick, and heavy rains falling every day, the roads (if they could be called such) became impassable for vehicles, and pack-animals had to be employed to carry food to the army, which, being extended to the right around Santiago, increased the distance from the coast every day and made the task more difficult. . . .

"Everything that human ingenuity could devise has been done to succor that army,—not the ingenuity of the Secretary of War, but the result of the combined counsel of those who have had a life-long experience in the field. That some men have been neglected on transports coming home there is no doubt,—all against positive orders, due, perhaps, to carelessness and negligence, but largely on account of not having the medical force to spare (many of whom were sick) from the camp at Santiago. Many medical officers sent with transports were taken ill on the way home."

This chapter may be suitably closed with the recital of an incident that formed part of the series of events described. On July 23 Colonel Roosevelt wrote to Secretary Alger, with the approval of General Wheeler, asking him to send the cavalry division, "including the Rough Riders, who are as good as any regulars, and three times as good as any State troops, to Porto Rico." This division, with the other regiments of Rough Riders, would make nearly four thousand men,

THE WAR WITH SPAIN.

"who would be worth easily any ten thousand national guards armed with black powder Springfields or other archaic weapons."

This communication brought a tart reply from the Secretary of War, sent in the form of a cable message, after the date of the "Round Robin." It said,

"Your letter of 23d is received. The regular army, the volunteer army, and the Rough Riders have done well, but I suggest that, unless you want to spoil the effects and glory of your victory, you make no invidious comparisons. The Rough Riders are no better than any other volunteers. They had an advantage in their arms, for which they ought to be very grateful.

"R. A. ALGER,
"*Secretary of War.*"

The sharpness of this rebuke was not uncalled for in the character of Colonel Roosevelt's letter, but the making public such a reply to a private letter exposed Secretary Alger to severe animadversion in the hostile press, which seemed disposed to attribute it to spite at Roosevelt's implied criticism of the War Department in his communication to General Shafter. However that may be, we cannot but look upon the outspoken colonel as the right man in the right place when we consider the quick and important effect of his action.

CHAPTER XIX.

THE INVASION OF PORTO RICO.

THE movements of the Spanish navy proved the dominating influences in the war with Spain. Had military considerations alone ruled, Havana would have been the main point of attack in Cuba, but the fact that Cervera's fleet took refuge in the bay of Santiago centred the movement of invasion about the city of that name. The city of Manila, through the presence of a Spanish fleet in its harbor, became a second central point in the war. And, thirdly, the movement of Camara's fleet from Cadiz to Port Said gave rise to a projected naval expedition against Spain. This was deferred on account of Camara's hasty return, but the purpose was not abandoned, and almost at the last days of the war a powerful fleet under Admiral Sampson was held ready to proceed against the Spanish coast. The only event in the war not dominated by naval exigencies was the invasion of Porto Rico. At an early date in the war the conquest of this valuable island became a settled purpose of the administration. The invasion was deferred from time to time for reasons connected with the Santiago campaign, yet the occupation of this island before the conclusion of the war was held to be indispensable.

As it was proposed to send an army to Porto Rico large enough to effect a rapid conquest of the island, its departure was delayed until after the surrender of Santiago, in order that a part of the experienced regiments

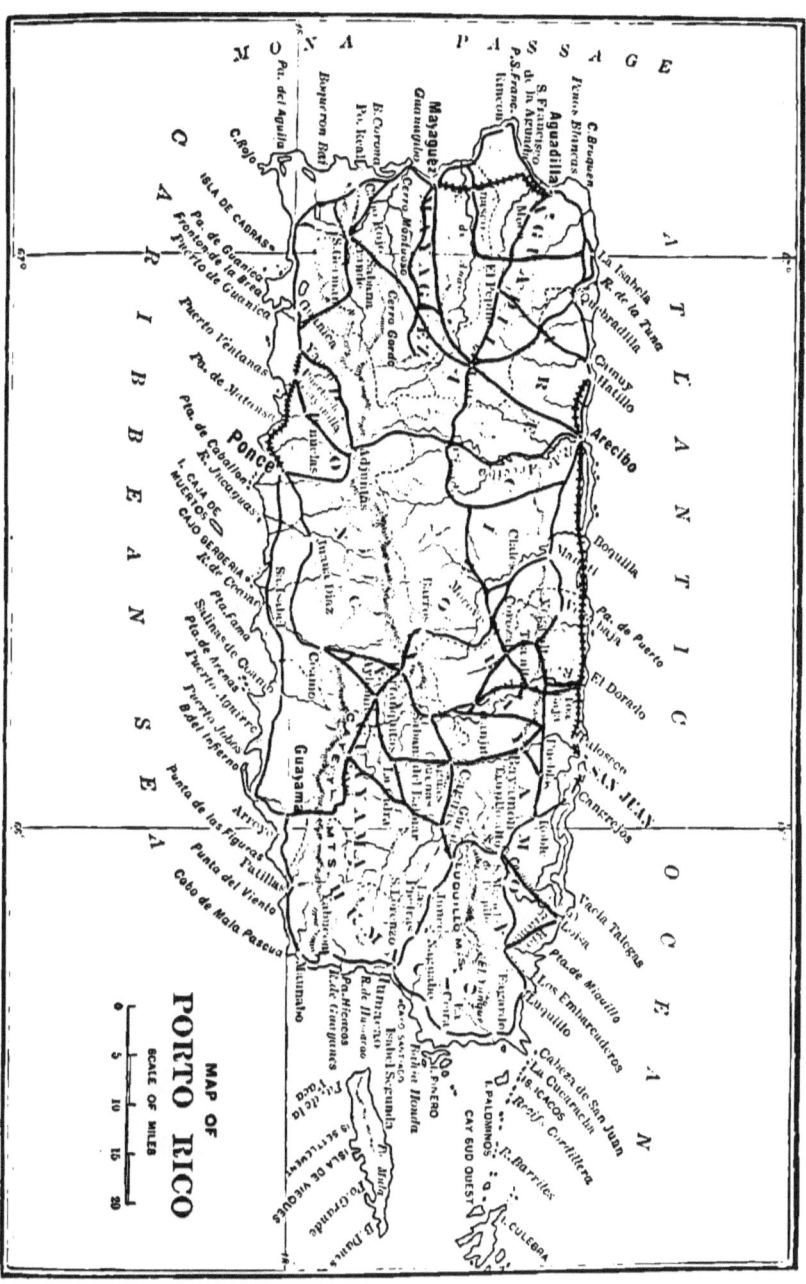

at that place might be employed. Those under Major-General Miles, commander-in-chief of the expedition, were ready to sail on July 18, but a detention for several days took place, due to delay on the part of Admiral Sampson in furnishing the requisite naval escort ; a remissness which, whatever its cause, brought him severe blame. To complete the expedition, a large body of troops were to be sent from the United States under the command of Major-General John R. Brooke, sailing from Charleston, Tampa, and Newport News.

For several days Miles's troops sweltered in the crowded transports under a tropical sun while waiting the promised escort. It was not until the 21st that they finally set sail, some four thousand in number. The expedition from Charleston, numbering about three thousand men, was already under way, and fears were entertained that it might reach the point of rendezvous in advance of the naval support. A similar force set sail from Tampa, while General Brooke, with five thousand three hundred men, left Newport News a week later. It was proposed that these should be followed by others, making a total force of about thirty-five thousand men. Supplies in abundance were forwarded with the troops, and a strong corps of engineers accompanied the army, with a large store of engineering machinery and equipment for road- and bridge-building. The authorities did not intend to repeat the mistakes which had so seriously imperilled the success of the Santiago expedition.

It was not publicly known to what port the expedition was directed, but general surprise was felt on learning that on Monday, the 25th, four days after sailing, Miles's transports had entered the harbor of Guanica, in the southwestern section of the island, and at almost the farthest possible remove from the port of San Juan. This was not the point originally determined upon, but the commander-in-chief, for satisfactory reasons, decided during the voyage to change its destination. In the lead of the escort was the Gloucester, the little converted yacht which had made so noble a record in sinking the Spanish torpedo-boat destroyers at Santiago. After her came the Massachusetts, the Yale, and the Columbia, escorting the transports, whose tardiness had kept the expedition so long upon the sea.

The harbor of Guanica is a picturesque place, a broad level of meadow land extending from the shore-line of its placid bay to a background of high mountains. The village consisted of about a score of prettily painted houses, with a sugar-mill on the right and a block-house some two miles distant on the left. The Spanish flag floated on a small log house upon the beach.

Sounding constantly as she went, the Gloucester pushed boldly into the harbor, from which there soon came back to the fleet the sound of her 6-pounder guns. On reaching the village, she had sent her launch ashore, with about thirty sailors and a Colt rapid-fire gun. Rushing to the house that flew the flag of Spain, in a minute the active tars had it down and the stars and stripes floating in its place, while a hearty cheer greeted the first display of this emblem on Porto Rican soil. In a few minutes more there came a sharp patter of bullets from a squad of soldiers hid among the houses of the town. The rifles of the Americans answered, and the guns of the Gloucester quickly joined in, following the fugitives with 6-pounder shot as they broke and fled towards the hills. The result of the skirmish was four Spaniards killed and not one American wounded.

The men of the Gloucester were warmly cheered for their useful service as the other ships came up the bay, and the landing of the troops was quickly under way, the men forming into companies and occupying points of vantage in the vicinity on reaching shore. A strong detachment was sent out to reconnoitre Yauco, a small place about five miles inland, which formed the terminus of the railroad from Ponce, fifteen miles due east. A high-road, whose condition was the reverse of promising, led to the latter place, but from Ponce to San Juan extended a military road, eighty-five miles long, in admirable condition, and thoroughly adapted for the passage of artillery and army wagons.

On the 27th, two days after Guanica was reached, Commander Davis set out with the Dixie, Gloucester, Annapolis, and Wasp to blockade the port of Ponce and capture lighters for the use of the army. Here no resistance was encountered, the Spanish having evacuated the place, which surrendered to Commander Davis on demand, the American flag being raised in the early morning of the 28th. Sixty lighters and twenty sailing-vessels were captured, and the people received the American troops with wild enthusiasm. Soon after General Miles reached the place, with transports conveying General Ernst's brigade, of Wilson's division, which was at once landed, and was received with an ovation by the citizens.

The scene, indeed, was among the most remarkable of the war. As the ships entered the harbor, they were surrounded by boats filled with citizens shouting "Viva Americanos." The flags of all nations but Spain floated from the houses, and the streets, balconies, and roofs were filled with joyous people, of every class of society, loudly cheering General Miles and the American flag. There did not seem to be a Spanish sympathizer in the town, and the people fraternized with the soldiers as if they were overjoyed at the idea of becoming citizens of the United States.

General Ernst's brigade at once started for the town of Ponce, three miles inland, which capitulated as readily as its port, the Spaniards retreating towards the mountains, and the people welcoming the troops with the warmest enthusiasm. Generals Miles and Wilson were cheered to the echo when they entered the town, in which they were received by the mayor and the British consul, who acted in behalf of the Spaniards in delivering the city into their hands. Stepping on to the balcony after the ceremony, they were received with such a roar of cheers that the modest conquerors hastily withdrew. "The island," said Mayor Colon, "would now enjoy peace and prosperity, and the best citizens were glad the Americans had come."

General Miles then issued the following proclamation:

"In the prosecution of the war against the kingdom of Spain by the people of the United States, in the cause of liberty, justice, and humanity, its military forces have come to occupy the island of Porto Rico. They come bearing the banners of freedom, inspired by a noble purpose, to seek the enemies of our government and of yours, and to destroy or capture all in armed resistance. They bring you the fostering arms of a free people whose greatest power is justice and humanity to all living within their fold. Hence they release you from your former political relations, and it is hoped this will be followed by your cheerful acceptance of the government of the United States.

"The chief object of the American military forces will be to overthrow the armed authority of Spain and give the people of your beautiful island the largest measure of liberty consistent with this military occupation. They have not come to make war on the people of the country, who for centuries have been oppressed, but, on the contrary, they bring protection, not only to yourselves, but to your property ; promote your prosperity and bestow the immunities and blessings of our enlightenment and liberal institutions and government.

"It is not their purpose to interfere with the existing laws and customs which are wholesome and beneficial to the people, so long as they conform to the rules of the military administration, order, and justice. This is not a war of devastation and desolation, but one to give all within the control of the military and naval forces the advantages and blessings of enlightened civilization."

The capture of Ponce was an important step towards the subjugation of the island. It is the second city of the island, with a population of twenty-two thousand, and a jurisdiction numbering forty-seven thousand. Playa, the port, has about five thousand population, and has a spacious harbor, into which vessels of twenty-five feet draught can enter. Ponce was founded in 1600 by Ponce de Leon, whose name it bears. It possesses a number of handsome edifices, and occupies one of the healthiest and most agreeable situations on the island.

The first opposition to our troops, beyond that of the skirmish at Guanica, occurred on the succeeding day at Yauco, near which the Spaniards ambushed eight companies of Massachusetts and Illinois regiments. The enemy was repulsed and driven to a ridge a mile away, from which a body of cavalry charged the advancing infantry. They in turn were driven back and retreated to Yauco, leaving four dead on the field. No Americans were killed and only three were slightly wounded. On the following day Yauco was occupied, and the troops from Guanica began an overland march upon Ponce. So far not a man had been killed on the American side.

The business of Ponce, momentarily checked, was soon in full tide again, those citizens who had fled to the woods and hills with their valuables quickly returning, and banks and stores being opened for trade. The competition of the merchants for the American dollar was matched by the competition of the people for the American flag, the stock of flags on hand being soon so reduced that General Miles felt it necessary to cable home, "Please send any national colors that can be spared, to be given to the different municipalities." On the 31st he telegraphed as follows:

"Volunteers are surrendering themselves with arms and ammunition. Four-fifths of the people are overjoyed at the arrival of the army. Two thousand from one place have volunteered to serve with it. They are bringing in transportation, beef, cattle, and other needed supplies. The custom-house has already yielded fourteen thousand dollars. As soon as all the troops are disembarked, they will be in readiness to move."

On the same day the town of Juan Diaz, eight miles from Ponce on the road to San Juan, was occupied, the people greeting the American flag with the same enthusiasm as at Ponce. A similar feeling was manifested at Yauco, whose mayor issued a grandiloquent proclamation, saying,—

"This is a day of glorious remembrance for each son of this beloved isle, because for the first time there waves over it the flag of stars, planted in the name of the United States of America by the major-general of the American army, Señor Miles."

He concluded with,—

"Citizens, long live the government of the United States of America. Hail to its valiant troops! Hail, Porto Rico, always American!

"El Alcalde, FRANCISCO MAGIA.
"YAUCO, PORTO RICO, UNITED STATES OF AMERICA."

Thus far the Spaniards had shown no disposition to make a stand against the Americans, though they might have attacked with effect some of the small American garrisons. Colonel Hulings held Juan Diaz with but two companies, who might have been flanked and cut off by the Spaniards; yet they were not molested, nor were any of the little detachments which he sent out for reconnoitring purposes, though the fields of tall sugar-cane bordering the roads offered abundant opportunities for ambushes.

There was reason to believe, however, that the Spaniards were preparing to give the Americans a warm reception at Aibonito, where the military road to San Juan crosses the mountains, a point which presents excellent opportunities for defence. General Miles received information that this road had been mined by the enemy, who had also hidden explosives in the wayside bushes. These defences lay between Juan Diaz and Aibonito, at which town was a considerable body of troops prepared to offer a stout resistance. Miles, therefore, determined to foil them by a change of plan, and to approach San Juan by a different route.

In pursuance of this new plan, movements were made in various directions, troops being advanced on lines east and west of the imperilled situation. Their outposts in a few days were twenty miles to the north of Ponce, the several movements being so co-ordinated that the Spaniards at Aibonito were likely to find themselves beset on every side, and in danger of capture unless they should make a hasty retreat upon San Juan.

General Brooke, with a force of twelve hundred men, proceeded on transports to Arroyo, whence his advance, on August 5, reached the town of Guayama, on the eastern side of the island, due south from San Juan. They found here a Spanish force of about five hundred men, but a mere skirmish sufficed to drive them out, the sole loss being one Spaniard killed and two or three on each side wounded. From there the line of march lay to Cayey, farther inland, a position from which the military road to San Juan could be seized beyond the points where mines had been placed.

This movement to the east was paralleled by one to the west, General Roy Stone occupying Adjuntas, to the north of Ponce, and reaching, by the 4th, the town of Utado, fifteen miles farther inland and near the centre of the island. The road between these places was not adapted to the transportation of wagons and artillery; but General Stone soon had a force of five hundred natives at work, making the way passable. His route lay towards Arecibo, on the northern coast, where transports could meet him with the guns and wagons, and whence a railroad and a good dirt road extended to San Juan.

The important town of Coama, midway between Ponce and Guayama, remained unoccupied, but the advance

was rapidly approaching it, a reconnoitring party of about twenty men advancing to the suburbs on the evening of August 1. Here they opened fire on the volunteer pickets, who immediately fled. The town was not taken, however, until the 9th, when General Ernst's brigade advanced upon it, while the Sixteenth Pennsylvania, under Colonel Hulings, made a flank movement through the mountains and struck the Aibonito road half a mile beyond the town, thus cutting off the retreat of the garrison. The Spanish force, one hundred and fifty in number, was captured.

Other events of passing interest took place elsewhere. An advance guard, reconnoitring northwest of Guanica, came upon a strong Spanish force in the hills near Hormigueros, north of Mayaguez. A sharp encounter took place, the enemy being dislodged with considerable loss. The American loss was two killed and fourteen wounded. From that point a march on Mayaguez, a place of some importance on the western border of the island, was contemplated. At Cape San Juan, the northeastern point of land on the island, a landing had been effected, and the light-house was held by forty American sailors, who were attacked by a force of eight hundred Spaniards before daybreak on August 9. They were driven back by shells from the Amphitrite, the Cincinnati, and the tug Leyden, suffering severely for their temerity.

Thus on the south, the west, and the east the American forces were pushing forward into the island, meeting with scarcely any resistance, and received by the natives with a flattering greeting at all points.

The Spanish leaders seemed to have based their sole hopes of a successful resistance on the garrison of

Aibonito, on which mountain stronghold General Miles was moving his troops from several directions. By the 11th a cavalry advance reached a point within three miles of the town, where it was fired upon by the Spanish outpost, strongly posted with artillery on a high hill that commanded the military road. A sharp skirmish took place, none of the Americans being injured. By the 13th the invading army had gained favorable positions in all quarters. General Schwan had reached Mayaguez, General Henry was within fifteen miles of Arecibo, General Brooke had advanced beyond Guayama, and was on the point of attacking a strong Spanish position on the road to Cayey. An artillery duel had just taken place with a strongly posted Spanish force near Coamo. At Aibonito the enemy's batteries on the heights had been shelled on the 12th. General Wilson was moving to turn the right flank of the Spanish, whose rear was threatened by General Brooke. All was ready for what might have proved a severe and sanguinary battle, when news reached the island and spread to the camps that put an end to all hostilities. "Cease action!" shouted Lieutenant McLaughlin, riding up to a battery that was about to fire on the Spanish works before Guayama.

"Why?" came the wondering question.

"The war is over," was the reply. "A peace protocol was signed at Washington yesterday, and all is at an end."

It came in time to save the Spaniards from inevitable defeat. In a week more the whole of Porto Rico would probably have been in American hands.

The tidings of the treaty of peace put a stop to several active movements of hostility elsewhere. At Manzanillo, in Cuba, a severe bombardment was in progress,

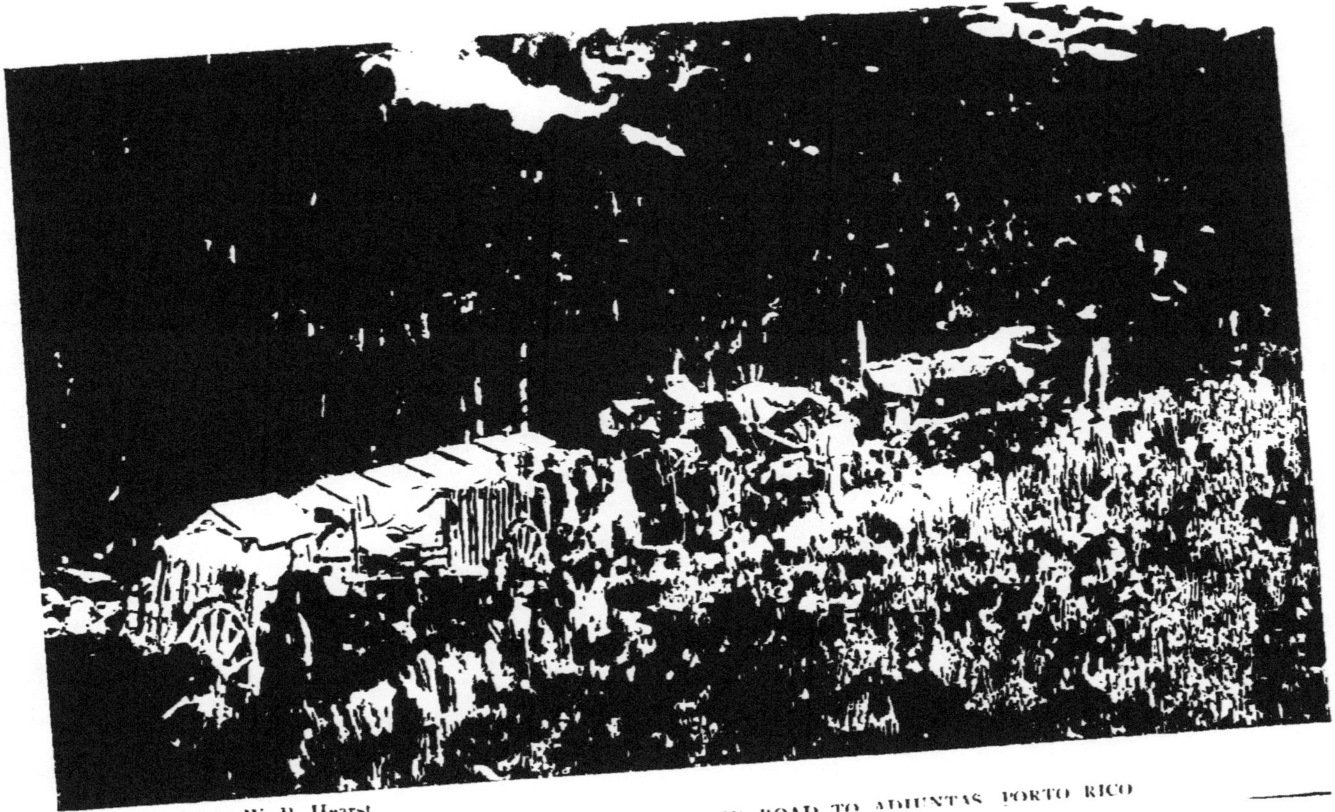

Copyright, 1898, by W. R. Hearst

AMERICAN SOLDIERS IN THE BOUGH MUD ROAD TO ADJUNTAS PORTO RICO

which continued through the afternoon and evening of the 12th, and was resumed on the morning of the 13th. The town was summoned to surrender, the authorities being given three hours in which to capitulate. When a flag of truce appeared on the Spanish side, the natural implication was that they were ready to treat. But when it reached the American ships, their commander was handed a cable message from General Shafter to the effect that peace had been declared and that hostilities must cease. The guns had fired their last shots.

Another engagement was in progress at the port of Caibarien, on the north coast of Santa Clara, whither the Mangrove had gone to protect the landing of a Cuban expedition. She found here the Spanish gunboat Hernan Cortes and a smaller gunboat, which were anchored near the shore in shoal water. The Mangrove had only two 6-pounders, while the gunboats were much better armed, and there were several pieces of artillery mounted on shore. Yet, in despite of this superiority of force, the little tug made an attack on the Spanish boats, reply being made from ship and shore with artillery and Mauser rifles. The Hernan Cortes carried two 4.7-inch guns, whose shells exploded all about the Mangrove.

Suddenly there appeared flags of truce, one on the small gunboat and two on shore, and a boat put off with a Spanish officer on board. On reaching the Mangrove, he announced, "Peace is proclaimed, and I have instructions for your commanding officer from the military commander of this district." This commander had been telegraphed information of the fight, and had at once sent word that peace was restored and the fight must cease.

The final and the most successful shots from Morro Castle, Havana, were fired on the morning of August 12 at Commodore Howell's flag-ship, the San Francisco, the monitor Miantonomoh, and the yacht Sylvia, then on blockade duty. The ships had orders not to attack the batteries and turned to get out of range. As they did so, a 10- or 12-inch shell struck the stern of the San Francisco, tearing a hole about a foot in diameter, and making a complete wreck of the commodore's quarters. His bookcase was smashed to fragments. No one was injured. Before the day closed, the peace protocol was signed and the long blockade was at an end.

CHAPTER XX.

THE SIEGE OF MANILA.

THE war with Spain had two widely separated fields of action,—the islands of Cuba and Porto Rico in the Atlantic and the Philippine Islands in the Pacific, nearly half the circumference of the earth intervening. In the former field warlike events were far more varied and continuous, and therefore we have given undivided attention to these after describing the great victory in Manila Bay. We must now return to the Philippines, where, though the American forces were quiescent, there had been no small degree of warlike activity on the part of the natives.

In the preceding chapters concerning the Philippines mention has been made of the compact that ended the rebellion at the close of 1897, and the rise of the rebels again in 1898. This second outbreak did not become active until after May 24, on which day General Aguinaldo and twelve others of the insurgent leaders landed at Cavite, having come from Hong-Kong on the despatch-boat McCullough. The return of this able leader at once gave vitality to the insurgent movement, and a bold advance against Manila was made. At that time there were said to be thirty thousand natives in the field, though they were poorly supplied with arms.

On the night of the 24th the insurgents made a reconnoissance in force against the Spanish outposts, and found them to be protected by guns which had been turned landward from the shore batteries. During the succeeding days they were actively aggressive, the principal engagement being on the left branch of the Zapote, which they waded during a typhoon, stormed the banks for several miles, and drove the Spaniards from their trenches with knives. Other fights took place around Manila, the insurgents apparently having an ample supply of arms and ammunition, given them in part by Admiral Dewey. One result of their operations was a large number of prisoners, about eighteen hundred in all, whom they brought into Cavite. In addition, two batteries had been taken and the whole province of Cavite was in their hands. By May 31 they had taken several places in the vicinity of the city, whose suburbs they were attacking, and which they encircled for a distance of seven miles. The Spanish authorities had offered a reward of twenty-five thousand dollars for Aguinaldo, dead or alive, an appeal to treachery which fortunately failed in its effect.

Admiral Dewey, fearing a massacre if the city should be taken, set limits to the advance of the insurgents, forbidding them to cross the Malolele River, seven miles south of Manila. They were told that if they should seek to disobey this order, the gunboat Petrel would be stationed there to bombard them. He was not willing to permit "hordes of passionate semi-savages to storm a civilized metropolis," and determined to hold them in check until the American troops should arrive. Meanwhile, the Spaniards felt themselves to be in a serious strait. On June 3 Captain-General Augustin cabled to Madrid:

"The situation is very grave. Aguinaldo has succeeded in stirring up the country, and the telegraph-lines and railways are being cut. I am without communication with the provinces. The province of Cavite has completely rebelled, and the towns and villages are occupied by numerous bands.

"I am striving to raise the courage of the inhabitants, and will exhaust every means of resistance; but I distrust the natives and the volunteers because there have already been many desertions. Bacoor and Imas have already been seized by the enemy. The insurrection has reached great proportions, and, if I cannot count upon the support of the country, the forces at my disposal will not suffice to hold the ground against two enemies."

Aguinaldo, on landing, had issued three proclamations. One of these based his return on the failure of the Spaniards to carry out their promised reforms and the support offered by the United States. He proposed to act as dictator until the islands were completely free, when a constitutional republic, with president, cabinet, and congress, would be established. The second proclamation forbade all peace negotiations with the Spaniards, and the third forbade robbery and acts of violence. The prisoners in his hands were well treated.

On the 12th a despatch from Dewey said, "There is little change in the situation since my telegram of June 3. Insurgents continue hostilities and have practically surrounded Manila. They have taken two thousand five hundred Spanish prisoners, whom they treat most humanely. They do not intend to take the city at the present time. The health of the squadron continues excellent. The German commander-in-chief arrived to-day. Three German, one British, one French, one Japanese men-of-war in port. Another German man-of-war is expected."

By the 20th of June the insurgents had taken four thousand Spanish and one thousand native prisoners, and had closed in on the city until it was very closely besieged. On the 12th they had proclaimed in Old Cavite the establishment of a provisional government, a declaration of independence of Spanish authority being read and General Aguinaldo elected president. The new president informed Mr. Williams, the United States consul, that this action was taken merely for purposes of cohesion, and that the insurgents desired to make an American colony of the Philippine Islands. He declared that no other country should possess the Philippines without fighting for them, and that if the United States declined the proffered gift, an independent republic would be founded.

Day by day the situation of the Spaniards in Manila grew more desperate. On June 23 Augustin cabled as follows to Madrid:

"The situation is still grave. I continue to maintain my position inside the line of block-houses, but the enemy is increasing in numbers as the rebels occupy the provinces, which are surrendering. Torrential rains are inundating the intrenchments, rendering the work of defence difficult. The numbers of sick among the troops are increasing, making the situation very distressing and causing increased desertions of the native soldiers. It is estimated that the insurgents number thirty thousand armed with rifles and one hundred thousand armed with swords, etc. Aguinaldo has summoned me to surrender, but I have treated his proposals with disdain, for I am resolved to maintain the sovereignty of Spain and the honor of the flag to the last extremity."

Yet, despite the confessedly desperate situation of

Augustin, he contrived to hold his own against the natives during the succeeding month, the Spaniards, though driven from their outpost works, holding on to their interior intrenchments with obstinate valor. It began to appear as if, despite the impetuosity of the natives, they could not succeed in their purpose without American aid. They were now, however, in possession of artillery, and had the city almost completely invested, while there was much sickness among the defenders and food had grown very scarce. On the other hand, anarchy appeared to have broken out among the natives, and Aguinaldo's position as dictator was by no means assured. The restraint exercised by the Americans over the insurgents was thought to have caused much irritation among the latter, and decreased their desire to become citizens or subjects of the United States.

Admiral Dewey, during these operations, maintained a position of masterly inactivity, keeping a controlling hand over Aguinaldo and his native forces, but desisting from any hostile movement towards the city other than that of the blockade. He was waiting, doubtless with impatience, the arrival of the troops, whose coming had been so annoyingly delayed, and his position was a very trying one, requiring the exercise of the highest judgment and discretion.

The first expedition of troops, conveyed by the cruiser Charleston, entered Manila Bay on the 30th of June. On the 20th it had reached Guahan, or Guam, the largest of the Ladrone Islands, a group belonging to Spain. The chief town of this island, St. Ignacio de Agano, was defended by two forts, which were summoned to surrender by a shot from the Charleston. Never was there a more amusing capture of a town. The commandant, who knew nothing of the war, supposed the shot to be a friendly salute, and sent off a boat to the Charleston with regrets that, being out of powder, he was unable to return the salute. He was soon undeceived, and the governor and other officials of the island were taken on board and brought to Cavite, a force being left in charge of the captured town. On July 6 the troops were unloaded from the transports at Cavite, and the first step was taken towards an assault on Manila by land.

Dewey, meanwhile, maintained the blockade, but not without a cause of irritation in the attitude of the Germans, who had sent thither a far larger fleet than any other nation, and were thought to have intentions of interfering in the settlement of the Philippine question. What seemed an open indication of such a purpose was manifested on July 6, when the insurgents informed Dewey that the German gunboat Irene had refused to permit them to attack the Spaniards on Grande Island, in Subic Bay.

Admiral Dewey had hitherto maintained an attitude of diplomatic friendliness towards the Germans, but this reported interference called for decisive action, and the cruisers Raleigh and Concord were at once sent to investigate the affair. On entering the bay, the Raleigh fired upon the forts, on observing which the Irene slipped her cable and steamed out by the other channel. No resistance was made by the Spaniards, and the garrison, thirteen hundred in number, was quickly surrendered. The Spanish seemed endeavoring to defend the bay by submarine mines, in order to hold it as a place of rendezvous for Camara's fleet, supposed to be on its way from Spain. On returning to Manila, the commander of the Irene explained that he had interfered "in the

THE WAR WITH SPAIN. 353

cause of humanity," and offered to hand over to Admiral Dewey the refugees he had brought from the island. These Dewey declined to receive. The action of the Germans created much irritation in the United States, where many considered it little short of an act of war. But this feeling subsided when later despatches gave the details of the affair. Admiral Dewey's despatch contained no indication that he considered the action of the Irene as important.

The second American expedition from San Francisco reached Manila Bay on July 19, and the disembarkation immediately began, the troops landing at Paranajo, two miles south of Manila, the cruiser Boston being detailed to cover the landing. The troops of the first expedition, under General Anderson, were still at Cavite, though on the 19th the First California Regiment was pushed forward to Janbo, two miles from the Spanish lines. General Francis V. Greene, the leader of the second expedition, took command of the advance, General Anderson remaining in Cavite. As regards the condition of affairs in Manila, reports came that the inhabitants were reduced almost to a state of starvation, new supplies of food, either by land or water, being cut off, and the old stock nearly exhausted. Abattoirs for the slaughter of horses and dogs were opened. Sickness, due to the wretched food and impure water, and aggravated by the rains, which fell daily in torrents, was said to be very prevalent, and Manila to have reached almost the extreme limit of its powers of resistance. The condition of affairs found on the surrender of the city, however, indicated that these reports greatly exaggerated the situation, the people showing no evidence of the work of famine.

Dewey still waited. A third expedition, under General Merritt, military commander of the Philippines, was nearly due, and the monitors Monterey and Monadnock were well on their way. He had no desire to capture the city till assured of his ability to hold it, and to control the natives if they should attempt to make trouble. On the 25th, Merritt arrived in the Newport, accompanied and followed by a number of transports, the strength of the expedition being about five thousand officers and men. He at once took command of the land forces, establishing his head-quarters in Cavite arsenal.

It was a season of storm. Rains of unusual heaviness fell daily, and high winds made the waters of the harbor so rough that it was impossible to land the troops, who remained on the transports for a week or more after their arrival. The Spanish commander in the city took advantage of this opportunity to make an attack in force on the American troops, perhaps with the hope of driving them back before they were reinforced.

The attack seems to have been precipitated by a movement of General Greene to extend his lines. On the 31st of July his trenches faced the Spanish works, extending some three hundred yards from the beach and joining the insurgent lines on their left flank. This, however, was a feast day of the natives, who, regardless of military considerations, withdrew into their camp, leaving the right flank of the Americans exposed. Two companies of the Tenth Pennsylvania and the Utah Battery were ordered to fill the gap, but before they could fairly do so the Spaniards were upon them, three thousand strong.

It was an excellent opportunity for a surprise, a tropical typhoon raging and the rain descending in blinding

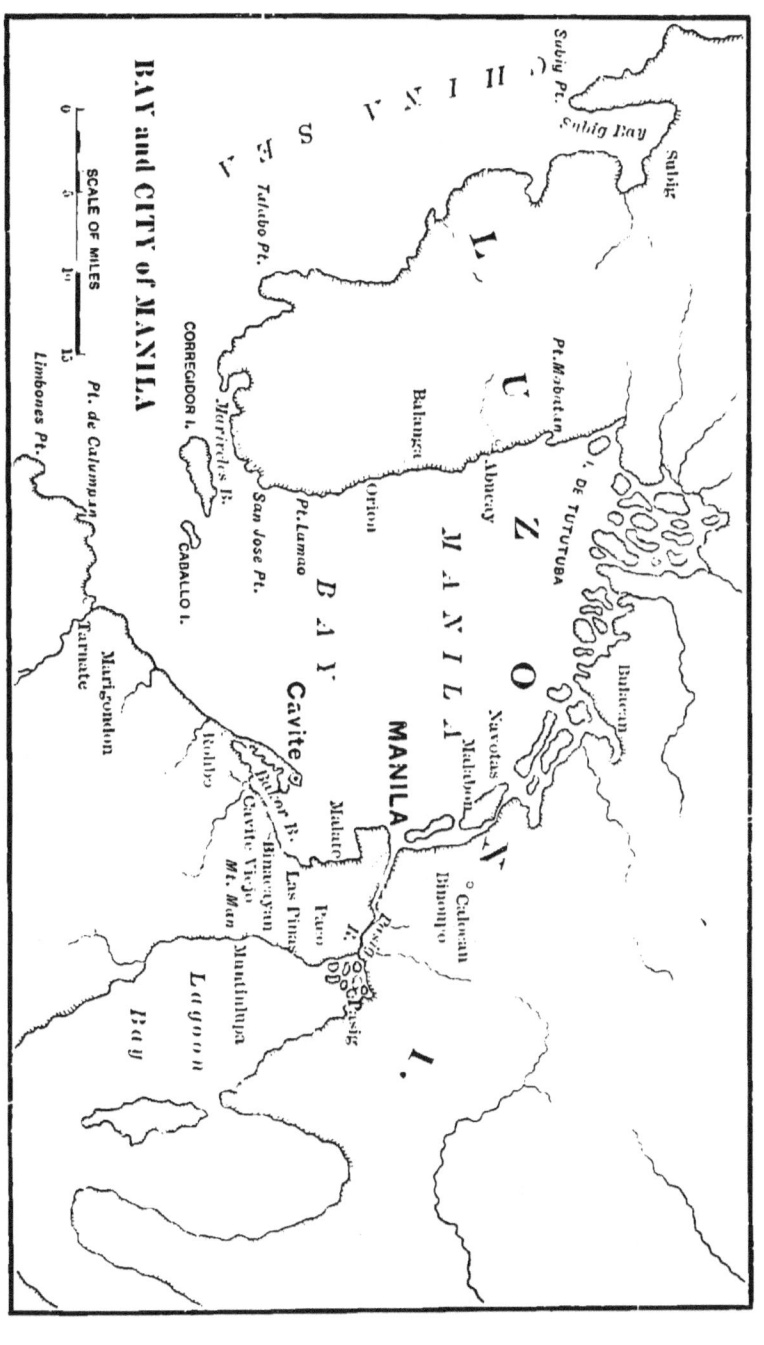

torrents, yet the Pennsylvanians stoutly held their ground in the face of a fierce fire, which they briskly returned. The Utah Battery was dragged to the front through mud axle-deep, and poured in a destructive enfilading fire on the enemy. The alarm rapidly spreading, the First California was rushed to the point of danger, with two companies of the Third Artillery, armed with rifles. The charge of the enemy had carried them to the top of the trenches by the time these reinforcements arrived, but the fire proved too severe for them to face and they fell back in disorder. Several desperate charges were made with the same result, and in the end the Spanish soldiers retreated into the bush, from which they kept up an incessant fire on the road leading to Manila, along which they seemingly expected the Americans to advance. But the latter had exhausted their ammunition and made no attempt to follow the enemy.

The fight was renewed on the night of August 1, and again on the succeeding night, but no infantry charges were made, the enemy confining themselves to the use of artillery, to which the Utah Battery replied. The loss in the three days' fighting was fourteen killed and forty-four wounded, the Spanish loss being much heavier, though the numbers were unknown.

This vigorous effort to check the American advance had proved an utter failure, and the fall of the city was evidently near at hand. On the 4th of August the Monterey entered Manila harbor. The Monadnock was expected in a few days, and the time had arrived to bring the long period of suspense to an end.

The final operations began on August 7, when Admiral Dewey and General Merritt sent a joint notice to the Spanish commander, giving him forty-eight hours to remove non-combatants preliminary to a bombardment of the city. They had a new man to deal with. Governor-General Augustin had withdrawn from military control on the plea that Spain was sending him no help. He was succeeded by General Jaudenes, from whom came a courteous reply to the American note, thanking the commanders for their humane sentiments, but stating that he had no place of refuge for the large number of sick and wounded, women and children, who were within the walls. During the interval, the German residents and many of those of other countries took the opportunity to leave the city on the war-ships of their respective nations.

On the 9th, at the end of the period granted, a second joint note was sent to General Jaudenes, demanding a surrender on the ground of the hopeless condition of the Spanish forces and the suffering in store for the sick and the non-combatants in case of assault. In reply, time was asked to communicate with Madrid by way of Hong-Kong; but this respite was refused, and the ships began to strip for action, a second respite being granted until noon of Wednesday, the 10th. All the boats and woodwork that could be spared from the ships were sent to Cavite Navy-Yard, splinter nets were spread, guns cleaned and oiled, and other preparations made. The foreign war-vessels in the harbor took positions to observe the action, the British and Japanese ships anchoring near our fleet, the German and French taking positions opposite. Thus they seemed to separate into two groups, the friendly and the lukewarm.

On Wednesday morning the ships were cleared for action and the men at their quarters, when a signal came from the Olympia, "Action postponed." General Merritt had found that the army was not ready. It was understood by this time that the Spanish resistance would be in form only, sufficient to preserve the honor of their arms, but the American leaders took no chances and prepared to meet a stubborn resistance if it should come.

The truce now continued until Saturday, the 13th. At 8.45 A.M. on that day the fleet got under way, the Concord taking her position on the north end of the line and the Monterey standing in close to the Lunetta battery. The Charleston, Baltimore, and Boston faced the same battery farther out, and the Olympia, Raleigh, and Petrel took positions opposite the Malate forts. With them were the McCullough and the Callao, the latter a gunboat captured from the Spaniards.

At 9.30 the Olympia opened fire, followed quickly by the Petrel and the Raleigh, while the little Callao, which had steamed close in shore, opened briskly from her single rapid-fire gun. The first shots all fell short, as if with the purpose of satisfying Spanish honor without loss. But no signs of surrender came, and the ships began to fire with better aim. Clouds of smoke, dust, and flying fragments rose above Malate, on which the whole attack was directed, and it was evident that the position would soon be made untenable. No reply came, and no shots were fired at the Lunetta and Pasig batteries, which continued silent. At 10.50 the Olympia signalled, "Cease firing," and the Spaniards were asked by the international code signal if they had surrendered. The result was not known in the fleet until 2.30 P.M., when the Olympia set the signal, "The enemy has surrendered," and wild cheers of exultation broke from the crews.

While the ships were thus engaged, a more sanguinary

contest was taking place on shore. The Utah Battery kept time with the ships in playing on the Malate works, which answered, though rather feebly. In less than half an hour after the bombardment began General Greene decided on an advance, signalling to the ships to cease firing. They kept on, however, the heavy rain rendering the signals invisible. All the morning rain had been pouring down in sudden gushes, but in spite of this the troops sprang forward at the word, moving swiftly along the beach, with colors flying and band playing. A creek lay in their way, but they plunged in it and waded across. At eleven o'clock the Malate fort was occupied, the Spanish flag hauled down, and the American flag waving above its walls.

The hardest fighting was done by the right wing, led by General McArthur, with the Astor Battery, his attack having no support from the guns of the fleet. The California troops, galled by a hot fire from Spanish sharpshooters in houses on the right, charged into the Ermita suburb, where a stubborn contest took place in Calle Real with the Spaniards, who had barricaded the streets. They were attacked and driven out with pistols, the clearing of Calle Real ending the assault. About noon a white flag was floating over the city walls, indicating that the struggle was at an end. The loss on the American side had been eight killed and forty wounded. The Spanish loss was much greater, though the number was unknown. Before the surrender the gunboat Cebu, in the Pasig River, was set on fire, and several smaller boats were destroyed.

Flag-Lieutenant Brumby went ashore about noon and had an interview with General Jaudenes concerning the terms of capitulation. General Merritt subsequently joined in the conference, the terms agreed upon being, in brief outline, the following :

Surrender of Manila and its suburbs.

Officers to retain their swords and personal effects, but not their horses.

Men to surrender their arms, prisoners of war being supplied from the treasury fund until exhausted, then by the Americans.

The safety of life and property of Spaniards to be guaranteed as far as possible.

The question of transporting the troops to Spain to be decided by the American government, and that of returning their arms to the soldiers to be left to the decision of General Merritt.

All public property to be surrendered and banks to continue in business under existing regulations.

Under these terms about seven thousand soldiers were surrendered as prisoners. The insurgents were not permitted to take part in the attack on the city, being kept in the rear of the Americans. After the surrender they were forbidden to enter Manila unless unarmed, fear of violence being entertained.

As soon as the terms of capitulation were signed, Lieutenant Brumby hastened to lower a Spanish flag, as an indication of the end of Spanish dominion over Manila. The flag lowered was a large one that waved over Fort Santiago in the northern portion of the walled city. As it descended, and the Stars and Stripes rose in its place, tears flowed from the eyes of many of the observers. It meant the end of a once vast colonial empire of the Spanish nation. The event was greeted by the guns of the fleet and loud cheers from all the Americans within view.

An event succeeded that roused some severe criticism in the United States, the departure of General Augustin, with his family and suite, on the German war-steamer Kaiserin Augusta, which left the harbor immediately after the surrender. It was looked upon as in line with the general discourtesy with which the Germans had been charged throughout the blockade of Manila. But later advices showed it to have been done with the concurrence of Admiral Dewey, and the feeling subsided.

With a proclamation by General Merritt, announcing a military occupation by the United States of the island of Luzon, the protection of all inhabitants in their personal and religious rights, and the retention of existing laws until notice of change, the circle of military affairs in the Philippine Islands ceased. The taking of Manila, indeed, was the final military and naval event of the war. The peace protocol had been signed the day before, and the war with Spain was at an end.

CHAPTER XXI.

FROM WAR TO PEACE.

THE war of 1898 was in some respects a singular one. It was fought entirely outside the two countries concerned,—that is, if we consider the colonies of Spain as no part of the country itself. It was fought almost entirely by the navy, there being but one battle on land in which large armies took part; yet throughout the war less than a score of men lost their lives on the ships of the United States, and not a ship was seriously injured, while the navy of Spain was practically annihilated. It was a war in which all the successes were on one side, all the failures on the other, and in which the entire loss of life in battle on the part of the United States was but a few hundred men. That of Spain it is impossible to estimate.

But while the war did not touch the mainland of the two countries concerned, its effects made themselves strongly felt there. To the United States it seemed to bring prosperity and glory. Industry advanced, commerce increased, values grew, and money and food became superabundant; while the eyes of Europe for the first time became fully opened to the greatness of the republic of the West, and came to look upon it as a new-world power, to be taken seriously into account in all future rearrangements of the status of the nations. Four months of war had surprisingly changed the relations of the United States with the great powers abroad.

To Spain, on the other hand, it brought loss and degradation. That country came out of it shorn of her most valuable colonies, overloaded with debt, virtually bankrupt, and greatly lowered in rank among the nations. While the United States obtained all the money needed in the war from her own people at a low rate of interest, and took a large part of it directly from her treasury, Spain sought in vain to borrow from the capitalists of the world, who refused to trust their money in such doubtful hands. Yet, if she could have borrowed millions, they would have been of little use to her; for, beyond sending one fleet across the ocean to be annihilated, she was obliged to let the war be fought by the forces in her colonies, the soldiers sent over in previous years to subdue the insurrections. These once conquered, Spain's power of defence in her colonies was at an end, for she was utterly unable to come to their aid.

Such were the respective conditions of the two countries. Some relation of the events that took place in each during the war comes here in place, as leading to the terms upon which peace was granted. In Spain a persistent system of falsification prevailed. The newspapers were not permitted to tell the truth, and it was only through indirect channels that a knowledge of the true state of affairs made its way among the people. The country was so deeply permeated with the elements of revolution, so many diverse factions—Carlists, republicans, anarchists—stood ready to rise against the government, that the rulers dared not admit the losses of their arms, lest they should be driven in disgrace from the land.

And yet the revolution that impended was not a result

of Spain's misfortunes in war, but of her misgovernment and oppression in peace. The majority of the people were said to be absolutely without interest in the war, being so affected by the misery that prevailed at home as to take no concern in the affairs of the colonies. Hunger and destitution were the controlling forces; the bread question was far more prominent than the war question, and the outbreaks that took place and the troubles that threatened were instigated by starvation rather than war. Spain was in a state of ferment which threatened every social and political institution of the land, and the government was in no condition to prosecute a war abroad while at home she seemed trembling on the verge of a volcano. Her wisest statesmen felt that the contest was hopeless, but feared the effect of a confession of defeat. And the fatal Spanish spirit of procrastination was by no means absent, uselessly protracting the struggle when every day added to the difficulties of the situation and the chances of a sterner penalty being imposed in the end.

A few words will suffice to indicate the financial ability of the United States to prosecute the war. As a preliminary to the contest, $50,000,000 were taken in one sum from the treasury to aid in the work of preparation. At the end of the contest the treasury held more than $200,000,000 in gold. The total direct cost of the war was about $130,000,000, to provide the funds for which, without disturbing the ordinary financial operations of the government a war-loan of $200,000,000 at three per cent. interest was offered to the people, care being taken that small subscriptions should be given the preference and that it should be in every respect a popular loan. The loan was taken with the greatest avidity, the offers made amounting to the vast sum of $1,325,000,000, or nearly seven times the amount of the issue. Nearly three hundred thousand subscriptions were received, the books closing on July 14, and the loan was distributed to the small bidders, the upper limit of allotments being $4500, while nearly half the total amount went to subscribers for $500 and under.

To provide funds for the repayment of this loan and the meeting of the war expenses a new internal tax law was passed by Congress, embracing stamp taxes on a great variety of legal and business documents, license taxes on places of amusement, bankers, and brokers, and taxes on legacies, fermented liquors, tobacco, tea, and mixed flour. The law went into effect, except in the case of the last-mentioned items, on July 1, 1898. It promised to yield in no great time sufficient funds to pay all the expenses of the war.

The ability of the United States to meet all demands likely to be made upon its resources, in war or peace, was shown in a statement issued in July from the Government Bureau of Foreign Commerce, whose statistics indicated an extraordinary development of American commerce during the fiscal year ending July 1, 1898. This statement showed that the exports of the United States during that year had enormously exceeded the imports, and that these exports consisted of articles of manufacture to a degree greatly exceeding those of any preceding year.

Mr. Frederick Emory, who prepared the report, referred to this trade development as "an American invasion of the markets of the world." In his view the United States was no longer merely the "granary of the world," since, while its export of agricultural products was extraordinarily great, its sales abroad of manufactured goods had greatly extended, in spite of obstructions and discriminations in foreign countries. "Notwithstanding," he said, "that organized effort to reach foreign markets for our manufactures is as yet in its infancy, the ability of the United States to compete successfully with the most advanced industrial nations in any part of the world, as well as with those nations in their home markets, can no longer be seriously questioned." We are being converted, he said, "slowly but surely from a people absorbed with the internal development of a virgin continent into one of the great commercial powers of the world, with the international interests and responsibilities which such a position naturally implies."

The war with Spain promised to add greatly in its results to our position and interests as a world power, by giving us valuable colonial possessions in near and distant seas. One of these new possessions, the Hawaiian archipelago, while not directly, was indirectly a result of the war. This important group of Pacific islands had for several years been waiting to be accepted or rejected by the United States. A request from Hawaii for annexation several years before had been declined by President Cleveland. The subject of annexation was brought up again in 1898, passed the House in the form of a resolution, and was passed by the Senate with a two-thirds vote on July 6. President McKinley immediately signed the resolution, and the long contest over Hawaii was at an end.

On the 7th Secretary Long gave orders for the departure of the cruiser Philadelphia from Mare Island for Hawaii with the important news. The Philadelphia had taken no part in the war, being under repair since its beginning. She was now given the distinguished honor of carrying the flag of the United States to those islands, and by this act including them within the American Union. The duty of hoisting the flag was assigned to Admiral Miller, then in command of the Pacific Station, the President appointing a commission to frame laws suitable for the new acquisition of the United States. The Philadelphia sailed on the 27th, and the ceremony of final annexation took place on August 12, by an interesting coincidence on the very day on which the protocol of peace with Spain was signed. The ceremony of raising the flag and formally proclaiming the Hawaiian Islands part of the United States was a simple one, Admiral Miller wisely not making it an occasion of ostentation, in view of the fact that the loss of their independence was bitterly opposed by the natives of the islands. Few of them witnessed the ceremony of flag-raising, and the small number who appeared turned their eyes, filled with tears, away from their flag as it came slowly down, to be replaced by the standard of the United States.

The ceremony took place at noon, in the presence of the authorities and all the people of Honolulu except the natives. As the Hawaiian standard fluttered downward to the earth, Admiral Miller gave a signal, the sound of a bugle was heard, and from the ground rose a magnificent American flag, hailed with cheers as it unfurled and floated out on the air, and the inspiring notes of the "Star-Spangled Banner" rang out from the band of the Philadelphia. The President's proclamation was then read, the oath of allegiance to the United States was administered to President Dole and his Cabinet, who for the time being continued in power, the Hawaiian National Guard took the oath at their barracks, and the ceremonies ended. The republic of Hawaii had become part of the United States of America.

Returning to affairs more immediately connected with the war, some reference to the attitude of the powers of Europe seems here demanded. Though these powers, in common with the other civilized nations of the earth, had declared neutrality between the warring nations, some degree of hostility to one or the other parties concerned seemed to underlie their sense of international obligations. The attitude of Germany appeared to indicate that a desire to share in the partition of the Philippine Islands was strongly entertained in that country, and many of the newspapers of Germany and France were strongly pro-Spanish in their comments on the war.

Rumors of a purpose of intervention on the part of the European powers were from time to time set afloat. and the statement was made that several of these powers had it in view to try and make a European question of the hostile relations between Spain and the United States, dealing with these powers as they had dealt with Crete and Greece. If such a design was seriously entertained, dread of how the United States might receive a movement of this character stood seriously in the way of an attempt to put it into effect. And the attitude of Great Britain was an equally serious obstacle to any such project. That country not only was not to be drawn into any scheme of interference, but could not even be trusted to remain neutral. There was the strongest reason to believe that it would aid the United States in resistance to Continental coercion, and the powers of Europe did not dare to array against them, in a transatlantic matter, the British fleet. However all this be, and whether or not such a project was entertained as has been asserted, no open indication of any such purpose was made, and the war remained strictly confined to the two powers concerned. In truth, the real sentiments entertained by Germany and France towards the United States remained undivulged, the views afloat being mainly based on newspaper utterances, not on official acts.

This being the case, and Spain being forced to depend on her own weak self, only one course stood between her and ruin, a request for peace. Such a request the United States had obviously no thought of making, and the continued series of reverses to the arms of Spain made it evident that the longer the war was permitted to continue the greater would be her final loss. It is the custom in modern wars for the conquering nation to make its defeated enemy pay the cost, and the "bill of expenses" was running up at a rapid rate. Spain's only hope lay in an immediate peace, yet she seemed to be the last of the nations to perceive this, and permitted the war to drift on long after wisdom dictated a yielding of her pride and a request for the most favorable terms she could obtain.

The first move of Spain in this direction was made on July 26, three months after the outbreak of the war, through the intermedium of M. Jules Cambon, the French ambassador to the United States. This gentleman called on President McKinley at three o'clock in the afternoon of that day, with the statement that he had been instructed by the Foreign Office at Paris to make a tender of peace to the United States on the part of the Spanish ministry. M. Cambon had been simply authorized to open peace negotiations, but his powers were soon extended to enable him to act as the repre-

THE WAR WITH SPAIN. 369

sentative of Spain in obtaining conditions from the United States.

After full consideration in cabinet meetings and in conferences with M. Cambon, a synopsis of the conditions upon which the United States would consent to an armistice, pending the conclusion of a treaty of peace, was formulated and transmitted to Spain. It was in effect as follows:

The President waived for the time being the question of demanding a pecuniary indemnity from Spain, but required the relinquishment of all claim of sovereignty over or title to the island of Cuba, and the immediate evacuation of that island; the evacuation and cession to the United States of Porto Rico and other islands held by Spain in the West Indies; and the cession of an island in the Ladrone group. The city, bay, and harbor of Manila were to be held by the United States until a commission, to be appointed by the two countries concerned, had decided on what should be done with the Philippines, and had concluded a final treaty of peace on the basis above indicated.

Spain dealt with these terms with considerable deliberation. On August 1 the Cabinet at Madrid held a long session, ending in a despatch to Washington for "further explanation of some difficult points." There was the best of reasons, however, for believing that the Spanish government had no intention of continuing the war, since that must result in the loss of all the Philippines, and possibly a demand for a large money indemnity, while if the terms were quickly accepted the United States would perhaps limit its demand to a coaling and naval station in the Philippines.

Later instructions to M. Cambon were to the effect

that Spain was anxious to retain possession of Luzon, the principal Philippine island, to have her troops depart from Cuba and Porto Rico with all the honors of war, and to have the right to remove all war material from those islands. She also asked to be relieved from paying the debt incurred on account of Cuba and Porto Rico. This last proposition, which would have saddled Cuba with a debt of $550,000,000, incurred in the effort to subdue its inhabitants, the United States was very little likely to accept, and the French ambassador was given to understand that this country would neither modify its propositions nor consent to enter upon peace negotiations until Spain had fully accepted the conditions proposed.

Finding that no better terms were to be had, the Spanish Cabinet, at a meeting held August 7, accepted those offered. Though this information was at once made public in the United States, the answer itself was two days in reaching Washington, it coming *via* Paris, and requiring to be twice translated, put into cipher, and again deciphered. As the paper was a long one, entering into considerable detail, all this took time, and it was not presented to the President by M. Cambon until 5.30 P.M. of August 9. As the answer proved to be a practical acceptance of the American terms, the President directed a protocol, or preliminary basis of a treaty of peace, embodying the propositions made, to be drawn up and submitted to M. Cambon as the representative of Spain. This decision was communicated by M. Cambon to the government at Madrid, from which came an immediate reply authorizing the French ambassador to sign the protocol on behalf of Spain.

It was expected that the protocol would be signed and

the war end on the 10th, but the French ambassador preferred first to transmit its full text to Madrid, that there might be left no room for misunderstanding, his request gaining force from the fact that a few verbal changes had been made in the text. Secretary Day assented to this request, and the protocol was converted into cipher and cabled to Madrid. Authority to sign came back by cable, and the final ceremony of signing took place about 4 P.M. on August 12, at which day and hour the war with Spain came to an end,—for no doubt was felt that the armistice would end in formal peace, Spain being helpless to resist any demands that the United States was likely to make.

The text of the protocol, the signing of which was immediately followed by a proclamation from President McKinley suspending hostilities, was as follows:

"His Excellency M. Cambon, Ambassador Extraordinary and Minister Plenipotentiary of the French republic at Washington, and Mr. William B. Day, Secretary of State of the United States, having received respectively to that effect plenary powers from the Spanish government and the government of the United States, have established and signed the following articles, which define the terms on which the two governments have agreed with regard to the questions enumerated below, and of which the object is the establishment of peace between the two countries, namely:

"ARTICLE 1. Spain will renounce all claim to all sovereignty over and all her rights over the island of Cuba.

"ARTICLE 2. Spain will cede to the United States the island of Porto Rico and the other islands which are at present under the sovereignty of Spain in the

Antilles, as well as an island in the Ladrone Archipelago, to be chosen by the United States.

"ARTICLE 3. The United States will occupy and retain the city and bay of Manila and the port of Manila pending the conclusion of a treaty of peace, which shall determine the control and form of government of the Philippines.

"ARTICLE 4. Spain will immediately evacuate Cuba, Porto Rico, and the other islands now under Spanish sovereignty in the Antilles. To this effect each of the two governments will appoint Commissioners within ten days after the signing of this protocol, and these Commissioners shall meet at Havana within thirty days after the signing of this protocol with the object of coming to an agreement regarding the carrying out of the details of the aforesaid evacuation of Cuba and other adjacent Spanish islands, and each of the two governments shall likewise appoint, within ten days after the signature of this protocol, other Commissioners, who shall meet at San Juan de Porto Rico within thirty days after the signature of this protocol, to agree upon the details of the evacuation of Porto Rico and other islands now under Spanish sovereignty in the Antilles.

"ARTICLE 5. Spain and the United States shall appoint to treat for peace five Commissioners at the most for either country. The Commissioners shall meet in Paris on October 1 at the latest, to proceed to negotiations and to the conclusion of a treaty of peace. This treaty shall be ratified in conformity with the constitutional laws of each of the two countries.

"ARTICLE 6. Once this protocol is concluded and signed, hostilities shall be suspended, and to that effect in the two countries orders shall be given by either government to the commanders of its land and sea forces as speedily as possible.

"Done in duplicate at Washington; read in French and in English by the undersigned, who affix at the foot of the document their signatures and seals. August 12, 1898."

The ceremony of signing was one of some interest, and its chief incidents may be given in a few words. The President, whose deep interest in everything relating to the war made him desirous of seeing its concluding event, had expressed a wish to be present at the signing, and was informed by Secretary Day that he had arranged with M. Cambon for the performance of this ceremony at four o'clock. In consequence it took place at the White House, instead of at the State Department, as had been previously arranged.

At five minutes to four o'clock the Secretary of State made his appearance, coming through a heavy downpour of rain. He was accompanied by the three Assistant Secretaries, Mr. Cridler bringing the two copies of the protocol which had been prepared. Ten minutes later M. Cambon and his secretary, M. Thiebaut, appeared at the north entrance, and were ushered into the Cabinet-room, where Secretary Day formally presented them to President McKinley and the others present.

There was no delay in the work to be done. The document, as stated, had been prepared in duplicate, the text being given in parallel columns, one English, the other French; one having the first column in English, the other in French. The latter was first signed, "M. Jules Cambon" on the upper line, "William R. Day" on the lower. In the other copy the signatures were reversed. The latter copy was to go into the archives of the State Department, the former to be transmitted to Madrid. When it came to attaching the seals, it was found that though wax had been provided, no means of heating it were on hand, and this was finally done by the aid of a candle found in a common candlestick in the President's bedroom.

President McKinley strongly expressed his satisfaction at the conclusion of the ceremony, and earnestly thanked the two French gentlemen for their useful services in bringing about the result. Congratulations were exchanged among all present, followed by the President affixing his signature to the proclamation announcing the armistice, and the passing around of a box of the White House cigars. As a souvenir of the event, Assistant Secretary Moore secured the pen with which the signing had been done. Within a brief period telegrams were being sent to Cuba, Porto Rico, and Hong-Kong ordering the cessation of hostilities, and before the day ended the news of peace had spread around the earth. From Hong-Kong a swift British steamer sped away at full speed to carry the welcome news to Manila, before which far-off city, a few hours afterwards, the final battle of the war was fought. The Hispano-American war ended with the falling of that city of the Eastern seas into American hands.

CHAPTER XXII.

FINAL CONSIDERATIONS.

OUR history is practically ended. We set out to describe the war with Spain, and have carried that forward to its concluding event. The signing of the protocol was equivalent to concluding a treaty of peace, for there was no question but that this would be its ultimate result. A dozen loose threads of consequences of the war remained floating in the air, but these we can merely name ; in what they will end is for the future to decide.

The conclusion of the war did not put an end to the hostile relations between the native inhabitants of the Spanish colonies and the Spanish soldiers and residents. The people of Porto Rico manifested the same bitter hatred against the Spaniards as animated the Cubans, and the close of hostilities between the contending parties was followed by violence on the part of the natives, largely instigated by reports of outrages committed by the Spanish soldiers in their retreat. The town of Cota was burned and the Spanish residents were obliged to fly for their lives, while throughout the surrounding country the terror-stricken Spaniards appealed to the Americans for protection. This was given where possible, and two newspapers which violently called for vengeance were suppressed, but it was not easy to prevent individual examples of persecution. The turmoil, however, could only continue until the evacuation by the Spaniards and the full American occupation of the island.

In Cuba the insurgents remained in arms, and it was evident that some degree of hostile relations would persist between them and the Spanish soldiers until the evacuation was completed and a temporary American protectorate established. Commissions were appointed by the President to proceed to these islands and arrange for them a form of government, to continue until their final status should be decided. The commissioners appointed for Cuba consisted of Rear-Admiral W. T. Sampson and Major-Generals M. C. Butler and James F. Wade; those for Porto Rico were Rear-Admiral W. S. Schley, Major-General John R. Brooke, and Brigadier-General W. W. Gordon. Captain-General Blanco headed the Spanish commission for Cuba and Captain-General Macias that for Porto Rico.

Congress had resolved that Cuba should be independent, but as the conditions there became better understood serious doubts were entertained of the ability of the insurgents to maintain a civilized form of government. Many of them were ignorant negroes. Knowledge of political affairs was sadly lacking among them, and a large number of the inhabitants, alike of Spanish and of Creole birth, fearing anarchy in place of settled government, were anxious for the United States to retain possession of the island. It seemed not improbable that, in view of the considerable depopulation of Cuba during the war, an influx of Americans might replace the vanished inhabitants, and the island in this way eventually come under American control. In any event an American protectorate would probably need to be long maintained, for the people were evidently unfit to govern themselves.

The disposal of the Philippine Islands was an equally

pressing problem, this, by the terms of peace, being left to the decision of a commission of five members from each country, who were to meet for consideration of the subject not later than October 1. The American commissioners, as appointed by President McKinley, were the Secretary of State, William R. Day, Senators C. K. Davis, of Minnesota, William P. Frye, of Maine, and George Gray, of Delaware, and Hon. Whitelaw Reid.

As to what should be done with the Philippines, a wide difference of opinion prevailed in the United States. Many called for a retention of the whole group ; many others opposed retaining any, looking upon an extension of American dominion to those distant waters as a dangerous experiment. The probability seemed to be that the island of Luzon would be annexed, while the remaining islands might be left to Spain to be governed under strict regulations devised by the Commission. The old unjust and cruel rule would certainly not be permitted.

As in the West Indies, so in the Philippines, there was a native element to be dealt with that was likely to give trouble unless its wishes were considered in the settlement. The reports of irritation of the natives against the Americans were exaggerated or unfounded, and at a conference with their leaders they expressed their full willingness to co-operate with the Americans and to surrender their arms if assured that the islands would remain an American or a British colony or protectorate. But they positively refused to remain under Spanish rule, and declared that they dared not disarm until they knew who were to be their future masters. Aguinaldo, in an interview held with him, said that he was in command not of an army, but only of an unruly rabble, and was earnest in his desire that the Americans should give the Philippines a free and liberal government, to whose establishment he would lend his full support.

On August 20 an imposing naval demonstration took place in the harbor of New York, the leading war-vessels of the West India fleet—the battle-ships Iowa, Indiana, Massachusetts, Oregon, and Texas, and the cruisers New York and Brooklyn—entering the harbor on that day, where they were received with an ovation that amply testified to the admiration of the people for the battle-scarred ships, their commanders and crews.

Rewards were dealt out freely to the heroes of the navy. Dewey, as already stated, had been early made a rear-admiral. The same reward was given Sampson, Schley, and Howell, Sampson being advanced eight numbers on the navy list and Schley six, so that Sampson outranked Schley, instead of being subordinate to him as previously. Rewards were dealt with a liberal hand to other officers of the navy and army, the three months of war giving to many worthy officers an advance in rank greater than they were likely to have attained in twice that many years of peace.

The very valuable service rendered by the navy in the war, and the disposition of European powers to add steadily to their strength upon the sea, could not fail to give rise to a desire to add largely to the strength of the American navy, and fit it for possible contest with stronger powers than Spain. Though five new battle-ships were nearly completed, and three more, with four monitors, had been ordered in the recent session of Congress, this was thought to be insufficient to meet the new requirements arising from the recent war. The Board of Experts, which includes the chiefs of all the bureaus of the Navy Department, agreed upon a general programme of additions to the navy to be recommended for consideration by Congress at its next session.

This programme embraced the construction of fifteen sea-going fighting ships. Three of these were to be battle-ships of greater tonnage and speed than any now in the navy, their displacement to be 13,000 tons and their average cruising speed 19 knots. Their main batteries were to be composed of four 12-inch rifles, and their secondary batteries to include fourteen to sixteen 6-inch rapid-fire guns. There were also recommended three first-class armored cruisers of 12,000 tons displacement and 22 knots' speed, to be covered with heavy armor from stem to stern, and to mount four 8-inch rifles in turrets and ten or twelve 6-inch rapid-fire guns in broadside. Nine other cruisers were provided for, three to be second-class protected and armored ships and six third-class protected ships. The building of a number of troop-ships for colonial service was also recommended, to be capable of carrying twelve hundred soldiers, with their supplies and baggage. These were deemed necessary in view of the newly acquired colonial possessions of the United States.

That the United States would need a larger standing army in the future was equally evident, though it was felt that great dependence would need to be placed on the National Guard, the latter to be much better trained and disciplined than heretofore. By this means a large and effective army could be made available at short notice and at small cost in case of exigency. As regarded the volunteer army raised for the war, steps were taken immediately after the signing of the protocol for disbanding a large number of the troops, though the requisites of garrison duty in the newly acquired territory rendered it necessary to keep a considerable contingent of them for some time under arms.

The suggestion was made that the United States should add to its official corps a General Staff, such as is employed by European governments, to take charge of military matters in times of peace and keep the army in a fixed state of readiness for war. In such a case the lack of material, awkwardness, and inefficiency displayed in the early days of the war with Spain would not be likely to recur in future conflicts, and even a hastily levied army could be put into the field more quickly and under far better conditions than in the instance here under consideration.

As regards the formation of a large standing army, which some advocate, the recent action of the Czar of Russia gives voice to the feeling which is widely entertained concerning the military establishments of Europe. He advocates a reduction of these immense armies as crushing and dangerous elements of the body politic and as threatening obstacles in the way of the development of settled conditions of peace. It is sincerely to be hoped that the international conference to this end proposed by him may yield the desired result. Whether it does or not, the movement of the Czar is a decided step in the right direction, and the disarmament which he suggests cannot fail in the end to come.

Complaints as to the treatment of the sick soldiers continued, severe blame being laid on the War Department, the chorus of detraction spreading until it affected the press of the country like an epidemic. To what extent this blame was deserved could not be decided in the heat of the moment, and needed to be left for later and cooler consideration and a possible official investigation. Much sickness prevailed, not only among the soldiers brought home from Cuba and encamped at Montauk Point, but also in the home camps at Manassas and Chickamauga, while the supply of food was said to be absolutely unadapted to the needs of the sick, the water to be contaminated with disease germs, and the other requisites lacking or inadequate to the situation. To overcome the difficulty new camps were established in healthier locations, to which the sick soldiers were removed, and steps were taken to provide them with suitable food and shelter. The lack of proper care and attention may have been in a measure unavoidable, but there was certainly much neglect and inefficiency, for which some one was to blame, and official red tape in many instances seems to have set aside the dictates of common sense and humane sentiment.

A few words on the probable effect of the war on the nations concerned and we have done. Spain has lost all, or nearly all, her remaining colonies, but whether this is likely to prove an injury or an advantage to her it remains for time to decide. The colonies of Spain for several centuries immensely exceeded in extent those of any other nation, yet history yields no evidence that any benefit was ever derived from this vast colonial dominion. Even in the early days, when gold flowed in rich streams into the coffers of Spain, this wealth served to enrich the commercial nations surrounding her, not herself. In fact, her colonies proved a deadly incubus, draining off her energy and yielding nothing of value in return. Absorbed in the government of these distant possessions, the home interests of Spain were sadly neglected, industry remained stagnant, commerce undeveloped, and while the nations around were making immense strides forward in prosperity, Spain, once foremost among them all, sank steadily into decadence.

It may be that the loss of her colonies will prove to her a blessing instead of a curse. Having no interests to care for abroad, she may devote new attention to her interests at home, and develop her natural resources until in time she regains something of her old rank among the nations. Whatever be the effect of the loss of her colonies upon Spain, it cannot but prove a blessing to the colonists themselves, who have escaped from the most severe and crushing of despotisms, and taken their place among the free and self-governed people of the earth. The colonial policy of Spain was from the first to the last a cruel and barbarous one, and the moral sentiment of mankind long ago demanded that it should be brought to an end. The United States has proved the evangel of liberty and prosperity to the manumitted peoples.

As regards the effects of the war upon the United States, they are likely to be much less important. The war was but a passing incident in the history of this country, not a vital problem. It has given us an increased knowledge of our strength and resources, and won us a new and high respect in Europe, but has added little to these powers and resources. It has given us island colonies, but what benefit these are likely to bring us it is too soon to say. We have stepped into what some designate a dangerous imperial position, but this simply means that our growing interest in the concerns of the world has been unmasked by the events of the war, not that these three months of hostilities have brought us any new strength or higher importance. They have but swept away the mist of misconception and revealed our real importance to the powers of the world. It must soon have manifested itself in any event.

Two results may be spoken of. The war has had a valuable effect in removing the shreds of ill feeling remaining between the North and the South, and welding the two sections of our country into one strongly cemented Union; and it has aroused a strong sentiment of affinity between the Anglo-Saxon peoples of the earth which may in the end prove a leading factor in the histories of the nations. The English-speaking peoples have grown mighty and all-pervading with the passage of the years, and with joined hands they would be all-powerful. But it is in peace, not in war, that the great republic of the West is destined to prevail. It is with the olive-branch, not the sword, that it should stand before the world. It may again be forced into war, as it has been forced by Spain, but peace is its mission, industry its interest, prosperity its goal; and the invasion of the world which in the future it is destined to make will be that of commerce, not of arms; of thought, not of force; of the beneficent products of the soil and the mill, not the direful harvest of fire and sword.

THE END.

www.ingramcontent.com/pod-product-compliance
Lightning Source LLC
Chambersburg PA
CBHW020536300426
44111CB00008B/685